The Unfinished Journey

The Greens and McGills

Searetha Smith-Collins

ISBN 978-1-64416-302-3 (paperback)
ISBN 978-1-64416-304-7 (digital)

Christian Faith Publishing, Inc.
832 Park Avenue
Meadville, PA 16335
www.christianfaithpublishing.com

Printed in the United States of America

To my father, Elbert Lee Green (deceased) and my mother, Oleatha Green (deceased on November 13, 2018), to whom I will be forever grateful for shedding light on what it means and feels like to be a part of a loving family; and to the Green and McGill family, especially the children, grandchildren, great-grandchildren, nieces, nephews, cousins, and the greats of generations yet to come, "Tell ye your children of it, and let your children tell their children, and their children another generation" (Joel 1:3, KJV).

"A people (family) without knowledge of their history, origin, and culture is like a tree without roots."

Marcus Garvey

Acknowledgments

Special recognition is given to Reddie Mae Pittman King, my cousin, whose research and drafts of the ancestral history provided the basis for the early chapters in the book. Reddie Mae Pittman Rosemond King passed on Friday, October 26, 2018, in Illinois. She was brought back home to Maysfield, Texas, by her family after her death. Reddie Mae was the former President of The Green – McGill Family Reunion Committee. She served faithfully for many years as President and also held several positions throughout the years.

Also, to Elnora Pittman Sullivan, Johnny Cunningham, Leana Taylor, Dr. Virgie Harris, Leslie Miles (deceased), Melloniece Fuller, Rosemary Freeman, and Jacqueline Flood, thank you for your contributions. Acknowledgment is given to James Bell, Dorothea Carter, Dr. Bettye Bellamy, Dr. Jacob Collins, Joseph Nickens, Wheeler Peavy, and Shirly Starke-Wallace for their stories, suggestions, and insights and support.

Contents

The Family Tree

Why do they call it a Family Tree?
My child curiously asked me.
I thought a moment, then tried to explain
How generations go on … their lives not in vain.
From roots buried deeply beneath the earth
Comes the very foundation of our family's birth.
Each root brings its own gift to help form the tree.
As our ancestors each left their legacy.
The trunk of the tree is our very core.
Holding life … love … and so much more.
Home base to return to when life gets too rough.
Support and acceptance when the world gets too tough.
From the trunk other branches grow,
Forming the beautiful tree that we know.
Each limb is different each plays a role,
Different strengths … yet sharing one soul.
If one branch is broken, the tree feels the pain,
Sap runs like tears until it heals again.
Families, like branches, spread out from the tree,
But, part of them remains through eternity.
Like leaves caught up in a gust of wind
Carried away … some come home again.
Nestling around the base of the tree
Close to the Roots that gave life selflessly.

—Author Unknown

Preface
A Personal Pilgrimage

> My great-grandmother told my grandmamma
> the part that my grandmamma didn't live
> through, and my grandmamma told my mama
> what they both lived through, and we were sup-
> posed to pass it down like that from generation
> to generation so we'd never forget.

—Gail Jones (1975) in *McKnight,*
African American Wisdom, 2000

What if you could know the exact history of your ancestry? It was
Ken Burns who said, "History isn't really about the past, settling
old scores. It's about defining the present and who we are." History
establishes human existence and activities in time and place. History
is the way we know how we have progressed and where we have been.
History is the way consciousness, traditions, and legacies are passed
on. History is the way we share memories—the eyes, ears, words, and
memories passed down by ancestors and the past.

For those who are aware, you are the fortunate ones. Like most
people of my generation and before, we had some notion of the people, sacrifices, and ideas about how hard-earned achievements were
acquired. We were lucky, in a sense, because as I recall life's situation
and past times, most of us had the benefit of resourceful mothers,
fathers and relatives; and strong ties with elders, relatives, and communities who invested in our being.

11

During 2016, I met Leanne King Devitt, M.A. (2016), an elder counselor and family mediator in Seattle, Washington. I was moved by her work and commitment to the elderly. One of the key messages on her website struck me as essential to the fore thoughts of my book, so I will share some of her words now.

Leanne said:

> "Stories ... I love people's stories. When I meet someone, I am most interested in their story, the story of their family, their culture and the times through which they have lived. I work hard to try to see the person as someone who embodies a lifetime of adventures, experiences, hopes and losses. It is in this context I hope to offer ideas and guidance in helping individuals and families make the next move or come to terms with where they are now."

Leanne went on to explain the value of elders as important to our ancestral journey. She stressed that in many cultures and settings elders are valued, listened to and honored. She explained that connections in our lives, such as family and community, give us value, and our connections should be honored and maintained. This book contains important stories of ancestors and elders who bridged connections to their family and their family history. Everyone has a story. For instance, on her website, Leanne displayed a picture of herself standing by a blue car. She said the picture was about "the story of her dad's 1941 Cadillac and how it came to live with her, which was one story she loved to tell. As a teaser, she added, "Ask if you are interested!"

The stories you will read in this book will describe the journey of a family that has similarities to most. Although each family is unique, their stories illustrate the significance of elders and the relationships that often are the only source of connections to the memories, events, and people who generated the pathway to today. An unknown person said, "If we fail to listen and record the voices, hopes, and experiences of elders, many clues to our family's existence, and how we were shaped may be lost of forgotten."

This book reflects the eyes, ears, and voices of ancestors who passed down the rich legacy of culture and family tradition. In addition, the book was written in concern for the preservation of our family history, generational continuity and consciousness, and the impact of the disintegration of family, in general, as we knew it. Documenting a family history, even in an incomplete form, can help keep history alive; however, this book will tell a family story centered around three major themes:

- The importance of the family unit;
- The preservation of culture steeped in continuity and wholesomeness; and
- The power of unity of purpose/togetherness.

Ancestors spent generations building and instilling the importance of identity, history, culture, traditions, family, and self-worth; therefore, the book, which is part memoir, part family history, part American history, and part a futuristic vision of the well-being of family, points out our family's pilgrimage, which parallels the socio/cultural history and relationships of America's past to the present. The book traces the twists and turns of change and constancy, specifically in the broader context of understanding how tensions of change and continuity influenced current generations.

The history of my paternal family, the Greens and McGills, started out as a desire to record what was passed down over the generations through oral history. Storytelling, oral history, and tradition help to interconnect literature, history, music, art, and knowledge from one generation to another. Some of the early accounts of the Greens and McGills evolved from knowledge, personal stories, and research by my cousin, Reddie Mae Pittman King, who died in 2018. Several years ago, Reddie drafted narratives, memories, facts, stories, and experiences from interviews with family members, and whatever sources could be found.

At the same time, I began to write stories about our family history and growing up in a family that reflected times that were very different from modern-times. Realizing that those family memories had significance to past family history, Reddie and I joined forces. Like a detective story, the ancestral search involved seeking related facts about family by full names, births, dates, places, deaths, marriages, and significant events.

After the initial draft manuscript of the book was completed, and read by family members and others, it was suggested that the contents had a greater reach than just our family members; so the project took on broader topics that would be of interest to a general audience. What was to be a simple family history became an expanded notion of a book on family and generational history, continuity, and consciousness. First and foremost, the motive was to document our paternal family history; then the theme broadened to linking and making connections to current generations during these times of rapid change and divisions between older and younger generations.

Let me loosely define what I mean by older, younger, rising, newer, and newest generations. Keep in mind there is great diversity among groups and individuals, and there is variation in and between individuals and generational periods and characteristics. Those born prior to 1965 are considered the older generations. Those born between 1965 to the mid-1990s are considered newer generations. People born in the late-1990s and at the millennium (the year 2000) to the present are considered the newest generation; and children currently ten years of age or so are considered rising generations.

Because of generational and American societal and life changes, many members of newer or rising generations do not know what it is like to have two biological parents in the home, nor have they experienced strong connections to a family. Some have not experienced or seen models of a family unit consisting of a mother and father living in the home; nor have they experienced family life that was grounded in communal and cultural support and traditions. This book was written as a voice of passion to get to the heart of what it means to grow up with strong family influences and models from childhood to adulthood, including gaining family and cultural health, and committed resources for family and community support.

It is well-known that attempting to account for decades and centuries of American or family history can never be all inclusive; therefore, there was no attempt to account for all families or family members, events or activities. The stories in this book connect to hundreds of years of known and unknown history of the Green and McGill family, spanning from the aftermath of slavery to the end of World War II, the Civil Rights Era, and the present.

Special emphasis was placed on five generations, popularly known as:

- The Lost/World War I Generation (Approximately 1883–1900) (Strauss & Howe)
- The Silent/World War II/GI Generation (Approximately 1923–early 1940s)
- Civil Rights (Boomers) Generation (Approximately 1943–1960)
- Post-Civil Rights Generation (Approximately 1960–Present)
- The post-modern groups include Generation X (Approximately 1961-1981), Generation Y (Approximately 1964-1985), and Tweeners/Generation Z (10 to 12 year-olds).

Society, as well as the character of our youth, have undergone tremendous change in the last decades, which has presented perplexing challenges for parents, schools, communities, and families. Much of what you will be reading will be about times when parents provided a path to growth and opportunity by investing in their children, which generated generations of powerful cultural, social, economic, family, and educational influences that secured a pedagogy of confidence.

Roots and Influences

Whereas I am an advocate for change, and making room for creating new experiences, I have a healthy interest in both the old and the new. It is natural to want to change or throw away old or outdated things, and replace them with something new; however, one of my favorite pastimes is visiting antique shops or rummaging through artifacts that often find their way into thrift shops, flea markets or yard sales. Oftentimes, I come across items that are symbolic of how people lived in different times. Exploring the past can unlock the present and serve as a catalyst for understanding differences in history, traditions, practices, and the vision of elders and ancestors.

Also, as a collector of Black memorabilia—the piercing symbols, remnants, and that tangible reminders of attitudes and biases that historically manifested themselves against African Americans in this country—I find that although they are distasteful and offensive, such images can help examine the painful past, and serve as a driving force for understanding legacies and perspectives that still are alive today. Incorporated in this book are stories, perspectives, and ideas that reflect many voices, experiences, efforts, memories, history, and thoughts about family, culture, heritage, legacy, struggles, and relationships that sustained so many of us over the generations.

Such thoughts were reflected in a historical artifact that I acquired as a part of my memorabilia collection. It is a picture of a group of enslaved black men, women, and children, who are gathered around an excerpt from the Introduction of a book entitled, *Now is Your Time: The African American Struggle for Freedom* (1991), written by Walter Dean Meyers. The message of the excerpt is a reminder of the worthiness of the legacy of hundreds of years of African-American cultural and lived experience that began in 1619.

The message as written below expresses the importance and senti-ments of this book that tells our family story and how we connect to a unique past.

> "The African American experience cannot be lived in one story or even a hundred, for it is a living experience, ever changing, ever growing, ever becoming richer. Events of the past cannot change, but they can change our perception of them, and ... our understanding of what they mean to us today. Some hundreds of years ago, an African was brought to the shores of North America. That African was my ancestor, and will always be a part of my heritage ... I claim the womenfolk, the quilts they made, the articles they wrote, their fear of having their children sold away, their art and songs ... I claim the darkest moments of my people and celebrate their per-severance. I claim the joy, and the light, and the music, and the genius, and the muscle, and the glory of these I write about, of those many more I know about, and of the legions who have passed this way without yet having their stories told."

Enslavement in North America is not a disconnected marker in the story of Africans in this nation. It is a part of the foundation which requires deeper reflection, introspection, and examination of how past experiences affected our current-day conditions, which includes cycles of poverty, violence, discrimination, lack of oppor-tunity, and disruption of families. Ancestors and sympathetic others "fought, bent, and broke" stereotypes, images, and issues of enslave-ment and racial injustice so that we could exist (Jesse Williams in *Mayo & Lemieux*, 2016).

Family is the starting place for finding out about our origins, well-being, and position in life. Every family has a rich history, and the family from which we were fortunately or unfortunately born is the starting place for finding out about our geneses, welfare, and lived experiences. As you read this book, you will be joining the pilgrimage of the Green/McGill family whose roots are in Navasota, Texas. The book shares the history and stories of people who underwent a distinct journey in America, as well represents a celebration and historical tribute to ancestors who formulated our journey from its humble beginnings to today.

Since the Greens and McGills are of African descent, much of what you will read is the result of curiosity about who our ancestors were, and what they did as enslaved and freed people. I was curious to know more about how they endured the treachery, hostility, degradation, and state of life throughout their journey. I wondered what life must have been like in 1865, specifically during and after the end of slavery in North America. I wondered how finding out about all of this would explain how our family individually and collectively evolved; and finally, I wondered what interest all of this would have to rising generations.

Seeking answers to such questions led to a greater understanding of the history of slavery from an African-American perspective. This consideration is critical now, because our family and life journey as African-Americans is once again at a perilous fork in the road. When at a crossroad on a journey, it has been suggested by an unknown source to consider four options—go straight ahead, turn left, turn right, or turn back. Of course, we do not want to turn back to past times, because there are some prior occurrences that need not be retraced, repeated or preserved.

Why is this book entitled, *The Unfinished Journey*? I believe that we are a part of a long journey or continuum to now, and the connections to that journey give us value and purpose. Our journey to now, and moving forward in the present, rests with the choices and decisions that we make today.

Because we are a family of African descent, the search of the Green and McGill family heritage started with three compelling queries: (1) What was the location of the slave trade site where the first known descendants of the Greens were traded or sold? (2) What was the name of the slave owner who fathered the children of the first known descendant of the Greens; and (3) Who were the ancestors, from where in Africa did they originate, and what did their journey entail for us to become who we are today?

Although the book concentrates on the family history of the Greens and McGills, special emphasis was placed on the impact and inheritance of three pivotal contemporary generations, the torchbearers of our continued legacy, commonly known in popular media as:

- Generation X: Born 1961–1981, currently ages 23–44;
- Generation Y or Millennials: Born 1980s–mid 1990s or 1982 or 1981–2000, currently ages 23 to the early 30s, and
- Generation Z or Tweeners: Born in the mid-2000s, children of Gen X, currently 22 or younger, or ages 2–19 (some define as born 2000–2025).

The Green/McGill legacy is based on the desire to maintain and sustain family roots, heritage, and connections; however, it is important to clarify upfront that the book is *not* suggesting that we simply turn or go back in time or saddle newer generations with old traditions and institutions. Rather, the book suggests that reexamining the past can provide insight into what was, and still is, needed to achieve family, individual, and collective success. The intent is to bring additional knowledge to the attention of those who are not familiar with the values of earlier periods, especially people who are not familiar with the time in our history when most families were functional, strong, and progressive.

It must be acknowledged also that there are no perfect families, and we are people with different family, cultural and generational circumstances, and experiences. As each family story was written, recurring themes evolved that generally defined common family ideals, such as communication, commitment to education, uplifting, love, continuity, and consciousness. The ideal of parenting surfaced as being of supreme importance to nourishing, bridging, and sustaining the life of family and children. Therefore, illustrations and thoughts were presented to pinpoint some of the important building blocks that prevailed overtime.

Change, Transmission, and Transference

As the saying goes, "Everything changes with time'" for instance, language and slang change, fashion trends change, dance and music styles change, hairstyles change, and the world as each generation knows it changes with new attitudes and ways of thinking. Change was an underlying theme in the book. Change that is not a continuation of existing beliefs and practices requires shifts in beliefs, practices, knowledge, skills, and resources; and often sparks a response to resist, assimilate, adopt, adapt, adjust or integrate new ways of living.

Ultimately the book is about good and bad changes from a family and child perspective. Much of what is behind the book are concerns about the tug, pull, and influence of certain changes and trends that create family and generational divisiveness. Transmission and transference of family knowledge and history require generational continuity; therefore, the book delves into changes over the past generations that had strong implications for families in the context of different times. This required identifying strengths and weaknesses over the generations, and pinpointing what families had to do to survive.

Then there was a need to consider if characteristics of past family life had relevance to those who are reared now, in very different times, under very different conditions.

Acknowledgement was given to newer generations who are experiencing a very different journey from childhood to adulthood than previous generations. Concerns were presented, such as how sometimes, newer generations are not aware of how the past relates to them individually or collectively. Also, there is a concern that the generation popularly coined as *millennials* (born in the 1980s–mid-1990s), is considered bright and successful, but oftentimes, seem a bit anxious about their future. Parental concerns center around questions such as, "Will they have jobs?"; "Will they have stable lives?"; "Will they find mates and start families?"; "Will they find the independence to live on their own?"; and "Will the institution of marriage and family survive?"

Similar questions existed in the past, but the difference now is there is less family and emotional strength, communal support or common thought about the value of family. In the past, there was a tremendous legacy of commitment by parents who made enormous sacrifices to ensure that children had better lives than previous generations spiritually, culturally, emotionally, economically, and psychologically. In turn, such thoughts raised current-day questions about parenting and family, like, "Has the potential for our children's success and happiness become so imperiled that it might not be possible to achieve more than previous generations?"; and "Can our legacy be preserved during what seems to be destructive family times that have fallen on many people?"

This led to a need to seek a deeper understanding about contemporary relationships between and among generations. It seems we are losing the value and impact of traditions and multi-generational continuity. The book took on the hope of providing insight to help older and younger generations look to the future within the context of understanding what came before, and what might come after, their time. Understanding family history and its relationship to now must translate into a connected vision of the future. Many experiences in the book are applicable to contemporary times and universal family circumstances and concerns.

The salient message throughout is that we exist because of the sacrifices, labor, unselfish acts, and commitments of ancestors and elders. We must know and honor the memory of ancestors and elders, because had it not been for the people who created the relationships, connections, and fundamentals upon which our evolution was built, we would not exist. Such a notion is relevant to the title of this book, because a new child is born each day, and a new generation is created.

New generations of youth, children, and young adults often subscribe to the notion that it is more important to shine headlights forward than look back through rearview mirrors. To further complicate matters, there are people who do not have the benefit upon which to draw or gain an understanding of family life in the traditional sense.

The major work rests with people who are thirty to forty years of age and younger. They are the torchbearers, along with the rising generations who must bring forth the continued progress that was built by culturally proud, functional people who journeyed before our time. Therefore, as you embark upon this journey, keep in mind:

> There are many more miles to travel and legacies to accomplish. The unfinished journey calls for continuing to fulfill our destiny and collective well-being, as well as become more comfortable in the continuity of our heritage and family connectedness. (Source Unknown)

Also keep in mind, there are those, both old and young, who evolved from generational and family experiences that presented toxic, dysfunctional issues that left unprotected feelings, which most would rather flow away with the tide to never return. Bringing forward the common work of family, understanding relationships between and among family, and engendering beneficial family and multigenerational continuity are aspirations of this book. Regardless of the good or bad, there are valuable lessons that can be gained from reflecting and revisiting roots, origins, connections, influences, and experiences that can help us heal, and transition into the future with greater strength and perseverance.

It seems that something in the ancestral plan to manage life and risks ahead went awry. John McWhorter (2005), senior fellow at the Manhattan Institute, pointed out a new reality: "Never has there been a time where children have been fearful of living their lives by simply living them."

As we consider the "unfinished journey" of life, all must keep in mind our connection and relationship to one another. The reflections below remind us that often, we are strained by generational shifts and transitions that divide the views of the old and new. Perhaps when people speak of "the good old days," they are longing for the sentiment of stability and predictability that seemed prevalent during earlier times and are critically missing today.

If you are at least fifty years of age or older, the lyrics to the following song, "Bring Back the Days of Yea and Nay" by Marvin Winans and CeCe Winans (1985), might joggle memories about a time when family was strong, and when things seemed a bit clearer:

Bring Back the Days of Yea and Nay

A time of innocence and love,
Could we go back to how it was?
I remember when life was so simple,
You did or you didn't, you would or you wouldn't,
But it ain't like that anymore.
I remember when life was so easy,
People said what they meant,
They were either for it or against,
But it ain't like that anymore
Somewhere, we lost the score.
Bring back the days of Yea and Nay
When we could plainly see the way,
Then it was up to us to choose
Whether to win or lose,
Bring back the times when we could see
What it was we were to be,
Caught in the midst of complexity
We searched for Yea and Nay.
I remember when life was so simple,
Parents were a light,
Through them, we saw what was right
But it ain't like that anymore.
I remember when life was so easy,
Boys grew into men

Little girls to women then,
But it ain't like that anymore
Somewhere, we lost the score.
We knew where we belonged,
What was right and what was good,
Need a simple yes or no,
Should I stay, or should I go?
Life has become so advanced,
Wish I had a second chance to go back if I could.
See what' was bad and what' was good.
Now, I'm here and what I fear,
Is we won't find Yea and Nay
Search for them all before,
Will we find Yea and Nay?

Introduction
What's in A Name?

One of the inherent tragedies of slavery is the fact that masses of black people often remain nameless in the historical record. The 1850 and 1860 United States Population Slave Consensus, for example, recorded the age, gender, color, and owner's names for approximately 7.2 million slaves, but failed to record the names of individual slaves.

—Digital Library of American
Slavery, 2000–2009

An important aspect of genealogical history is that it produces interests in knowing the significance of how one acquired a name, because a name signifies a distinct representation of a person or a connection to identity or heritage.

Thoughts about writing this book probably started long ago, before it was even a part of my consciousness. The seeds were planted and rooted early when I became curious about how I came to be who I am. Like many inquisitive children, I wondered how I came to have my maiden or unmarried name, which is Green. For a long time, the derivation of my surname, and its relationship to the history of enslavement in America, was the extent of understanding my family's origins; but there was so much more to the story.

The actual search for the origin of my surname started while attending elementary school. There were a few classmates who had the same last name, Green, so thinking in the mind of a young child, I wondered if we were all somehow related. Of course, the logic did not follow, because some of us had variations of the spelling of the name, Green and Greene, and others came from Jewish or Irish backgrounds; and certainly, they did not look like they were a part of my family.

I recall looking up the derivation of my surname in the encyclopedia (back in the 1950s and 1960s, every thinking family had a set of encyclopedias in the home). A Google search on the Internet or logging onto websites such as Ancestry.com as information sources were unheard of in those days. I learned from the encyclopedia that the surname "Green" originated in earlier centuries in Europe. The name was very common in England and Ireland. Realizing that I was neither English nor Irish, I was a bit confused about how I came to have the surname, Green.

Being of African descent, my early ancestors were among the enslaved who were given a surname of a slave owner of European descent. My family's history is intertwined with the story of Africans who were captured and transported to the colonies of North America during the European Slave Trade; therefore, my paternal family, the Greens and McGills, exemplify a social, cultural, and historical interconnection to general American history.

Sometime between the sixteenth and nineteenth centuries, captured Africans were sold or traded, and enslaved to work as free labor or servants in the homes or coffee, cotton, and sugar plantations of slave owners. Others labored in gold and silver mines or in timber and construction industries to help build the foundations of this nation. Enslaved Africans were stripped of their original name, and not allowed to retain or speak about their African name, language or origins. They were given a name, and assigned the last name of their slave owner indicating property ownership. Others were given or gave themselves a single name or initials without a surname.

Most Africans, and African-American early ancestors, were forbidden from going to school, therefore many could not read or write. Consequently, few if any written family records or documents were generated about the past journey, their roots or their surnames.

To complicate matters even more, initial records were not kept on slaves and slave owners, so there were voids in ancestral data about descendants. Accounts of early family beginnings were lost, so it was not possible to pinpoint exact information about the life of the early ancestors of the Green/McGill family or ascertain where they originated.

Such concerns led to a Boolean search (keywords and phrases on the Internet) and inquiries on Ancestry.com that surfaced information that was cross-referenced with American and oral family history and stories. Personal narratives and facts were discovered from news clippings, church and funeral programs, and newly found relatives who surfaced during the process of writing the book. Such discoveries and information are significant because, at some time in life, usually during the teen years, most people want to know about their identity. They want to know such questions as: "Who are my parents? Where did I come from? Who am I? Answers to such questions require getting people to talk and share information that will help understand oneself as a product of family experiences. Answers help the understanding of being a member of a generation, the coming of age, and how that plays out in the larger world. Further such knowledge can help re-evaluate our path, take stock in life, and move forward with a sense of purpose and belonging.

Bringing It Forward

Bringing the matters forward to contemporary times, as people search for meaning and significance to relationships to the past and present, it is important to examine current and future conditions. There was an attempt to write about our family history in a way that would affirm what younger generations knew, and apprise them of what they may not have known about universal truths, and what sustained individuals and families over time.

In my work as a seminar presenter, I had many conversations with young adults, who repeatedly expressed the concern that they felt abandoned by their parents, and had received little to no information about generational and family transitions or why what happened in the past was so important to them today. For instance, in my work with young adults (Gen X), I have had many conversations where, repeatedly, they expressed feelings of loneliness and abandonment by their boomer generation parents. In contrast, their parents often express feelings they have invested a great deal of effort in their children to ensure that they could continue the inheritance of progress and success. The book seeks to explain why there is a general disconnect and facilitate the ability to apply past information to present predicaments, which has potential for both young and old as they engage in conversations about how to achieve societal, generational, and family cohesion.

Demographers have predicted that in twenty years, marriage and the traditional family as it was known in the past (a mother, father, and children) will entirely disappear. If indeed that prediction is correct, it is important to fully consider the impact of that prediction, and our personal connection to such an outlook based on the cycles of history from enslavement to now. Despite our horrid past, generation after generation produced families and children who were achievers and survivors; however, there is a new threat to our future.

Vast generational differences about family now complicate our collective thinking like no time before. Sadly, there are those who have little knowledge or desire to know what and how ancestors and descendants overcame so much in their life. That was then, and this is now. The problem is complicated even more by the fact that the current state is the only reference point for many of the young. It is important to gain a deeper understanding of what and why something was good in the past, why many of the things that were good did not survive the present, and in the case of the traditional family as we knew it, why it may not survive the future.

When trying to determine the good, previous generations often view the preceding times through "rose-colored glasses," where everything is deemed good or better. A concerted effort was made to not be entirely nostalgic; however, some of the views in this book might seem a bit "rose-colored;" but I am not entirely of that character. I believe that many modern-day advancements are more beneficial, and we can learn a great deal from the perspectives and new thinking of younger generations.

Likewise, we can enlighten children, youth, and young adults in ways that can help improve upon some of the mistakes and miscalculations of the past to now. At the same time, some achievements have retrogressed to the extent that we are losing many important values and foundations in the modern-day landscape. An example is the absence of generational and family strength, especially in African-Americans families. Multigenerational and family strength starts with strong roots, strong foundations, and strong families.

As you will see, family strength, like that of the Greens and McGills, was carved out by culturally proud people who functioned and based efforts and accomplishments on principles such as strong family ties, legacy, responsibility, respect, culture, quest for education, effort, preparation, and unity. The ancestors believed that the progress of each generation had to be better than the one before; therefore, they had a commitment to continuity and responsibility to produce relentless progress and advancements during every generation.

This family pilgrimage will take you through passageways for examining the roles and responsibilities of family that are increasingly shifting. The expedition will lead you through several generational crossings that will help examine the futuristic question, "Is there a need or can the traditional family survive or be revived in the present and future?"

It is my hope that this book will help readers understand more deeply how the past relates or applies personally, and collectively. I hope the stories and information will strengthen the Green-McGill family, and serve as food for thought to strengthen our family as well as others. I hope the book will inspire younger generations to listen, record, and discuss how critical history and information shared by elders can help inform their vision for the journey yet to come.

May this book serve as encouragement to elders and newer generations to do a better job of connecting and preserving treasured memories. And finally, may the information and ideas lead to a deeper appreciation for the connections of our family and ancestral history, because as noted by the late Maya Angelou (1972), "No man (woman) can know where (s)he is going unless (s)he knows exactly where (s)he has been and exactly how (s)he arrived at his/her present place" (African American Wisdom, p. 1).

With that thought in mind, our pilgrimage now begins.

What is a Pilgrimage?[1]

A pilgrimage is the act of deliberate travel; traveling outside while traveling within.

It is a chance to reconnect with the earth, to listen, to face your inner self, to actively commune with a greater power.

A pilgrimage is a refuge from the din and clutter of the outside world.

It is a unique dimension to appreciate life's wonder and revel in minutiae. It is the heady aroma drifting from fields of thyme or the drone of bees in a sun-dappled forest.

---

[1]   Reprinted with special permission from Brian Wilson (2013, February)

It is autumn frost blanketing a multihued trail, and the rough grain
of your walking stick rubbing against your palm.

A pilgrimage is time devoted purely to the present.

There is no past, no future, only now. Your world is your breath, a
heartbeat reverberating in your ears, and a Zen-like placing of
each footstep along a well-trodden path.

A pilgrimage is a trampoline for the mind, a purging of the soul.

It is a thousand small moments. It is unexpected acts of kindness and
fleeting revelations.

It is surrendering to fate, spontaneity, absolute unknown and small
arrows that mark your way.

A pilgrimage is a solitary journey.

Yet as you traverse this portal between past and present, you pay
homage to those who have gone this way before while leaving
your essence for those who pass long after you are gone.

A pilgrimage is traveling lightly.

Just as you leave most of your worldly belongings behind, on the trail
there is a gentle unraveling of fears, emotions, desires, and demons
as you surrender unwanted psychic baggage to the universe.

A pilgrimage is letting go, the discovering, and in truth, be found.

A pilgrimage is peace personified one deliberate step at a time.

When serenity is found within, how long can our world remain without?

Each pilgrim's journey is unique. It can never be repeated.

Yet it continues long after we return home to distant shores.

It is my passion, my reason for being. This is one pilgrim's journey.

—Brian Wilson (2012)

Chapter 1
The Journey Begins

Writers are the custodians of memory. If not documented, memories can die ... the past looms
over all ... decisions in a thousand fragments,
defying them to impose it on some kind or order.

—William Zinner, 2006

Some people say I have a gift for seeing patterns and parallels, and synthesizing information to bring together the sum of the parts of a given situation or issue. If that is so, this book is the result of pondering questions and gathering many pieces of information to bring together, in one place, the story of my family's origins. It is the result of reading and hearing about generations of history, wisdom, and experiences, which includes the intelligence, common sense, respect, drive, and spirit of those who journeyed before us.

This family journey is the outcome of probing into the will of past generations to pass on certain cultural values, traditions, and institutions from across the Atlantic Ocean, spanning to slave plantations to periods of great migration, through eras of racial segregation to struggles for civil and human rights, and to the disintegration of the family today. It is the result of taking all the pieces that have been discovered about the Green and McGill family, and weaving the sum of the parts into the whole of our understanding about our family, and the institution of family in general.

Most of my generation and before had some notion of the preceding achievements that were earned. As I recall, most of us had the benefit of strong ties with elders and resilient, resourceful mothers, fathers, families, and communities that invested in our being. Past generations were fortunate to witness events and people who were responsible for shaping the present, as well as enjoy memories of cross-generational experiences that built critical connections to family life and success.

In a sense, writing this book allowed me to be a "tour guide," providing a glimpse into the life of several generations of family, friends, and others. One of the biggest challenges was deciding how to structure and organize the contents of the book. Zinner's words above took on special meaning as I deliberated how to seamlessly deliver the fragments of our family history, and communicate related thoughts and ideas about generational and family significance, past and present. It was important to document triumphs, challenges, and roles that family played in shaping our history and family; however, pulling together all the pieces presented a tremendous undertaking.

The design of the book took on a mixture of history, recollections, reflection, information, perspectives, and thoughts from my point of view, and that of others. I was challenged to decide how to bring together information about our family history, as well as incorporate generalized thoughts about current issues and change. The hardest part was to decide how to tie together a family history with elements of personal narrative, research, information, and past and current questions and concerns. I grappled with questions such as, "What should I include as a part of family history? What should be left out? Where should I start? Where should I stop? How should I make the contents relevant to young people in a contemporary sense?"

Frequently, I paused to reflect, explain, illustrate or touch upon truths and other thoughts that brought deeper meaning to family and generational life. Initially, I wrote chapters with no specific order in mind. I recorded whatever memories seemed significant or whatever was shared that related to our family; or paralleled experiences from friends, relatives, and others. I relayed accounts that seemed to explain the general influences of family, such as demonstrating the essence of close-knit relationships and co-responsibilities that were a part of the traditional family cultural model that was specific to generational periods over time.

As suggested by Zinner, I had to make decisions about what might be interesting to the reader—what was too emotional or too sensitive, what was important, what was unusual or unique, and what was humorous. I pondered what was universal and what was not, what was worth investigating and expanding, what answered some of the pending family questions and mysteries, what offered sources and models for multigenerational and family support, and what was needed to illustrate how to strengthen the security of family life in this new generational landscape.

A pattern emerged that began to deliver our family history. Primarily, I decided to structure the book in a way that would tell children, grandchildren, and children to come about the family in which they were born. As mentioned, sources for the book took many forms including extractions from notes and narratives written by my cousin, Reddie Rosemond King. The initial idea of writing the book was generated when Reddie and I decided to co-author a book about our family. Fortunately, Reddie provided handwritten notes that documented what she experienced, researched, and discovered about the early history of the Greens and McGills.

Unfortunately, as time went by, Reddie was unable to complete her investigation or participation in the project due to illness and memory loss. Her charming, folksy, "down-home" narratives and conversations generated thoughts about my own family experiences growing up in the Green and McGill family, so I incorporated those experiences in the book. I decided to broaden the emphasis of the book by including personal memories and experiences of friends and others to give homage to the legacy of family life in general.

Initially, I had limited knowledge about the background of my paternal family, but I had grown up around many of my father's brothers, sisters, my cousins, and other relatives. Accordingly, from a personal perspective, I wrote about what it was like to grow up with family based on the traditional family cultural model, in both the southern and northern regions of the country, during different generational times.

The organizing framework involved identifying family episodes that seemed important enough to illustrate universal truths, memories, and experiences that readers could recognize and relate to from their own family or individual experience. I recalled what it was like to grow up in a divided society, contending with different family, generational, and societal circumstances; and different motivations in different regions of the country.

A storytelling style developed with added comments and reflections that explained the relevance of our early ancestry to each level of development, from childhood to adulthood. This was followed by sharing related generational and personal experiences written from the viewpoint of growing up with a wiser perspective in my older years. The initial aim was to provide a history about the lineage of our paternal family. However, as I looked at the evolution and expansion of our family over time, the purposes and goals evolved and broadened to understanding the impact and influences of generational and cultural change, continuity, and consciousness—past, present, and future.

The Author's Aims

I came to understand the magnitude of Zinner's words, that "fragments of history inadvertently span across time," which required unveiling and explaining what ancestors and descendants did to survive under harsher and more unjust conditions. Tracing our family roots, footsteps, and stories across several generations was a monumental endeavor. It was challenging to characterize our family in its entirety, because of its size; therefore, some information is incomplete or no longer current, because during the process of writing over the years, babies were born and family members died.

Upon searching through my electronic files, I was surprised to discover that I had started writing and revamping this book in 2005. Now one might ask, "What took so long?" I knew that documenting lineage of a large family by full names, births, dates, places, deaths, marriages, and significant events was going to be complex; but I did not realize that this undertaking would become such a long-term endeavor. Some people can extract genealogy information from wills, diaries, inventories, bills of sale, depositions, court records, petitions or other such documents; but I relied on gaining information from oral history and oral tradition.

The work of uncovering the Green/McGill story was like a mystery that has yet to be solved in its entirety. The tumultuous impact of the past and present required uncovering and tracing generations of political and social change. It was difficult to identify who begot whom for all family members; or fully know names, timelines or which people belonged to which descendants with full accuracy; therefore, a disclaimer is offered.

Information that was known to be not factual was presented as speculation, guesswork, or not fully verified. The family lineage that is accounted for was checked by different sources, but still, there may be some inaccuracies or omissions in perceptions, people, dates, events or reporting. Apologies are offered in advance for any unintended errors in information, speculation or omissions. The family lineage in this book is intended for personal family use only; therefore, names, relationships, and information about our personal family may not be used for any other purposes.

The title of the book, *The Unfinished Journey*, indicates there is a need to continue to uncover the origins of our family heritage; therefore, current day sources and tools will be needed to continue exploring our family roots and associations including incorporating DNA testing and other sources for tracing genealogy. As I expressed previously, the book *is not* suggesting that we hinder newer generations with old traditions and institutions, nor should we be closed to new ways and thinking. On the contrary, the hope is that the information will bring to the forefront the benefits of times past when families, especially African-Americans, were purposeful, solid, enlightened, independent, and respected.

Common Terms

It is important to take some time to define and clarify some of the terms in the book. There were references to generations, older and newer generations, generational continuity and discontinuity, generational shifts, intergenerational divisions, generational cycles or patterns, generational diversity, generational intersections, etc.

A *generation* is commonly defined as a cohort of people born over a specific time, based on a date of birth to a death year or to all people born during a lifespan of the same time. Murphy (2007) indicates that a *generation* is a span of time when a specific group of people share a common set of formative interests, beliefs, attitudes, values, events, and trends; or the time it takes for people to grow and produce their offspring. The generational sequences focused on in this book are three contemporary generation timeframes of the most recent torchbearers:

- Generation X: Born 1961–1981, currently aged 23–44;
- Generation Y or Millennials: Born 1980s–mid-1990s or 1982–2004, currently aged 23 and younger; and
- Generation Z or Tweeners: Born in the mid-2000s, children of Gen X, currently 22 or younger, or aged 2–19 (some define as born 2000–2025).

Generational continuity refers to the permanence, stability, endurance, and unchanging quality of experiences that remain consistent or uninterrupted overtime. Generational continuity has a lot to do with staying power of traditions, values, heritage, and feelings of responsibility to carry on the investment of those who came before. In contrast, generational discontinuity indicates struggles with a sense of legacy, identity, belonging, and connection to family, history, tradition, and culture.

Change is a significant topic in the book. The world around us changes, and each generation changes with new attitudes and beliefs. Change requires new resources and ideas, but not all change is good. Change can create "discontinuity" or disruption as the previous generation knew it, such as now there is a breakdown in traditions and institutions, such as family and parental responsibility.

Generational cycles are inherent in the saying, "History repeats itself." Theories of generational cycles represent the occurrence of historical patterns that repeat themselves every twenty-five to thirty years (Strauss & Howe, 1997). Generational cycles explain events during specific generational time spans, such as wars, social revolutions, and catastrophes. They represent a continuum that encompasses similar and different outcomes and experiences, involving joys, trials, pain, and suffering that were etched in a period of history.

Generational life cycles of humans include childhood, young adulthood, midlife, and old age or the elder years. The life cycles intersect with historical, social, economic, family, educational, and political trends.

The journey of each generation involves differences, similarities, and tussles with beliefs and attitudes from the preceding generation. For example, now there are generations of young people who do not seem to listen to elders or parents or anyone who is not among their peers. Certainly, these conditions do not apply to all, but we have far too many young people whose principles are modeled after popular culture, music, and media that often engenders disrespect for self and others. At the same time, there are youth and young adults who managed to gain the principles and virtues of family and achieve as expected; but the numbers are decreasing.

Forward and Backward Thinking

Family is a major theme, because it is of extreme importance to most of us. Families provide networks—aunts, uncles, cousins, play cousins, nieces, nephews, close friends, play sisters and brothers, grandparents, and others who influence our lives and give love and support.

Now there is a trend toward deterioration of the makeup of the family unit, and the contemporary vision is not in alignment with the historic view of a nuclear family.

Wetzel (1990) provided a definition of the traditional or nuclear family: "Throughout human history, the nuclear family has been the basic institution of raising children, providing for their needs, passing on culture, and providing models for shaping their understanding of what it is to be an adult. The nuclear family has historically been defined as a mother, a father, and their children."

Because of multi-faceted generational change over the last few decades, it is now common for more people to not be exposed to intact, traditional family life experiences. This dilemma brought forth the need to examine insightful recollections of the strength of ancestors—what they did to sustain as family in the wake of forced separation and massive adversity—and what can be learned that could guide the contemporary journey.

Although much has changed, family roles, responsibilities, and the need for a traditional family model has remained constant. Economist Reinhard Selten (2005) suggested that many people are guided by experiences without knowing their history or really understanding why something worked or did not work in the past. He suggested two processes for examining modern-day complexities—*optimization* (forward looking), and "*ex post rationality* (backwards looking).

Optimization or "forward looking" entails trying to anticipate the range of possibilities that might occur in the future. *Ex post rationality* (backwards looking) is guided by hindsight, which offers a way to consider what could have been done differently in the past, only had we known. Consideration must be given to how current problems and experiences resemble past problems and events.

Such thinking was applied to explore and reexamine universal family practices, virtues, truths, beliefs, attitudes, and needs that were present during times when families were considered more fruitful and sustaining. Characteristics were identified that bred and transmitted cultural and historical knowledge; generational stability; and the accumulation of familial, social, cultural, economic inheritance over the generations. Cultural and social capital includes values, expectations, life goals, character, education, and family assets, including money and property, which were passed down from one generation to the next.

As noted, society has undergone significant changes in the past few decades. Somehow, multi- generational families managed to maintain until now. Perhaps, generally, African American parents of the past few decades have failed to arm the current generation for the continuous struggles they would evidently face to maintain social and civil justice in this country. Consequently, we have new generations who are not poised to carry forth the legacy of progress; or have the where-with all to maneuver through current situations and hurdles that are rooted in past occurrences. To maneuver through these changes and those to come requires an examination of where we have been, where we are trying to go, and how to survive the fallout and tremors from the continuous powerful cultural, social, racial, economic, and political shifts, forces, injustices, and obstacles that continue to rekindle the flames.

The family environment is where we are initially taught behaviors and consequences of our actions. Detrimental forces or disparities, such as racial, and cultural biases, insensitivities, and inconsistencies are usually taught and learned in the family the environment. The stories that follow illustrate how family roles and responsibilities were performed during past times, how shared elements of life stories can unite people, and allow others to examine their humanity and struggles, and see how resilience can demonstrate a path to success (EducationDive,2018).

Harry Passow (1960, p.3), provided the following words of wisdom as we prepare to embark on this journey: His words provide a reminder that history intersects with our understanding of the past, present, and the future:

> It is possible, in going on an important journey, to fix our eyes firmly on a distant goal, and become so intent upon our pursuit of it that we take a little stock of where we are and lose sight altogether of where we have been. In doing so, we may be spending our time rediscovering what is already known and repeating past mistakes.

Chapter 2
Generations Adrift

The stories that follow illustrate how family roles and responsibilities were performed during times when there was more of a traditional sense of family. For example, families reared children and taught them how to dress, behave, use manners and self-control, and to understand their boundaries, such as when a parent or family member said to a child, "Mind your manners;" or "Come on in here and sit down, and act like you have some sense!"

As mentioned, generational experiences and transitions shared in the Green and McGill family journey span five generations, popularly referred to as:

- The Builders—prior to 1946 (Ages sixty-two and above)
- The Boomers—1946–1965
- The Busters—1965–1983

    - Children of Boomers
    - Grandchildren of Builders

- The Bridges—1983–present (twenty-five years and under)

    - Children of Busters
    - Grandchildren of Boomers
    - Great Grandchildren of Builders

A shift in foundations and traditions gradually evolved to influence the contemporary vision. Approximately between 1945 and 1965, the dramatic cultural shifts in family, and societal foundations and traditions, started to take hold, involving new employment and migration patterns that offered new opportunities for living. Although generational, multigenerational, and family connections are the most reliable sources for helping families and individuals understand their value, now, for the first time in modern history, rather than connecting to family and strong multi-generational relationships, we have offspring, grandchildren, and others who are a part of the present generational trend to connect primarily through other sources, such as iPhones/Smartphones, iPads, Skype, texting, Facebook, Instagram, Myspace, Tweets or anyone willing to respond.

As you will see, the significance of family sense began to fluctuate, starting with the Boomer Generation, which created a departure from the traditional, family cultural model, especially for African-Americans. Over the last few decades, the trend began to reconstitute what is normal like no other time. The question is, how did we get here as a disconnected family institution? And how can we correct the error of our ways? In hindsight, as parents and a member of the Civil Rights Boomer Generation, perhaps for a great number of us, our capacity was greater than past generations, especially since many of us moved successfully into solid middle and upper middle-class lifestyles.

Consequently, many offspring developed a sense of entitlement as opposed to the historical, cultural rootedness that had been transmitted by elders and parents. As children, the historical prescription went something like this: "You are not given anything. No one owes you anything, you earn it;" "Get as much schooling as possible;" "Work hard, work smart, and rise above."

Such an upbringing was the experience of most of us who grew up prior to or during the Boomer Generation. Perhaps in our eagerness to give our children everything they wanted and did not need, we took away some of their power and armor to connect to a generational, cultural, and family sense. Perhaps we took away some of their capability to develop inner, spiritual, and emotional strength, as well as core values such as grit, sense of community, belonging, and independence.

More important, we took away the transmission of experiences that brought forth the significance of family. Such skills and attitudes begin and take place initially in the home as family, then in the community and school as influencers of common understanding. Ultimately, many of the changes dissolved experiences that taught generations of people (especially black children) how to learn, adapt, survive, and compete in the society under adverse circumstances.

Consequently, children and grandchildren of the Boomers (the newer generations popularly known as the millennials and younger) are experiencing a very different childhood. Many times, there is no parent or committed adult to raise children, and no neighborhood, black community or strong educational support system in place to bolster family or successive generational well-being.

Our challenge now is to adjust to fast-paced change; but sadly, we are trying to navigate through tough uncertainty without the benefit of wisdom and guidance from elders, and those who passed before us. Instead, we find more disconnection from roots, origins, and a moral and cultural center. Many suffer from a detachment from spiritual and religious beliefs, or cultural consciousness or continuity at a time when our journey is even more uncharted.

It has been said by an unknown source that "you may know the destination of where you want to go, but the journey is the issue." As you journey into the lives of the Green and McGill families, in retrospect, hopefully clues will be found to answer the following questions:

In hindsight: (1) How were resources gained and used by past generations? (2) How were experiences crafted to learn, care, and act in spirit and unity? And, (3) how was the family environment structured to provide and teach love, sharing, security, discipline, safety, joy, respect for self and others, confidence, and agility in the face of turbulence?

And in foresight: (1) How will we know where we are if we do not know where we or those before us have been? And, (2) who will create the history, culture, conditions, continuity, and legacy for our children and their children's children?

Chapter 3
The Road Traveled

Historians have written about the importance of families. Other than oral history, US federal census records became the starting point for this genealogical journey. As for the Green family, my father, Elbert Lee Green, provided some information about his mother, Sirlina McGill Green, but I did not record or know much about my grandparents. Most of us who were born in and after the 1940s did not have the opportunity to know our grandparents, James Sr. and Sirlina McGill Green, before they died in 1941.

I knew that Grandmother Sirlina had a heart attack, and died while "getting happy" at church (having an emotional, spiritual experience) when my father was a teenager. Also, my father explained he named me as a combination of his mother's name, *Sir*lina, and my mother's name, Ol*eatha*, thus I was named Searetha. What is known about the Green/McGill family spans from the eighteenth and nineteenth century America to the present, and much of the family history is about the people who made strong impressions on our lives.

As noted, our family history parallels American history, including accounts of slavery in this country. In the beginning, I had a superficial understanding of the history of African and African-American enslavement in America. As I became a student of history, I developed the awareness that slavery was not unique to Africa and North America. The roots of slavery were embedded universally throughout American and world history. There were century-old accounts of African influences and slavery in Europe, Spain, South America, and other parts of the world, starting even in biblical times.

I knew the origins of slavery in North America evolved out of European models and societies that had a history of a caste system of persecution and enslavement. In North America, slavery and the cycle of oppression and suppression were rooted in ideas of power, control, and domination that stemmed from the benefit of free labor, economic business, and personal profit of slave owners. However, there were additional motives.

Sometimes enslavement involved conquest, power, and control as African nations. African tribes were complicit in the sanctioning of the slave trade business through seizing enemies during warfare, then selling or trading their captives to other traders in exchange for goods. Not only were Africans among the enslaved people in North America, economically poor whites were sent from England to North America and other places to engage in seven years of labor as indentured servants.

For a period, both freedmen and white settlers lived among one another, and worked as indentured servants for the early North American colonies. If their masters figured out how to keep them as workers, they were not freed after the seven years. If they were freed, the slave master was required to provide them with fifty acres of land (WGHB Interactive: PBS Online 2007). According to the Public Broadcast Service's (PBS) program, *Africans in America: The Terrible Transformation* (WGHB Interactive 2007), the indentured servant system changed to racial slavery.

In 1624, records indicated that the first twenty or so Africans who were transported to Jamestown, Virginia in 1623, were listed as servants as opposed to slaves. Sometime in the 1600s, laws were changed to declare, "All servants (who were) imported and brought into the country who were not Christians in their native country … (were accounted for as slaves) (WGHB Interactive: PBS Online 2007)." Henry Louis Gates Jr. (2013), an African American Harvard University professor, scholar, and writer, pointed out that a small number of freed African-Americans and Native Americans owned slaves as well.

Freedmen sometimes used enslavement as a method to free relatives and family members from the clutch of white slave owners or offered safe harbor until it was feasible to free them. On the other hand, some free black people bought relatives as slaves for personal benefit and profit as did white slave owners. The emancipation of slaves in the south in 1863, the end of the Civil War in 1865 (1861–1864), and the Reconstruction period of 1865–1870 created additional problems for millions upon millions of freed slaves. They had no money, schools, educational opportunities, work or places to call home.

Many freedmen were forced to participate in the free labor economic market in southern states, such as sharecropping that accommodated southern landowners and merchants who were left in need of labor. The free labor market broadly and harshly influenced the enactment of unlawful and unjustifiable ways to accommodate southern slave owner's needs for free labor. For instance, in Alabama, Louisiana, Georgia, and Mississippi, the Convict Leasing Program (1865–1868) imprisoned slaves (black men and women) who were forced to work in chain gangs on railroads, in mines, and fields (WGHB Interactive: PBS Online 2007).

Others were forced to work as sharecroppers who rented land from white landowners and merchants where they raised crops in exchange for working the land. Most often they worked without receiving wages. Sharecropping lasted until the early 1940s during World War II and beyond, when jobs were created in factories. Because there were unfair working conditions and arrangements, blacks who did not earn or profit enough money to pay off their debt to the landlords and merchants had to remain as sharecroppers with no pay or way out.

Such conditions served as extended forms of oppression and slavery even though slaves were declared free. During the Civil War through the 1930 and 1940s, law and order was manipulated to benefit property and business owners. Imprisonment and sharecropping was performed under these circumstances for many years, inclusive of violence, injustices, and poor working conditions (WGHB Interactive: PBS Online 2007).

Reviewing this period of history brought forth the realization that there was something unique about being a descendant of African-American ancestors who were entangled in enslavement and its aftermath in America. They managed to journey through injustices, setbacks, disappointments, and lost hopes and dreams. It was intriguing to learn more about the motives, intellect, common sense, and gifts, of those, who oftentimes were uneducated, undeveloped people who managed to survive.

The stories of ancestors who survived this horrid past revealed the level of courage, pride, shrewdness, ingenuity, and survival tactics that often were used to outwit captors and slave masters so that opportunities were created for us to exist today. Even under the cruelest circumstances, their collective and individual strength prevailed across generations. That is the significance of the background of our past as African-American families.

In contrast to that past, I often wonder about the long-term fate of newer generations today, especially those whose main source of knowledge is the worldview of peers, the Internet, multimedia, and other such sources. Without deep-level fortitude, courage, substance, relationships, and appreciation for historical knowledge, how will youth, young adults, and children progress and survive the current day perils in the long-term?

When considering the catastrophic destruction of enslavement (inclusive of destroying families—uprooting the seeds, roots, and branches of family, and strewing family members over several continents), it is no wonder the aftershocks can still be felt today. As we consider African-American families and the struggle they endured to maintain important ties and cultural traditions, the value of family takes on true meaning, especially for families such as the Greens and McGills.

The Green-McGill's early family history is somehow entangled in the sordid history of enslavement in this country. The weight, intensity, and impact of this background, and early journey of African-Americans such as my family, boil down to a poignant point made by Henry Louis Gates (2013): "Owning another human being by males, females, black, white, Native American or any others was, and still is, evil business."

Chapter 4
A Journey Back in Time

The story begins with a voyage. It was not the Spanish maritime expedition to the New World led by Christopher Columbus. It was not a family reunion or vacation on a cruise ship or yacht. It was not a fishing trip or underwater expedition. It was not a deep-sea vessel in search of unexplained missing persons. It was not migrants rescued at sea in a shabby boat. It was a commercial ship transporting goods—unwilling humans from Africa to the New World. We know very little about our family's roots, only that our ancestors were among the millions upon millions of slaves brought from the African coast to North America.

The fact that Africans were a part of the largest forced migration in history, often called the Middle Passage, is common knowledge. The dreadful journey involved triangular slave trading in slave ships that moved human cargo from the vast African continent to Europe, North, Central, and South America, and other world ports. The confused travelers had no say about their destination or the conditions of travel. There were no security checks, passports, electronic ticketing or a self-determined itinerary. The journey was imposed with no choice.

The rickety ships were filled with dazed, caged passengers who were forced into slave ships for the destination of providing free labor for economic gain of others. The future work of these passengers entailed laboring in tobacco, cotton, sugar, and coffee fields, and providing for the comforts and needs of slave owners and their families. They had no control over their lives or their futures. Some rebelled, some fought off their aggressors; others died from starvation, illness or ill-conditions, and some took suicidal jumps into the treacherous seas rather than participate in their captivity.

According to historical records, the voyages initially began with the intent of profiting Europe and colonies in North and South America. The first ships arrived in Virginia sometime around 1619, with the involuntary cargo of a small number of Africans (Simonson 2008). As indicated by the National Park Service (2012), approximately 12 million Africans were shipped as slaves to North and South America between the sixteenth and nineteenth centuries. Approximately 645,000 were sent to North America (Simonson 2008). Simonson also explained that by 1860 and the time of the Civil War, the population of slaves had progressed to almost four million in the United States of America.

The Africans were disconnected from their origins and roots. Their family heritage and history simply were destroyed during the slave trade voyages. In turn, hundreds and hundreds of years of intrusion and disruption of family, cultural, and history relationships, and knowledge resulted. To be more specific, the impact of this event created the inability of African-Americans to link to the epicenter of their family of origin even today. Few of the enslaved could write, so few written records were left to document this period of their journey. However, some of the horrifying accounts were provided by slaves who survived the dreadful voyages.

Life as the Enslaved

Providing this accounting of early history might shed a bit of light on possible conditions under which the Greens and McGills evolved in this country. For many African-Americans, embarking upon a journey into the past requires imagining life from generalized descriptions documented by others. One such accounting was provided by an American Defamation League (ADL) curriculum, entitled *A World of Difference, Americans All* by Bruce, Laparte, and Tolbert (1992).

The authors provided a historical accounting of African and African-American life, and the cultural traditions and practices that were transmitted during and after the Slave Trade journeys across the

Atlantic Ocean. Bruce, Laparte, and Tolbert (1992) reported on the devastating life of the African slave trade, and the circumstances and conditions of chattel enslavement. Although the historical story of enslavement is an integral part of the Green and McGill family story, it was not the beginning of their life journey.

Prior to enslavement, many generations ago, our ancestors originated from life in Africa; however, the exact origins and lost beginnings prior to coming to this country are yet to be discovered. Enslaved Africans were taken from their home with no idea where or what was to come when they landed in the New World. They were treated as property that was to be bought and sold. As slaves, they were forced to work without compensation under the harshest conditions. Frequently, elderly Africans did not survive the voyage or the demands of plantation labor. Significant to current thinking, this created an absence of elders, and the interruption of continuity and transference of cultural values from older to younger generations.

For many centuries, European ships transported captive people from their homeland to various parts of the world, including America. The significance of this event to the past and present is that newly purchased African slaves were not allowed to maintain family ties and cultural traditions. Families passed knowledge from generation to generation as a source of determination, pride, and self-esteem; however, since African slaves were not allowed to learn to read and write, they devised ways to communicate and survive in the new land during atrocious times of enslavement. Traditions, knowledge, and cultural traits were passed on through folktales, songs, and storytelling from generation to generation in oral tradition. Somehow, they found ways to maintain self-respect, as well as cope with cruelty, anger, terrorism, and the insanity of being treated as inhuman. Some ran away, some led rebellions, and some sacrificed their lives fighting against slave conditions.

Despite that history, even under the horrendous conditions, strong families evolved and produced successful offspring up until the 1980s. As explained in Chapters 24 and 25, this fact begs explanation as to why families evolved and produced strong offspring and legacies in the past under such adverse conditions as opposed to the present state.

Roles and Relationships

Family and extended family always was a strong component of the culture and traditions of African and African-Americans. Perhaps the modern-day shift away from traditions that started in slave communities occurred because newer generations were not made aware of the origins of family roles and relationships, and the powerful forces and practices that sustained us through our present. As we look at the American slave system, we can begin to isolate the early beginnings of family relationships that affected the roles of African-American families, such as the Greens and McGills.

African-American male and female relationships evolved from the historical background of slavery that was thrust upon families. Most African slaves lived in large groups, and as much as possible, private lives were safeguarded in the slave quarters. They devised coping mechanisms, which to the initial eye created an impression of openness and harmlessness to captors. They carefully guarded their feelings and families, and provided emotional support to one another. The interest of African and African-American women was to find relief from the demanding male and female roles that had been thrust upon them.

There were relatively few distinctions made between the work of men and women in the slave fields. Work gangs included women and men. There was no public uproar or interest in the protection of black women as females. They were expected to work like men, and there was no notion of the weaker sex in this system. Maximum production from each slave was the order of the day. Black women carried out the duties as mothers and homemakers after doing the work of the slaveholder. Women's work included spinning, knitting, washing, housekeeping, quilting, and other such tasks. This was all expected to be done after long hours of physical hard work in the fields. Because of the tremendous demands on them, women developed the habit of cooperating in child-rearing and managing the home.

Folk beliefs and skills were passed from generation to generation through cooperative efforts that took place in the slave quarters. For instance, child-rearing practices were about preparing and teaching children how to survive in an unjust, hostile environment that offered no justice or room for discussion or error. Slave women were not allowed much time to spend with their children, so they had to use opportunities wisely to prepare children for the harsh life that eventually they had to face.

Slave mothers went to the field early in the morning, leaving the children who were too young to work in the slave quarters in the care of the older women. When they returned from the fields at night, the children were ready for bed. As soon as children turned six to ten years of age, they qualified to become slaves and worked on the plantation. Since young children did not bring high prices at the slave market, sometimes they could be sold with their mother. However, frequently, child-bearing teen girls and strong teen boys were sold away from their parents.

Family and extended family made a strong imprint on their children's lives. Mothers were often thought of with great affection and respect by the children when they became adults. The aftermath of physical slavery and ancestral experiences established longstanding disadvantages, including splintered and lost family members, bruised and separated children, and sacrifice and loss of elders, parents, and siblings.

Such a historical past explains why there was a strong link to the significance of family. Modern-day forms of assimilation caused the forfeiture of historical knowledge and family relationships. Out of necessity, the link between respect and affection for mothers, grandmothers, and women and men who cooperatively took care of children in the communal sense that was a strong past family asset is now missing for far too many.

Enslaved Africans brought a unique culture to America that developed distinct and integral characteristics that influenced African-American culture. The effects of that culture remain in the minds and souls of many African-Americans still today; however, now there are different attitudes about the pivotal role that mothers, women, and men should play in the survival life of family. Perhaps, over the last few generations, the change occurred because values such as high respect for women, in general, was not collectively modeled or transferred to newer generations.

Legacies were formed by passing the torch to newer generations in honor of ancestors and family across generations. An unknown person once said, "If you don't know where you come from, you won't know when something is taken back." In other words, if you do not understand your legacy and the historical, pivotal role that mothers, grandmothers, grandfathers, men and women played in the survival of families, it will be easy to fall victim to your own demise. Family as a strong component of African-American culture and traditions is a major theme in the stories of the Greens and McGills.

As you meet the first known ancestor of the Greens and McGills in the next chapter, keep in mind the origins, background, and significance of life that sustained our family strength overtime.

Chapter 5
The Young Slave Girl: Granny Fannie[2] (Estimated 1822 to the late 1920s)

As far back as can be remembered from conversations around the fireplace in the winter or when the family just sat around on the front porch in the summertime eating watermelon, there were stories told about a young slave girl who was only known as Granny Fannie. She is the first known link to the Green family whose roots are in Navasota, Anderson Grimes County and Maysfield, Milam County, Texas. Different members told different stories. Siblings and family members such as Ruth Green Pittman, Charlie Mae Green Parhms Moten-Mathews, and Cousin Lucinda Allen Smart Watson (Cousin Cindy) reported information about the Green family. Maggie Jane Rosemond Holloway (Aunt Kossie) shared information about the McGill family. Regardless of the source, there were vivid memories of times when Granny Fannie told family stories to the children.

Granny Fannie's parents were slaves whose names are unknown. Based on conjecture and oral stories, it is believed that she might have been born around 1822. According to 1870 U.S. Federal Census Records on Ancestry.com, Fannie was born in Alabama, sometime between 1827-1832. Her residence in 1870 was Precinct 3, Grimes County, Texas USA. Fannie, the young slave girl, got separated from her parents when they were brought from what is believed to have

---

[2] A Narrative by Reddie Pittman King; Edited by Searetha Smith-Collins

been South Carolina (it was common practice in those times for slave owners to sell children, parents, and siblings to different owners, so perhaps that is what occurred).

The young slave girl, Fannie, was taken by an unknown slave master to a place only known as the Johnny Stone Plantation in Georgia or Mississippi. While living on this plantation, Fannie worked as a "live-in" maid for the slave owner who was reportedly "an old-town white judge." Fannie stayed in "The Big House" where, in those days, they were called "house girls or "call girls." As was the case during that time, slave labor was separated into field and house-work, so female ancestors were forced to work as slaves to survive and help feed their families.

During the years Granny Fannie stayed and worked for the slave owner, she tended to household chores and cared for his family, during which time she bore sons for the old slave master. Years later (date unknown), as Fannie grew older, she met and married a young man who worked on the plantation, whose name was Dagg Green. He and Granny had courted and later married. Dagg gave Fannie's children his last name (Green), but there was no further information on how he acquired his surname.

Sometime later (date unknown), the Green family left Georgia or Mississippi, and settled in Grimes County, Texas, in a place called Stoneham, near Anderson and Navasota, Texas. Information about Stoneham could not be verified, because all records were destroyed when the courthouse in Stoneham burned down years ago. There, Granny Fannie and Dagg worked as sharecroppers for many years, and Fannie worked as a maid and caregiver for some of the white people in Stoneham also.

They stayed in the area for several years, working and saving what money they could. Eventually, they purchased a small parcel of land in an area called Piney Woods near Anderson, Texas. Later, my mother, Ruth, frequently took us to visit cousin Lucinda (Lucinda Allen Smart), and cousin Maude Ester in Piney Woods. When Uncle Elbert Green was a small boy, he went with us a lot of the times. Piney Woods was a beautiful place with a lot of tall pine trees surrounding the area. Like many African-Americans, unfortunately, property taxes could not be kept up, so the land was lost sometime in the late 1970s, a few years before my mother died.

Granny Fannie and Dagg moved to Milam County in the 1900s to a place called Black Ridge near Calvert, Texas.

According to the legends, Granny Fannie lived to be 100+ years old (some said 110; others said 112 years of age). Reportedly, she grew a new set of teeth, and was still picking as much as 125 pounds of cotton a day at that age. Granny Fannie was very active, and was known as a good dresser who cared about the good things in life. Also, many reported that when it came to dancing, Granny Fannie could really "dance a jig," even in her later years.

Notes from the Author

It is unclear how many children Granny Fannie had by the slave master. There are discrepancies in oral stories shared by Reddie, and information provided by a historian, who studied the history of families in Navasota, Texas. Reportedly, Fannie had several children: Riley Green, Sr., Lymus Green (Uncle Dude), Landis Green, Willie Green (Uncle Pig), Jeremiah Green, Robert, Jack W. Green (Uncle Jack), and perhaps a daughter. I was told there was another child by the name of Columbus Green, but information cold not be found about him.

As another aside, there were parallels to information discovered about the early migration of settlers and their slaves, which, somewhat, verifies stories shared in Granny Fannie's oral history. According to The Texas State Historical Association, Charles Christopher Jackson (2018) explained that as early as 1822-1825, settlers from slaveholding southern states, mainly Alabamians, migrated to Grimes County and brought their slaves along with them. They sought this area because of the rich bottomlands, which were prime for timber and farmland. It is believed that Fannie was among the slaves brought to Grimes County sometime during that time.

Jackson (2018) further reported that between 1900-1910, there was a black exodus out of Grimes County, so like many others, in the 1900s, Granny Fannie moved to Milam County to a place called

Black Ridge near Calvert, Texas. I was informed by Wheeler Peavy, who considers himself "an amateur Navasota historian", and as well as discovered in U. S. Federal Census Records, in 1920 that Fannie (Green) Bradley (Granny Fannie) lived with her son, Jack W. Green. They lived on Anderson and University Street, Justice Precinct 1, in Anderson, Grimes County, Texas.

Granny Fannie was a widower, and 98 years of age at that time. She was not accounted for in the 1930 U.S. Census, so it was assumed that she died sometime between 1920 and 1930. Wheeler Peavy, the historian, knows Jack W. Green's granddaughter, and indicated that Granny Fannie married several times, but there was no account of additional marriages in oral stories. It was discovered in the Texas Select County Marriage Index, 1837-1965, that Fannie married Derry Bradley on February 5, 1878 in Grimes, Texas. It is unclear what happened to Dagg Green or Derry Bradley, and there was no information about additional children. Further research and clarification is needed to trace Granny Fannie's early and later life journey.

The following is an accounting of Granny Fannie's children who represent the first known offspring of the Green family. There may be children who are unaccounted for, and verification of some names and known siblings still lack clarity. There are many sets of the Green family that branch from Granny Fannie. This family history narrowly accounts for her children reported in oral stories predominantly in relation to the Greens and McGills from the Milam County, Texas area. Information originally was provided by Reddie Mae Pittman King, other family members, and updated by Wheeler Peavy, who was knowledgeable about the history of black families in the Anderson and Navasota, Grimes County Texas area. Emphasis in this book was placed on Granny Fannie and her sons, Riley, Sr. and Jack W. Green; and grandsons, Riley Green Jr., and James (Jim) Green, Sr. and his family, and the McGills who united with the Greens through James Green and Sirlina A. McGill.

Granny Fannie's Children and Their Children

Riley Green

Riley Green, Sr. was born in Alabama date unknown. Oral stories report that he was born on the Johnny Stone Plantation when Granny Fannie was enslaved; however, there are no records to pinpoint with accuracy his birthdate or the slave master who was Riley's birth father. Reportedly on February 21, 1878, Riley married Oney (Ona) (Annie) Jackson Green. Oney was born in Alabama around 1861. The parents of both Oney and Riley were identified on U.S, Census Records as born in Alabama, which identifies the birthplace of Granny Fannie.

Riley and Oney were the parents of *James (Jim) (Jimmy) Green, Sr., Riley Green, Jr., Mary Green, Harriet Green,* and *Robbert (Robert) Green*. There may have been other children who were not identified. As noted in the 1900 U.S. Federal Census on Ancestry.com, Riley, Sr. and Oney had 4 of 6 children living in the home, inclusive Riley Green (age 44), Ona Green, and children, Jimmy (19), Robbert (age 22), Harriet Spain (age 17), Daniel Spain (son-in-law, age 24), Riley Green, Jr. (age 12), Mary Green (age 11), and grand-daughter, Eloise Spain who was Harriet's daughter (age 1). Riley's occupation was a farmer, and based on property tax records for Texas, he was a share-cropper. Riley Green, Sr. was my great-grandfather.

Riley's son, *James (Jim)s Green, Sr.* (my grandfather) was born in 1873 in Branchville, Texas; however, on "Find a Grave Memorial" for Texas, he was born on September 28, 1881 in Grimes County, Texas. He died at the age of 59 on April 21, 1941 in Maysfield, Milam County, Texas. James (Jim) Green married Sirlina A. McGill, reportedly on December 31, 1908 in Milam County, Texas. They raised seven children, daughters: *Ruth, Juanita, Charlie Mae (May) Dorothy,* and *Maggie Samantha James*, who was Sirlina's daughter from a previous marriage whom Jim raised as his own child. Jim and Sirlina had two sons: *James, Jr. (Jim) (Uncle Buddy),* and the young-est, *my father, Elbert Lee Green (Uncle Elbert).*

According to the Thirteenth Census of the United States: 1919-Population, Department of Commerce and Labor—Bureau of

Census, Riley Green, Sr., was 53 years old, and head of the household with his wife, Oney (age 49), at that time. Children who lived in the household were, son, Riley Jr. (age 22), and daughter-in-law, Julia (age 20). Riley, Sr.'s son, James Green was 29 years of age, and head of his household, living with wife, Salina (Sirlina) (age 27) and, daughter Maggie (age 6). Also, they had a five-month old daughter (Ruth). You will read more about James (Jim) Green, Sr. in Chapter Ten.

Riley Green had another son, *Riley Green Jr.,* born on December 18, 1888 in Navasota, Grimes County Texas. According to Milam County Texas World War I Draft Registration Records, 29-year-old Riley, Jr. noted his race as "African," and had one dependent son and wife. Riley Jr. had a son, *Jasper Green, who* was born on August 10, 1910 in Baileyville, Texas. Jasper died on November 20, 1986 in Monahan, Texas. His mother, *Teary Franklin,* was born on January 2, 1892 in Robertson, Texas, and died on December 14, 1973 in Stamford, Texas.

Riley, Jr. married Julia Whatley on February 17, 1910 in Milam County, Texas. Julia was born on January 18, 1894 and died on June 27, 1966 in Houston, Texas. Riley and Julia had a daughter, *Charles Ruby Green*, who was born on December 1, 1919 in Branchville, Texas. Charles Ruby died on May 22, 1975 in Houston, Texas. Riley Jr. was a farmer. There was not much known about diabetes in those days, but it was suspected later that Riley Green, Jr. lost his sight and died from diabetes on December 13, 1937 at 48 years of age. He is buried in the Branchville Cemetery in Maysfield, Milam County, Texas.

Harriett Green

Riley Green, Sr.'s daughter, Harriett Green, may have been also called Aunt Hattie. Reddie Mae Pittman King remembered that Harriett or (Aunt Hattie) lived with her parents for many years. Harriet's date of birth and death are unknown. She married Daniel Spain and they had five children, daughters: Samantha Warren, Eloise, and Ondy (The Dass); and sons: Isiah, and R.G. Spain (Dooley). R.G was killed in Dallas, Texas in 1966 or 1967. According to the 1920 U.S. Census,15-year-old daughter, Onie (Ondy) lived in the home, along with, sons, S.P. Spain (13 years of age), and R.G. (10)

Willie Green

Willie "Greasy" Green, date of birth and death unknown, married Lucinda Stafford in Grimes County. Lucinda was born on February 2, 1982 and died on March 1, 1964. They had children, Pig Green, and Lula Lawrence.

Lymus Green

Lymus Green's date of birth and death are unknown. He married Elvira Hodges, and they had children, *Sally Green Chatman, Emma Green Johnson, Lucinda Green Allen (Cousin Cindy), Jack Green, Mary Jane Burns, Sarah Green Johnson, Fannie Green Cole, Lymus Green, Isaiah Green (Peacock)* who served in World War I, and *Elvira Green Larkins, who had two children and lived in San Francisco, California.*

Lymus' daughter, Lucinda Green Allen (Cousin Cindy) was born on December 27, 1875 and died on December 8, 1951. She married Rev. Carson Lawson Allen and they had eleven children: *Israel, Elvira, Myrtle, Lawson II, Paul Durbar Allen, Emma Allen, Robert Allen, Lucinda Smart, Maude, Dudley Allen,* and *Willie Allen.* They all lived in Navasota and migrated to Houston. Son, Israel Allen, was born in 1893 and died in 1962 at the age of 69. Lucinda was 46 years of age in the 1920 U.S. Census; Carson was 59 years old. Living in the home was grand-daughter, Mystie (18 years of age), Lawson (17), Rebecca (13), Robert (10), Lucinda (8), Maria (7), Dudley (5), and William (2) all born in Texas.

Emma Jean Allen Creeks Bradley (Cousin Emma), was born on July 14, 1906 and died on June 25, 2002 at the age of 95. Lucinda and Emma are buried in the Coaxberry Cemetery in Navasota, Texas. She married Lewis Creek, and they had ten children: *Sarah, Myrtle, Andrew, Allen, Joseph (Joe), Dorothy, Lymus, Clifford, Douglass,* and *Emma Jean. Myrtle Maude Ester, Emma's daughter,* had four sons: Israel, Robert, Willie, and Dudley Allen Green.

Isaiah Green (Peacock) was born on February 1, 1892 and died on December 2, 1957. He was a Sargent in the 165th Depot Brigade in World War I.

Jerimiah (Jerry) Green

Jerimiah (Jerry) Green was born in March 1865 and was 34 years old according to the 1900 U.S. Population Census for Grimes County, Texas. He was single and lived in Texas. His mother, Fannie Green was listed as born in 1831, was 68 years of age, a widower, who was born in Alabama (This was a discrepancy in Granny Fannie's age as reported in the 1900 U.S. Census data for her son, Jack W. Green, which noted Granny Fannie was 98 years old at that time). According to Wheeler Peavy, "amateur historian" on Navasota families, Jerry had at least three children by three different mothers. One mother was Julie Subbs, who had a child, Mary Ann Green, who had a child, Sally Bradley. Another mother was Wincie Wiggins, who had a child, Luella Wiggins. Still another mother, Mariah Henry had a child, Adelaide Green Ruckett, who married Jack Ruckett.

Jerry Green's daughter, Adelaide was born on September 15, 1889 in the Community of Bethel Grove, which is near Stoneham and Anderson, Grimes Count, Texas. She attended school in Grimes County. She died on April 17, 1979 in Galveston, Texas. Adelaide married Jack Ruckett and they "accepted a child into their lives and heart" by the name of Thelma Wade, who married Francis Wade of La Marque, Texas. Adelaide had a sister, Mary Bradley of Oakland, California, and several grandchildren in La Marque, Texas. While in Grimes County, she worked with the County Demonstration Agency and was a Matron of the Heroines of Jericho of Blackberry County, near Anderson, Texas. Adelaide was buried in the Coaxberry Cemetery in Plantersville, Texas. She served as the church secretary in the Coaxberry Baptist Church for many years.

Jack Wilson Green

Jack W. Green, also known as Prof. J.W. Green, was born in Anderson, Texas on July 12, 1867 in Grimes County, Texas. He married Hester Chambers from Shreveport, Louisiana. and they had several children, including *Sally Green Fair*, who had one child, Hester Bowens Lewis, who lives in Houston, Texas. According to the 1900

U.S. Census records, other children include; Maco Green who was born in Texas on January 23, 1903 and died at the age of 52 on June 24, 1955 in Texas; Robert, Julius, Roosevelt, Jackson, Jack Jr., Hobsey, and Frederick (Fred) Green. In the 1920 U.S. Census, Jack was listed as age 61, and wife, Hester was 56.

As noted, Jack's mother, Fannie (Green) Bradley was found to be living with him in 1920. She was 98 years of age and listed as a widower. Jack W. died on October 10, 1957, and is buried in the Coaxberry Cemetery, in Grimes County, Texas. You will read more about Jack W. Green, a noted motivational speaker who spoke to large audiences in various states in Chapter Nine.

Landis Green

Uncle Landis Green's date of birth and death are unknown. He had two daughters, Lula Green and Millie Green, who lived in Baytown, Texas.

Robert Green

Robert Green's (Uncle Jack) date of birth and death unknown. He married Marie Holmes, and they had a daughter and son whose names are unknown. It has been said that Robert Green had another daughter, Rebecca Green Howard (cousin Beck), who operated a beauty shop in Cameron, Texas. For many years, cousin Beck and her sister, Anna Jane, operated the Dorsey Keith Funeral Home in Cameron.

Columbus Green

Columbus Green was mentioned as a sibling in Bible records; however, there is no further information about him.

Chapter 6
Clues and Theories

Before going more deeply into the family lineage of the Greens and McGills, there were several compelling queries that motivated the writing of this book. Questions centered around searching for a deeper level of knowledge about our family history and background, such as (1) where did the first known descendants of the Greens originate? (2) What was the name of the slave owner who fathered the children of, Granny Fannie, the first known descendant of the Greens; and (3) who were the ancestors, where did they originate in Africa; where did they land, and what did their journey entail?

Realizing that Granny Fannie, my great-grandmother, and James (Jim) Green, my grandfather, and his father, Riley, Sr., were directly linked to the history of enslavement in this country, the connection to that heritage became very personal. Consequently, I sought more research and information through online documents, which produced potential insight into potentially identifying the plantation, slave ownership, and ancestral life in Stoneham, Texas.

Although it was impossible to pinpoint exact information, speculation and guesswork led to the conclusion that the location of the Johnny Stone Plantation was narrowed to Georgia, Texas, or Mississippi. The following serves as a background for understanding potential answers to some questions, and conditions under which ancestors of the Greens and McGills lived and evolved during early times in Navasota and Milam County, Texas.

Life in Grimes County

The Texas State Historical Society (Jackson 2013), Grimes County, indicated that Grimes County Texas had a colorful history. The earliest residents were the Bidaai Indians who lived there until their population declined in the late eighteenth and nineteenth centuries. In 1854, the surviving Bidaai were sent to reservations by the US government's removal program (Jackson 2013).

The resettlement of Grimes County was very suitable for the farm industry. Established as the first known stagecoach stop of Nolansville, the name was changed to Navasota in 1858 (Jackson 2013). Slave labor was a large part of the local economy in Navasota. African slaves were imported, sold, and used to work on many cotton plantations, and for labor during the early population boom that occurred from cotton, sugar, and timber and construction businesses. Nearby Anderson, Texas, was the source of guns, gunpowder, and shoe businesses that produced marketable goods as well.

In the 1880s, most people who migrated to Grimes County came from Alabama, Georgia, Louisiana, and Mississippi. Through exploration of the history of Grimes County, a potential, historical link to plantation and slave ownership of the Johnny Stone Plantation surfaced. A family by the surname Stoneham lived in Stoneham also, and they had history of plantation and slave ownership in Virginia, Georgia, Navasota, and Stoneham, Texas. Without exact information as to when Granny Fannie was enslaved and lived on Johnny Stoneham Plantation, much of the connection is conjecture.

Documentation was found to confirm that African slaves were imported to Grimes County, Texas, where they were sold and used to work on cotton plantations located in the area. US Census records confirmed that there was slave ownership in Grimes County by owners who had the surnames of "Stone" and "Stoneham." Some of the information discovered paralleled family stories about Granny Fannie's journey to Grimes County, Stoneham, Texas, but the information as a direct link to the history of Granny Fannie as a former slave is inconclusive.

Navasota had its boom eras, but it had bust periods also. There were disasters and epidemics of yellow fever and cholera that killed many people, causing numbers of people to flee the town in 1867 (Jackson 2013). After the end of the American Civil War, Blacks began to leave the area of Grimes County. The exodus continued for many years until about 1990 when reportedly less than 4,000 African-Americans remained. According to Jackson (2013), Navasota was a wild, lawless, boomtown where Confederate veterans roamed, torched, and killed black freedman. Uncontrollable militias, such as the Ku Klux Klan (KKK), flourished during the Jim Crow Era, which resulted in horrendous violence against black people.

Blacks were regularly threatened, assaulted, and killed in Navasota and nearby Anderson, Texas, which gave reason for the exodus that took place before and throughout the Civil Rights Movement through the 1990s (Jackson 2013). Based on oral stories, after living in Navasota, Granny Fannie and Dagg moved to Black Ridge in Milam County, Calvert, Texas. Some of the Green clan remained in the Navasota/Anderson area, while others migrated to Milam County.

Life in Milam County, Texas

There were no documented records of life in Milam County, because the courthouse burned down and country records were destroyed by fire in 1874. Due to the economic effects of the Great Depression of the1920s, life was very hard for the family, especially during the late 1800s and early 1900s. That period involved some of the most arduous, brutal, demeaning, and disparaging times in America, and those periods were even bleaker for black people.

In addition to social, environmental, and economic conditions, the country was torn apart by internal war, legalized "Jim Crow" terrorism against black people, racial segregation and discrimination, and disparate, inhumane treatment. African-Americans had no control over their destiny whatsoever. They experienced and suffered even deeper impacts of poverty. Family efforts involved recovering from the throes of slavery, and building a life as farmers in the direct aftermath of slavery and life in the segregated rural South.

People had to make ends meet, find creative ways to raise their families, and reconstruct life as free people with no assets. Despite the economic, racial, social, and environmental conditions, Granny Fannie and Dagg Green managed to create a life for themselves and their family. Before meeting the next generation of the Green/McGill family, stay tuned as you are introduced to some of the theories about Granny Fannie's associations and her early life.

Chapter 7
The Stoneham Family

The Meyer and Sargent Notes file by Pat West (Ancestry.com 2013), and other historical narratives and Internet records, led to speculation about a family called the Stonehams who are suspected as possible slave owners who bought Granny Fannie as a young slave girl. The Pat West files correspond to oral accounts of Granny Fannie's life in Stoneham in Grimes County, and Navasota, Texas. As mentioned, it is not clear whether Granny Fannie moved to Stoneham, Navasota, Grimes County, Texas before or after the Emancipation Proclamation in 1863. What is known is that she and Dagg lived there as sharecroppers for several years.

It is feasible to think that possibly one of the members of the Stoneham family who lived in Stoneham, Texas, was the slave master who purchased Fannie as a slave child, namely Henry John, George or John H. Stoneham (George's nephew). It is inconclusive, but a member of this Stoneham family could have been a town judge who was referred to as the "old white town judge" in oral family stories. Historical records indicated that one family member, John H. Stoneham, was an influential benefactor and founder of the town of Stoneham, Texas. He was involved in town politics and legal matters, so he might have had a connection to the law profession.

In addition, there may be a connection to George Stoneham or his nephew, John Stoneham, who both owned and had productive cotton plantations in Texas. In any event, more research is needed to verify which plantation was owned by which Stoneham, as well as their location and periods of slave ownership, if records still exist.

Henry John Stoneham

As reported in the Meyer and Sargent Notes, Pat West file (Ancestry.com 2013), Henry John Stoneham, the father, was a Revolutionary War veteran of five years, having served on the Virginia Line. According to Jackson, Texas State Historical Association (2013), he was born in Virginia around 1786. Henry ran away from home at age fourteen to join the Continental Army. In 1800, he and his wife, Jane Dillard, sold land that she inherited from her father to William K. Diggs. The land adjoined that of George Stoneham, Henry's brother.

Henry John and Jane Stoneham moved from Amherst County, Virginia, to Sparta Hancock County, Georgia, in 1801. Henry's unmarried brothers, Bryant and George Stoneham, moved with them, along with his uncles, Bryant and James. Henry and Jane had eleven children born in Virginia, and four more born in Georgia. According to War Pension records, Henry was wounded by a musket ball at the battle of Guilford's Courthouse. Obituary records of the *Georgia Gazette*, Athens, Georgia, indicated that Henry Stoneham died on January 17, 1815, at the age of fifty-two, at his home in Jackson County, Georgia. He was survived by his wife, Jane, and fifteen children (Pat West file: Ancestry.com 2013).

According to the Georgia County Census (Ancestry.com 1830, p. 345), Jane Dillard, Henry Stoneham's wife, was sixty to seventy years old when she lived in Jackson County, Georgia. According to the 1849 US Census, she lived in Conecuh County, Alabama. Jane was listed as head of the household along with two white males, two white females, and six slaves. This information is a possible link to Fannie's birthplace, which was Alabama.

Jane lived with three sons, John, Erastus, and Bryant, and a daughter, Susannah, before she moved to Grimes Prairie, Republic of Texas in 1845. According to the 1850 US Census (p.373B), Jane was ninety-two years old and lived in Grimes County, Texas, with three of her children, Susan, Bryant, and Erastus. Jane Stoneham lived to be one hundred years of age, and was buried in the Stoneham

Cemetery in Stoneham, Grimes County, Texas (The Pat West, Meyer and Sargent Notes, Ancestry.com 2013).

George Stoneham

George Stoneham (Stonam, Stonum) was a pioneer and cotton planter who lived in Jackson County, Georgia. According to the Texas State Historical Association (2013), George—named after his father's brother, George—was the oldest son of Henry and Jane Dillard Stoneham (Texas State Historical Association, Jackson 2013). George's family moved to Jackson County, Georgia, when he was fifteen years of age. Around 1819, he along with his brother, Joseph, moved to Conecuh County, Alabama. Again, this fact can be connected to the birthplace of Granny Fannie, especially since her sons, listed her birthplace as Alabama in the 1910 and subsequent US Census records.

George and Joseph successfully started a boating business that transported large bales of cotton down the Conecuh River from Alabama to Brooklyn and Pensacola, Florida (Jackson 2013). Joseph (George's brother) and his wife both died of fever in 1836, which is a connection to the yellow fever epidemic that was noted in the 1880s in the previous chapter, so George became the guardian of Joseph's four sons. In 1844, he took his nephews and many slaves to Grimes County, Texas, where he purchased a large tract of land from Margaret McIntyre in Grimes Prairie.

The Texas State Historical Association (Jackson 2013) indicated that the tract of land that was purchased is now known as southern Grimes County. The rest of his family joined George in 1845. He was a successful cotton planter who raised hundreds of bales annually. According to the Handbook of Texas Online, by 1860, he owned 115 slaves. George was one of the wealthiest men in Grimes County, with an estate worth more than $150,000, which was a great deal of wealth at that time. He gave land and slaves to each of his nephews as they became of age.

As noted, slave ownership did not come without consequences. Financial and legal aftermaths were created by the Emancipation and the Civil War. As a slave owner, George Stoneham was a perfect example. By the end of 1865, his cotton farming business was in ruins. Reportedly, by the end of the Civil War, his remaining property was worth only about $28,000, which was still a considerable amount of money during those times. After 1869, there were no additional county tax records recorded for George Stoneham, so apparently he died sometime before or during 1869 (Taylor 1982).

John Henry Stoneham

As stated, John Henry Stoneham, George Stoneham's second nephew, was very prominent in the town of Stoneham; in fact, he is frequently mentioned in historical accounts as being a founder of the town of Stoneham (Taylor 1982). According to accounts in the Wood & Torbert Family History on Ancestry.com, John H. Stoneham was born on December 29, 1829 and died on at the age of 64 on August 3, 1894. His father, Joseph Dillard Stoneham, was born on August 8, 1787 and died on March 28, 1836. John's mother, Rebecca Crowder was born around 1790 and died around 1836. According to the U.S. Federal Census of June 1, 1850 for Grimes County, Texas for George Stoneham's household, John H. Stoneham was among the family members, along with Augustus Stoneham, James Stoneham, Margaret Stoneham, Henry Stoneham, Robert Stoneham, Elizabeth Stoneham, Albert Stoneham, Levina Stoneham, Henry Bryant Stoneham and Joseph D. Stoneham.

John married Elizabeth Eveline Greenwood, who was the daughter of Franklin Jarvis Greenwood (a colonist) and Mary Jane Montgomery. According the Wood & Torbert Family History, John and Elizabeth had several children, namely, Joseph F. Stoneham, born in 1854, Edwin B. Stoneham born on May 20, 1855 and died on June 8, 1865, John Oscar Stoneham born on April 19, 1858, and died on May 28, 1906, David Stoneham born in 1859, William Stoneham born on May 12, 1861 and died in July 1868, Mary Ida Stoneham born on April 12, 1863 and died on September 26, 1867, George Stoneham born in 1865, Henry Stoneham born in 1867, Howard R. Stoneham born on March 2, 1869, Infant Stoneham born on January. 22, 1878 and died on February 24, 1878, and Gernice Stoneham born on July. 8. 1878. (All names, births and death dates are approximate).

John established a general mercantile store near the rail line in Stoneham, which was purchased by the Gulf, Colorado, and Santa Fe Railway in 1885. Also, he established a post office in Stoneham in 1890, in which he was postmaster. According to the *Handbook of Texas Online*, Charles Christopher Jackson (2013) in 1879, the Central and Montgomery Railway acquired a right-of-way and land was commissioned from local landowner, John H. Stoneham. In recognition, of that deed, the town of Stoneham was named in John's honor. He was buried in the Stoneham Cemetery in Grimes, Texas.

Consistent with the above findings, according to a post by an unidentified person only known as "Shirley" on Ancestry.com, who was searching for her family connections, information was provided about the Stonehams on a Message Board on Ancestry.com. According to the information, enslaved ancestors and their family and friends migrated with some of the Stoneham family, first from Virginia at the turn of the nineteenth century when they moved to Jackson, County, Georgia. After the death of Henry John Stoneham, the sons moved into Brooklyn Conecuh County, Alabama. The Stonehams migrated into Texas around 1844 when George Stoneham migrated to the Grimes/Montgomery County area. The remainder of the Stonehams arrived from Alabama around 1845, where they purchased land in Grimes County at that time. It is believed that the African Americans traveled this same pattern with the Stonehams as slaves.

Further information was posted from oral history of Shirley's family. On the Message Board, she explained that the older slaves were Virginians by birth, with later births in Georgia and Alabama. If that is factual, it could be concluded that Granny Fannie's parents possibly were among these slaves and could have been born in Virginia or Georgia. The online poster, Shirley, went on to say:

> "...Our [her] great grandmother {no reference
> to Granny Fannie] remembered her folks saying
> that they traveled overland as part of a large group

of slaves, many of whom were related. After slavery ended, many of this same group of folks, left Grimes County, a substantial number of them moving to Parsons, Kansas…. Some who didn't make it to Kansas, moved in the late 1880s to Denton/Red River and Milam County, [Texas], where there are still members of the Stoneham family living."

Given this information, it is conceivable to think that Granny Fannie may have been among those who traveled this journey to Grimes and Milam County, Texas.

Hypothetical Conclusions

After the Emancipation of Slaves in 1863, financial and legal consequences were faced by slaves and slave owners and their "mixed race" children, who suffered also. Documents acquired from the Augusta County, Virginia, Chancery Causes 1974–1912, indicated that George Stoneham Sr., as well as other slave owners, had a trail of "mixed race" children who were fathered in Virginia, Georgia, Texas, and other places.

The fact that George Stoneham fathered several children of color was confirmed by several processing notes that were recorded in the Augusta, Virginia, County Courts. As noted below, before he moved to Georgia, a person by the name of William Stoneham filed a lawsuit in Virginia in 1814 (Augusta County, VA. Chancery Causes 1874-1912; Processing Notes for the Library in Augusta, County and Virginia, Case 1814-097).

William Stoneham

Plaintiff, William Stoneham, a freeman of color, filed a lawsuit against the administrator of George Stoneham. The administrator of George Stoneham's estate was his son-in-law, who also was named William Stoneham. He claimed that while George Stoneham was alive, he "emancipated several of his children of color." One of those children was William Stoneham. According to the court documents, a Deed of Emancipation was made for William in 1806. As noted in court records, after a period of six years, George was "to have time to pay off any claims that might be made against him." In addition, time and provisions were to be given for the children to "learn an industry to enable the possibility of making their way through the world."

It appears that William sought to collect the promises of George Stoneham, his birth father. The finding of the claim was unclear as to whether his case was won, because the conclusion of the ruling was not documented (Augusta County, VA. Chancery Causes 1974-1912; Processing Notes for the Library in Augusta, County, and Virginia).

Eliza Stoneham

In 2014, there was representation of another court case of Eliza Stoneham that was posted online for auction by Scott Winslow Associates, Inc. The starting bid for the Eliza Stoneham's court case documents was $400,000. A lawsuit (1816-074), *Administrator of George Stoneham versus Henry Stoneham*, was filed against George Stoneham by the former slave woman, Eliza Stoneham, after his death in 1868. It claimed that for many years before the death of George Stoneham, "he had a strong connection with a woman of color who was his slave." Eliza claimed that she and George "had a number of children" (Archives, Library of Virginia, Augusta County, Virginia, Chancery Causes 1746–1912).

On October 26, 1879, claimant Eliza Stoneham, a former slave woman, filed the unique court case in Grimes County, Texas. She claimed that she was George's wife, and had the legal rights to control his estate. George's brother, Bryant and nephew George Jr., contested the validity of the claim made by Eliza. In accordance with the online document that was posted by Scott Winslow Associates, Inc. in 2014, the Administrators of George Stoneham's estate, Bryant and George Jr., responded by indicating that the deceased George

Stoneham "left little or no estate except the female Negroes aforesaid, and her children all of whom he emancipated."

Court records introduced in the Texas Supreme Court traced the lawsuit filed by Eliza Stoneham to the point of appeal. The documents apparently certified that the initial court case was tried before probate court in Grimes County Texas. The online document indicated that Eliza was the legal wife of George Stoneham, but his nephews, Bryant and George Stoneham Jr., claimed that the slave woman was never the legal wife or widow of George Stoneham.

Bryant and George Jr. maintained they were the nearest relatives, and should control the estate of George Sr. Additionally, they claimed that Eliza was a slave prior to the freedom of the "Slaves in the Southern States," and was indeed the property of George Stoneham. Their summation was that she was "a Negro, of ... African blood, and not his wife (Slave Claims to be Plantation Owner's Wife, Scott Winslow and Associates, Inc. 2013)."

On October 1, 1868, the lower Grimes County Court ruled that "Eliza Stoneham was never the wife of said George Stoneham" and his nearest kin, Bryant and George Jr., were entitled to his estate. Eliza Stoneham appealed to the District Court. After many lengthy delays, prompted by motions from the lawyers of Stoneham's blood relatives, in 1870, the District Court overturned the previous ruling, and declared that Elizabeth Stoneham (Eliza) was the lawful wife of George Stoneham at the time of his death, and was entitled to his estate. The District Court ruled also that Bryant and George Jr., had to pay Eliza's court costs. George and Bryant appealed the case in Supreme Court.

As to whether Eliza won the case was not documented. She may have had strong evidence for her claims, but as was common during the era of the Emancipation, Reconstruction, and Civil War, many court cases were filed by freed slaves who sued slave owners. Most cases took the same path as Eliza Stoneham's lawsuit. The lower courts usually ruled for the whites, regardless of evidence. The higher courts tended to reverse the rulings of the lower courts, which often infringed on the rights of slaves (Archives, Library of Virginia, Augusta County, Virginia, Chancery Causes, 1746–1912).

Questions Remain

The court cases and records cited against George Stoneham documented that he and other slave owners had a history of fathering children of enslaved women. However, it cannot be said with certainty that the slave owner associated with Granny Fannie and her sons, was among the Stoneham family of Virginia, Georgia, Alabama, and Grimes County, Navasota, Texas.

According to Eleanor Colson (2007)—who transcribed numbers, ages, sexes, and color of slaves held by slave owners for the 1850 Slave Census for Grimes County—both George Stoneham Sr. and George Stoneham Jr. owned slaves who ranged from three months to seventy years of age (Texas Grimes African-Americans, Rootsweb. Ancestry.com). Consistent with the theme of the unfinished journey, our family history will require additional steps to either verify or refute this potential connection to Granny Fannie.

Leading questions that require more study include, "What is the exact name of the 'old town judge and slave master' who fathered Fannie's sons? And what is the exact location of the Johnny Stone Plantation that is attached to Granny Fannie's history? What was the pathway of Dagg Green (Fannie's husband), and where and how did he acquire his last name 'Green'?" Additionally, other questions remain about the Stoneham family. "Was John H. Stoneham the 'old town judge' and slave owner who was referred to in oral stories about Granny Fannie? Was the Johnny Stone Plantation named after John H. Stoneham? Was Granny Fannie among the unnamed slaves recorded in the Grimes County US Census of 1859 where George Sr. and George Stoneham, Jr., and John H. Stoneham were lucrative slave owners?"

There is a tangible association of Granny Fannie and the Stoneham family. It was reported that after the Emancipation Proclamation and slaves were freed, John H. Stoneham bequeathed five acres of land to Granny Fannie, which became the site of the historically black Coaxberry (Cokesberry) Cemetery and the Coaxberry Baptist Church in Anderson, Navasota, Texas. Granny Fannie and many members of the Green family are buried in the Coaxberry Cemetery. According to Jerry Green's daughter and Granny Fannie's granddaughter, Adelaide Green Ruckett, who served as church secretary of the Coaxberry Baptist Church for many years, as a part of the annual church report, she customarily provided the history of the Coaxberry Baptist Church. Adelaide often reported that John H. Stoneham bequeathed land to Granny Fannie in 1865.

That information sheds a great deal of light on some of the initial ancestral questions. In addition to providing a direct link of John H. Stoneham and Granny Fannie, perhaps another conclusion can be drawn. Given there was a John H. Stoneham Plantation in the Stoneham, Texas area, possibly, the Johnny Stoneham Plantation that was referred to in ancestral oral stories, was misnamed in translation throughout the generations. Instead, in actuality, it may have been the John Stoneham Plantation where Granny Fannie lived as a slave and had children. Therefore, it is highly suspected, but not verified, that John H. Stoneham may have been the slave master who fathered Granny Fannie's children.

Since there is no family source to provide additional information, further clues and possibilities must be uncovered and verified through other sources. What is known thus far is life was very hard for Granny Fannie, Dagg, and their children as they grew from childhood to adulthood. As mentioned, experiences and effects of slavery, the Civil War, the Emancipation of Slaves, the Reconstruction, Post Reconstruction Period, and the Great Depression of the early 1920s were some of the most arduous, brutal, demeaning, disparaging times in American history; and they were even bleaker for black people like the Greens and McGills.

In addition to the social, racial, and economic conditions, and the inhumanity of slavery and its aftermath, the country was torn by internal war, legalized segregation, and the "Jim Crow" Era (inhumane treatment and racial discrimination against black people). During those times, there was no control over circumstances of those who had been enslaved. There were even deeper impacts of severe poverty, especially since enslaved people had no source of income or resources for themselves or their families.

The Greens, and those who had similar experiences, had to make ends meet, find creative ways to raise their family, and reconstruct life as free people with no employment or assets. It is mind-boggling to fathom how they could somehow make the miraculous evolution of survival under such hopeless circumstances. Despite the conditions, Granny Fannie and Dagg Green managed to carve out a life for themselves. Stay tuned as you meet some of their children, succeeding generations of children, and their children's children.

Chapter 8
Riley Green, Sr.[3]

As noted, Riley Green, Sr., the son of Granny Fannie was born on the Johnny Stone Plantation around 1881. His date of death is unknown. According to the 1900 U.S. Federal Census, Riley and Ona (Oney) (Annie) Jackson were married in 1878. Riley indicated in census records that his father and mother (Fannie) were born in Alabama; however, in the 1930 U.S. Federal Census, he and Oney both listed their parent's birthplace as Texas. In 1900, they lived in Justice Precinct 1, Grimes County, Texas. At that time, Riley was 53 years of age, and Oney was 44 years of age. Riley's son, Riley Jr., age 22, and daughter-in-law, Julia, age 20, lived in the home during the 1900 U.S. Census.

1900 Census records indicated that Riley, Sr. could read and write, had attended school, and his occupation was a farmer. Census records for Ona Green, included Riley Green, Sr, Jimmy Green (19 years of age), Robert Green (22), Harriett Spain (17), son-in-law Daniel Spain (24), Riley Jr. (12), Mary Green (11), and grand-daughter, Eloise Spain (1) as living in the household. You will read more about some Riley Green, Sr.'s children below.

Riley Green, Sr.'s Offspring
Riley Green, Jr.

---

[3] Co-writers Jacqueline Marie Voss Flood and Leslie Maria (Rea) Amos Miles were the great-granddaughters of Riley Green, Sr. Most of their memories are about their great grandfather, Riley, Green Jr. Rea died in 2016.

Although there is not a great deal known about Riley Green, Sr., there were memories of Riley Green, Jr. Cousin Reddie Mae Pittman King recalled that Riley Green, Jr. (Uncle Son) often went along with she and her brother, Isaiah, on cotton-picking trips, when her daddy, Andrew Pittman, contracted for acreage. They met and picked up Uncle Son when he traveled from West Texas to Branchville on the train to go to pick cotton, where they brought back loads of watermelon to sell also. Riley Green (Uncle Son), the brother of James (Jim) Green Sr. was born on December 18, 1887 in Texas.

Since updated technology and testing equipment did not exist in those days, there was not much knowledge about treatment for diabetes or "Sugar" as it was called then. Eventually, Uncle Riley went blind and died from diabetes in 1936.

As mentioned, Riley's Green, Jr.'s son, Jasper Green (deceased), was born on August 10, 1910 in Baileyville, Texas, and died on November 20, 1986, in Monahan, Texas. Jasper's mother, Teary Franklin, was born on January 2, 1892, in Robertson, Texas, and died on December 14, 1973, in Stamford, Texas. Riley Green married Julia Motley, who was born on January 18, 1894, and died on June 27, 1966, in Houston, Texas. Riley and Julia's daughter, Charles Ruby Green, was born on December 1, 1919, in Branchville, Texas.

Jasper Green married Katie Lee Gregory on October 14, 1927. Katie was born on November 14, 1909, in Bremond, Texas, and died on February 1, 1992, in Arlington, Texas. They had six children, Verda Mae, Verneda (Sister Baby), Roger Mae, Robert O'Neal (Squeaky), Katie Marie (Lady,) and Charlie Lee.

Verda Mae Green Henry Harris Johnson Batiste (deceased) was born on September 5, 1928, in Mexia, Texas, and died on June 3, 2002, in Houston, Texas. Verda had two children, Jamaal Nyerere, (James Willis Henry) and JoAnn Susan Harris Johnson. She had one grandson, Brandon Johnson.

Verneda (Sister Baby) Green Stalling was born on June 19, 1930, in Coolidge, Texas. She married Robert D. Stalling (deceased), who was born on April 5, 1928, and died on July 18, 2011. They had five children, Willie Mae (deceased), Rudolph (Rudy), Michael Wayne, Beverly Ann, and Nell Yvvonne.

Willie Mae Stalling Malone married Billy Ray Malone, and they had three children, Belinda of Waco, Texas, Billy Jr. of Plano, Texas, and LaTonya of Waco, Texas. She had six grandchildren, Demacun, Desrich, Daffine, Chance, Raven, and Reginald; and seven great-grandchildren, Demacun Jr., Sharavion, Ri, D'Erick, and Journey.

Rudolph (Rudy) Stalling of Austin, Texas, married Carolyn June Wydenra. They had three daughters, Dina, Catherine, and Jessica. Rudy has eight grandchildren, Jazmyne (deceased), Elijah, Tyler, Xavier, Donovan, Braylen, Jordan, and Jeremiah.

Michael Wayne Stalling of Houston, Texas, married Betty Griffin, and they had three children, Michael Jr., Robert, and Michelle; and five grandchildren, Taylor, Evan Michael, Ethan Edward, Vernesia, and Shania. Beverly Ann Stalling Wilson of Waco, Texas, married Clarence Wilson. Beverly has one daughter, LaShonda, of Arlington, Texas. Nell Yvonne Stalling Love of Waco, Texas, married Robert Love and had four children, Robert, Deodrick, Vernetria, and Nikoyle of Waco, Texas. Nell has six grandchildren, Vernesia, Shania, Ambraneq, Odision, Mathis, and Madison.

Roger Mae Amos Aaron Baker Allen (deceased) was born on October 6, 1932, in Branchville, Texas. She died on January 27, 2013, in Arlington, Texas. Roger had one daughter, Leslie Maria "Rea" Amos Miles (deceased). Roger and her husband, and two grandchildren, often attended the Green McGill Reunions. She created the programs for the family reunions during Reddie Mae's tenure.

Leslie (Rea) married Horace Miles, and they had two sons, Roderick O'Neal and Leon Anthony. Rea lived in Grand Prairie, Texas, until his death in August 2016. Roderick, Rea's son, has two children with Shelia Scott, DeMarcus DeShae and Lesley Jean Miles. He married Chrystallia Jones and has two children, Daneshia Dionne Jones and Alundis Asean Jones; and a stepdaughter, Brittanne Jones. Roderick has two grandchildren, Landen and Markel Johnson, and one step-granddaughter, D'Zariah Nichole Lee. Leon Anthony Miles Sr. has one child with Dursha Smith, Jonathan Miles; and one son with Dana Mays, Leon Anthony Miles. He married Wilneshia Cooper, and they have three children, Anthony, Leona, King Miles; and two stepchildren, Avion and Alexius.

Robert O'Neal (Squeeky) Green (deceased) was born on July 12, 1937, in Milam, Texas. He died on June 9, 2003, in Arlington, Texas. Robert married Alice Wigging, and they had two children, Robert Jr., and Trina Green. Squeaky has two grandchildren, Dominic and Brianna.

Katie Marie "Lady" Voss Toliver Hicks was born on born June 30, 1939, in Milam, Texas. She died on May 12, 2014, in Houston, Texas. Katie married Ross Voss (deceased) and they had three children, Russell Lawrence of Temple, Texas; Kathy Lenore of Waco, Texas; and Jacqueline Marie of Baltimore, Maryland. Katie later married William McArthur Toliver, and had one son, Harlan Keith of Houston, Texas.

Russell Lawrence Voss had five children, Tiswona, Brandon, Joshua, Alexander, and Alexandria Jackson. He has three grandchildren, Xavier, Anaya, and Amiyah. Kathy Lenore Voss Bogas has three children, Akil, Carlton Steele (deceased) and Brittany. She has seven grandchildren, Akil Jr., Arnett, Shen, Demacus Jr., Tomorrow, and Nafla.

Jacqueline Marie Voss Flood married Earl Flood (deceased). Jackie has five children, Dameon Griggs, John and Kyle Carter, Kiana and Willie Jr. Walker (deceased). She has eight grandchildren, Dameon, Dyamon and Dameris Griggs, Xavier, Jontel, Kanyiah, Kyle Jr., Carter, Elijah Walker; and one step-grandson, Christopher Flood.

Harlan Keith Toliver does not have children. Charles Lee Green was born on March 13, 1942. He married to Tillie Antoine (deceased) of Houston, Texas. They had a daughter, Deidra Green, and granddaughters, Shomare and Jasmine of Houston, Texas.

Charles Ruby Green married Clarence Jones, and they had no children. She was manager of the Dowling Theater in Houston, and often allowed family members to watch movies at the theater. She died in Houston, Texas, on May 22, 1975.

Chapter 9
Jack W. Green

Imagine it is the early 1900s and you are sitting in a large hall as part of the audience who is anxiously awaiting to hear the speaker who is known as one who "stands without a rival on a practical lecture!" Meet Professor, Jack W. Green, Granny Fannie's baby son.

Despite racial tension, oppression and coping with discrimination and challenges that were common in America before and after the turn of the century, blacks had to find ways to deal with their circumstances. There were those like Jack W. Green, who somehow found ways to ascend as a first-generation freedman. Some of his accomplishments were highlighted in an August 3, 2014 Blog by Russell Cushman, a sixth generation Navasota, Texas landscape painter, sculptor, photographer, writer and historian who covers the history of the Brazos Valley, Texas. Russell gave permission to share a brief portrait of Jack W. Green's uniqueness, as well as images of him as published in his Blog in the eNavasota Current (2014):

Jack Green: The "Tex Electric and Jubilee Speaker"

"Grimes County has produced or been the home for famous Texas singers, actors and lawmen. But before most of them came to their fifteen minutes of fame, we gave the world a great motivational speaker.

"Jack Green was born in Anderson, Texas in 1867. One of the first freeborn blacks in Grimes County, Jack became the archetypal "boot-strapper," making his life and love the fields of inspiration and education. He went to the little one-room schoolhouse provided for him and the other children of recently freed slaves, whenever there was not planting or harvesting to do. He became a Christian when just a boy, and he finished High School at age 16, something very rare for a black youth, in 1883. He must have had wonderful encouragement from his family and the community, because the next year he attended Prairie View A& M College in 1884, when just 17 years old. Soon he was back in Grimes County teaching what he had learned. For most of his life he was known as "Professor" J. W. Green.

I am trying to find out more about Jack Green, as he must have had a fascinating career. I have two posters about him made around the turn of the Century, and they tell us that he was active in his church, the Masonic Lodge, and other religious organizations. He advertised that he was a member of the Masonic Lodge, F.H.N.M., Prince Hall affiliation, whatever that was. Sounds important. But more significantly, he became a popular public speaker, traveling in eleven states throughout the South. From Texas to Indiana to Tennessee, Jack Green was called the "Tex Electric and Jubilee Speaker."

One poster touted that this "well known" lecturer had taught school in Grimes County for several years, and had been active in many church building programs, and had served for 41 years as Worshipful Master of his lodge. Another poster claimed apologetically that he was "without a rival on a practical lecture." His last place of service was noted as Deacon and Supervisor of Coaxberry M.B.C.W.M., of Ulmer Lodge, in Richards, Texas.

And perhaps most noteworthy, considering the racial tension and oppression which defined those times for this first- generation freedman, was the thin notation at the very bottom of the poster;

"All are invited regardless of race, denomination. There will be nothing said to offend anyone present."

Printed with permission from Russell Cushman (eNavasota Current, 2014)
Images of Posters of Jack Green Referred to in Cushman's Blog

Jack W. Green

Photo of Jack Green recently (2014)
discovered for sale on eBay (and restored).

COMING!

PROF. J. W. GREEN

Of Auderson, Texas

Known as Tex Electric and Jubilee Speaker

He stands today without a rival on a practical lecture. Lectured in the principal parts of eleven states to large and enthusiastic audiences. He is so well known in the state of Tennessee he is often referred to as a map of the state.

Prof W. G. Haynes, Nashville—I always go out to hear him, I learn something.

Peter Barksdale, Mail Service—He is speedy but speaks clear.

R. J. Huges, Evansville, Ind.—Listen at him, he has a voice like a white man.

He is one of our own—Mrs. Irine Winn, Past Grand Matron H. O. J., Dallas, Texas.

He has held many special positions. Special Deputy, Grand W. M. Masonic Lodge; Deputy G. H. P.; Secretary of the Board of St. Paul Association; Now Deacon and Supervisor Coaxberry M. B. C. W. M. of Ulmer Lodge, F. A. M. No. 349, Richards, Texas.

Well Known Lecturer

HEAR HIM

All are invited regardless of race, denomination. There will be nothing said to offend any one present.

Will Lecture At

....

.... 19....

Jack W. Green

JACK W. GREEN
ANDERSON, TEXAS

Born July 17, 1867. Joined the church in his early life, finished high school in Anderson in 1883; I. M. Terrell, principal. Ex-student of Prairie View. He is now the Senior Student of Prairie View A. & M. College.

J. W. GREEN

Anderson, Texas
Born July 12, 1867

Attended the Rural Schools in this Community

Finished High School in Anderson, Texas 1883
Prof. I. M. Terrell
Principal

Ex-student of Prairie View A. & M. College 1884. Taught school several years in his home county. Joined the church in his early life, and was active in many building programs. Active in the Masonic Lodge, F.A.N.M., Prince Hall Affiliation. Traveled extensively, through eleven states, forty-one years W.M. of Masonic Lodge, F.A.N.M., P.H.A.

Baytown, Texas
Sta. A, Box 3247
Phone H21061

Chapter 10
James (Jim) Green, Sr.

Grandpa James (Jim) Green Sr., Riley Green's son and my grand-father, was known as a consummate horse breeder. As noted in the Sixteenth Census of the United States 1940 (Ancestry.com), he was born in 1873 in Branchville, Texas. At first glance, it appeared that his exact birthdate was located; however, as I searched a bit more, the information remains questionable, because there were different dates and ages recorded in different US Census records.

For instance, the Thirteenth United States Population Census (1910) found on Ancestry.com listed Jim as a mulatto born in Navasota, Texas. If that information was correct, his birthdate would have been 1881. The 1930 and 1940 US Census Records indicated that Grandpa Jim was born in Branchville, Texas in 1873. In the 1920 census, he was registered as fifty years old, which was not con-sistent with data noted ten years earlier. According to the Sixteenth Census of the United States, 1940 (Ancestry.com), he was born in 1873 in Branchville, Texas. If Jim Green Sr. was fifty years old in 1920, his birthdate would have been around 1870. His daughter, Ruth Green, listed his birthdate on his Texas Death Certificate as born on September 28, 1881 in Grimes, Texas, the son of Annie (Oney) and Riley Green.

My grandfather, James (Jim) Green, Sr., was known as a very handsome man. Grandfather Jim married Grandmother Sirlina A. McGill (date uncertain), and they raised seven children: four daughters, Ruth, Juanita, Charlie Mae (May), Dorothy, and Maggie Samantha Holloway. As mentioned, Maggie was Sirlina's daughter from a previous marriage, however, she was raised as Grandpa's child.

Grandpa Jim and Grandma Sirlina had two sons, James (Jim) Jr. (Uncle Buddy), and Elbert Lee Green, my father. According to data on Ancestry.com, he had three daughters and two sons with Sirlina A. McGill between 1910 and 1923. James Green, Sr. died on April 21, 1941 in Maysfield, Texas, at the age of 59. He was buried in Milam County, Texas.

According to census data and oral history, Grandpa Jim did not attend school or college, and his occupation was recorded as a farmer. In the 1920 US Census records, he lived with his wife, Sirlina Green, in Justice Precinct 2, District 0119, Milam County, Texas. In the 1930 US Census, James Green Sr. was listed as fifty-six years old. Given that information, again his birth year would have been around 1873.

The 1920 US Population Census reported that there was another child by the name Susie Green, aged seven, who lived in the home. However, she was not living in the home in the 1930 census. It was reported that Grandpa Jim had children in the area prior to marrying Grandma Sirlina. There was mention of a child by the name of Lesley Green, who was buried in the Providence Cemetery in Branchville, Texas, but there is no additional information about him.

Grandpa James (Jim) Green's Children
Aunt Koosie's Family

Maggie Samantha James Rosemond Hollaway, my Aunt Koosie, was known throughout the area for her famous homemade teacakes. She always had a crock of teacakes on her stove, and "they were to die for." I do not know why she was called Aunt Koosie, but for a long time, I never knew her by any other name. Maggie was born to Sirlina McGill James and Henry James in Grimes County, Navasota, Texas, on August 13, 1900. Aunt Koosie died in Cameron, Texas, at the age of ninety-five on November 1, 1995.

Maggie met and married Wade Rosemond on what is believed to have been May 29, 1982. They had five children, Lawrence (Bubba), Everlonia (Sister), Robert D. (RD), Johnny, and Esther Rosemond. Maggie later married Carson Holloway in 1984. Carson was called "Popa" by the children and grandchildren, and he raised Wade and

Maggie's children as his own. Maggie was known as "Big Moma" to her grands, great grands, and great-great grands. As you will see, the branches of the family tree that sprung from Aunt Koosie were sizeable.

Lawrence (Bubba) Rosemond married Maenishie Young (both deceased). Maenishie had one son, Vernell Kemp (deceased). Lawrence and Maenishie had twelve children together, and thirteen combined: six daughters, Rosel, Vella D., Princella (Mama Nae), Geneva (Moot), Dorothy (June), and Celestine (Sue); and seven sons, Vernell Kemp, Lawrence Jr. (Man), Raymond (Sweet Papa), Waymond (Son), Leroy, David, and Johnny Rosemond.

Lawrence (Bubba) raised Vernell Kemp as his own son. He married Betty Jo Brown and they had nine children, Vernell (Tampa) Kemp Jr., Jerry, Linda, Barbara, Diane, James Earl, Theresa, Randy, and Cheryl Kemp. Vernell (Tampa) Kemp Jr. married Beverly Thompson, and they have three children, La Chaundra, who has two children; Cheree, who has two children; and Portia, who has two children. Jerry Kemp married Joyce, and they have two children, Jeremy, who has two children; and Christy, who has one child. Linda Kemp married Danny Johnson (deceased). They had two children.

Barbara Kemp who married George Mitchell, has three children, Sharva, who has one child; Katricia, who has three children; and Camille. Diane Kemp married Willie Webster, and they have three children, Lakeisha, who has three children; Kimberly; and Kassadi, who has two children. James Earl Kemp married Gloria Brockington (divorced). They have five children, Kristi, who has one child; Daryl, who has three children; Ashley, who has three children; and (twins) James Jr., and Janika Kemp.

Theresa Kemp married George Sims, and they have two children, Kendral, who has one child; and Ketric who has two children. Randy Kemp married Goldie Fletcher and they have three children: Lamar, who has five children, Devin, and Shanequa Kemp. Cheryl Kemp married Phillip Bivens and they have three children, Tamecqua, who has one child; Breyan, who has one child; and Chericia.

Lawrence (Man) Rosemond Jr. (deceased) married Mary Louise Simmons, and they had one daughter, Renea Davis, who has four children, NyQuithia Washington, Maskeshia Washington, Billy D. Davis, and Elantra Davis. Rosel Rosemond Randle married Hurl Randle, both deceased. They had children, Joyce Ann, Hermon Jr., and Charles L. McGee, all deceased.

Son, Roy L. Collins, and Temple J. James (deceased) had two children, daughter Lesa Martinez, and son Waymon James. Lesa Martinez had a daughter, Jaylen Martinez. Waymon James has two daughters, Tiara, and Kyra James. Mary Ann McGee has two daughters, Machelle Mathis who has two sons; Vontrea, DeVonte Mathis, and Monica Orona, who has two sets of twin daughters, Tyra and Jyra, and daughter and son, Alexsus and Antqwon Griggs.

Linda Kay Witherspoon has three daughters, Shayla, Sabrina, and Shervett Witherspoon.

Shayla's children are Rodney Green Jr., (deceased), Rodrick Green, Raheem Green, Mercedes Green, Rashawn Green, and Jaden Green. Sabrina's children are Christina Witherspoon, Nicholas Edwards, Natasha Darnell, and Quinterious Darnell. Shervette Witherspoon has no children.

Barbara Smith has a daughter, Linda Rosemond who has two daughters, Zaria and Zamya Darnell; and sons, Morris Randle (Kaleigh), Morris Jr, Serenity, and Faith Randle. Depatrick Rosemond has a son, De'Andre Rosemond. James Lester Randle has a son, Justin White, and daughter, Mackeish Moore. Betty Jo Rosemond has a son, Charles L. Rosemond, who has two children, Marcquis Rosemond, and Raquel Green.

Dewon Rosemond has children, Alajia Rosemond, Gia Bree Rosemond, and Cashious Rosemond. Mitchell's children are: Zy'Qutintavia Mitchell, Javion, Joshua Smith Jr., and Ja'Zyrion Smith.

Vella D. Rosemond Pinkston married W. T. Pinkston and they have seven children. Vella Dee later, married Amos Jefferson (Cuttwright), and they have two children. Later, Vella D. married L.C. Alexander, and they have one child. Altogether, Vella D. has ten children. Betty Pinkston has six children, Kyrone Pinkston and Tyrone have four children; Randy Pinkston, who has eight children; Darrell Pinkston, who has three children; Edward Pinkston, who has three children; Jonathan (PeeWee) Pinkston has two children; and Brnesha Pinkston, who has four children.

Willie (Fatso) T. Pinkston (deceased) had no children. Larry D. Pinkston (deceased) had four children: Treadean Williams, who has one child, Latonya (Lorraine), LaQuita Davis, Shannon Whiterspoon, and Terry Lee Pinkston and Shakesha. Terry has twins, Brenda Lee Pinkston Durand, who married Adrian Durand and had two children, Meosha and Mesha Pinkston Smith. Mesha married James Smith III and had two children, Shakesha (Wookie) and Gipson, who has one child.

Margie Ann Rosemond (deceased) had four daughters: Martha, Noressa; Lanett; and LaTasha. Martha Collins married Nathaniel Collins and they have a son, Joel Collins. Noressa has two daughters, Mosiah, and Kyiana. Lanett has a daughter, Kamry, and son, Tyrone. LaTasha has four daughters, Alexandra, Rashia, Ashanta, and Alicia.

Lawrence Charles Rosemond and Gloria have five daughters, Nastasia, who has seven children: Charlqwaindrick; Sha'terria; Naziya; Charlevon; Lawrence II; Cleresia; and Deriah; Tiearea has four children: Lezaria, Dre'Terria, Sa'Nyah, and Juan III); (Little) Princella, Tameka, and Lashawn do not have children. Lawrence Charles and Gloria had one son, Charles Green, deceased. Sara Ann Long McConic married Rickey McConic, and had two sons and a daughter, Joel Williams (deceased), Cedric Long, and LaToya Johnson, who has five children, Joelishia, Kebra, Myjae, DJ; and Chyra.

Jo Ann Dancer Wright has two sons: Dameon, whose children are Shawn; Tyler and Abcde Dancer; and son, (Little) Will Jr., who has three daughters, Kiara, Brittani, and Lex Wright, who has a daughter, Lakina (Kina) (deceased). Lakina has a daughter, Kyra. Betty Ann Dancer Riddley has three daughters, Kenica, whose children are Kehonia and Dewion: Karen, whose children are Denaisha, Deniya and Tay'Voisha, and Julian; and daughter, Debra Ann Dancer, who has a daughter, Shaquetha, who has twin boys and a daughter, Shavonder and Devondra (deceased), and Khalie. Johnny Otis Dancer Jr. has three children, Samera, Alexus, and son, Johnny Jr.

Waymon (Son) Rosemond (deceased) and Shirley Stephens (deceased) had a daughter, Angela who married Robert Finley.

They have two children, Latausha Finley, and Paul Anthony Finley. Latausha Finley has three children, A'Niya, Guthinji, Sa'Miya Finley, and Paul Anthony Finley. Sa'Miya has one child; ADeAndre LaMont Greer Jr. Paul has two children: Kaiden, and Karson Finley.

Geneva (Moot) Rosemond Simmons married Andrew Simmons (deceased) and has nine children, Jealdine (Jearl) Simmons Witherspoon (deceased), who married Roosevelt Witherspoon and has children, Tyron (deceased), and Andrew Witherspoon, who has three children, Demetrius, Jazlyn, and Mekhi Witherspoon. Willie Simmons (deceased) had three children: Willie Simmons Jr., Tremaine Simmons, who served in the U. S. Army, and Mariah Simmons Salinas.

Vella Simmons Kelly (Dee Dee) married James Kelly and they have one son, Robert Parrish, who served in the US Air Force. Janet Simmons Love married Andrew Love and they have two children, Jenica Simmons, and Charles Austin (deceased). Jenica has two children, Alyjae Graves, and Jacorien Wilson. Debra Simmons Smith married Stevy Smith, who served in the US Navy. Combined, they have six children, Derick Twitty (deceased); Gary Parson, who served in the US Air Force and has three children, Aniyah, Nehemiah, and Jasiah Parson; Shakira Conwright, Kendra Conwright, who has child, Aaliyh Hodge; and Kasheena Conwright who has two children, Michael Hightower, and Abran Jackson.

Carol Simmons Harris, married Michael Harris, who served in the US Army. Combined, they have four children, Erric Simmons, who has one child, Zariyah Simmons; Dominique Simmons, Jasmine Harris; and Micah Harris. Donna Simmons has six children, Darquinton Cleveland, who served in the US Marines and married Addie. They had children, Nia, Nalia and Navah Cleveland; Denzail Cleveland, who has one child, Kierre Cleveland; and Dejanaria Simmons, Deondra Cleveland, Daquandra Simmons, and Dejearl Cleveland. John Simmons, who served in the US Army, married Beatrice Simmons, and they have one daughter, Raven Simmons.

Pamela Simmons-Alexander married Shan Alexander, who served in the US Army and became the First Black Director for Lubbock County. Combined they have four children: Mikale

Alexander; Darrius Simmons; Marquise Alexander; and Kirsten Alexander.

Raymond (Sweet Papa) Rosemond married Helen D. Moore, and they had sons, Roderick and Jeffrey D. Rosemond. Raymond has two other daughters, Tamiko Douglas, and Kia Bolding. Roderick Rosemond is single with no children. Jeffrey D. Rosemond has two children, son Deterrance Williams Rosemond, who has a son and daughter, Shambi Rosemond. Shambi has two children. Tamiko Douglas, who has two children, son Kadri Walker and daughter Zorie Douglas. Kia Bolding married John Bolding II, and they have three children, Barrick Hodge, Ma Kya Riddley and Jimmy Riddley Jr.

Lee Roy Rosemond had two children, daughter, Annetta Rosemond and son, Lee Roy Rosemond Jr. Annetta has a son, Trent Fluellen, who has three children: Trenton, Alyla, and Sienna Fluellen. Lee Roy Jr., and wife, Rhonda Reyna have no children. Lee Roy Sr. had a stepdaughter, Michelle Johnson Rosemond (deceased).

David Rosemond and Thelma Fluellen had three children, two daughters and a son. Daughter, Natica married Bam Dean and they have four children, Nyeisha, Tnnique, DataeJa Dean, and Diamond Byrd. Daughter, Yemika Fluellen has a daughter, Kenda Reed; Son, David Rosemond Jr. married Cynthia Williams (divorced) and they had a daughter, Monique Rosemond. Monique married Robert Thomas and they have two children: son, Caden and daughter, Ryleigh Thomas. Later, he met Patricia Ransfer, and they had a daughter, Lahketha Ransfer (NaNa), who has a son, Quinton Taylor.

Johnny Earl Rosemond (JR/Johnny) and Glenda Marie Smith (deceased) had six children, Johnny and Peggy Ann Wilson who had a daughter, Teresa Ann Wilson. Johnny and Annie Smith had a daughter, Le'Nisha J. Rosemond. Johnny has eight children: Derrick Smith, an Army Veteran, married Ivanna Lewis, and they have two daughters, D'erica and D'anna Smith. Shlonda Smith; Martindale married Kendrick Martindale and they have two sons, and a daughter, Tykendrick, Keshaun, and Shaizae Martindale; Tyronza (Ms. Nish) Smith Johnson married Ellis Johnson, and had no children. Le'Nisha J. Rosemond has no children.

Twin, LaTosha Smith (deceased), had two daughters, Aaliyah and Shakyha Moore (deceased). (Twin) Joshua R. Smith has three daughters and son, (twins) Janiece and Janella Smith, Faith, and Joshua Smith Jr.

Erica A. Rosemond Chambers married Tony Ray Chambers and they have three children, Tyjae, Aaron, and Tijae Chambers. Teresa Ann Wilson married Jeffery Mitchell and they had a daughter, Monica Mitchell. Teresa went into the service in 1996, and she and Jeffery are currently serving in the US Army.

Everlonia (Sister) Rosemond Walker married Ervin Walker, and they had one child, Gloria Mae (Van) Walker. Also, Everlonia married Dave Westbrook, Durwood Bullard, and J. B. Bush, of which they had no children together. Following her grandmother's tradition, Gloria Mae (Van's) teacakes are a "must have" at the Green-McGill family reunions. She married Willie Lee Sullivan Sr. (Dub) (deceased). Willie and Gloria (Van) had six children, Wade, Mary Louise; Willie Lee Jr.; Kenneth; Glenda Faye, and Robert Earl. They lived in Houston, Texas, until retirement and then moved back to Branchville, Texas.

Wade Sullivan married Bernadine Lewis Sullivan (deceased), and they had children: Michael Sullivan Meade; Julian Sullivan (Stephanie); and Kimberly Sullivan. Julian has a son, Tyriq. He is currently married to Beverly Cox and they live in Houston, Texas. Mary Louise Sullivan Anderson (Mary) married Booker Anderson, and they have three daughters: Latresia Sullivan, who married Kevin Johnson, whose children are: Andrea Anderson; Monica Thomas, who has three children: Ashlynn Thomas, Matthew Thomas; and Nia Thomas. Latresia Sullivan Johnson's husband (Kevin) had one daughter, Dominique Johnson, who has two children: Jamarion and Brooklyn Murchison.

Willie Lee Sullivan Jr. (Jr.) married Treva Booker, and they have three daughters, Kristin Sullivan; Angela Sullivan Gilmore, who married Antonio Gilmore; and Danielle Sullivan. Kenneth Sullivan is single and has no children. Glenda Faye Sullivan Lee married Tony Lee and they have one child, Nigil Lee. Robert Earl Sullivan is single and has no children.

Robert D. Rosemond (RD) married Ella Philpot (both deceased). He has an adopted a son, Robert Darrell Rosemond. Robert has three daughters: Rokeshia, Shemeka, who has one child, Jelessia, and Derion Robinson.

Johnny Rosemond married Addie Marion (Mear) Brown, (both deceased). Johnny and "Mear" (Addie) lived in Branchville, Texas, where they did domestic work and share cropping. They had ten children, Rosetta, Joyce, John L. (deceased), Henry, Marion (Tump), Dennis, Lucene, Cheryl, Timothy (Tim) (deceased), and Victoria.

Rosetta Lee Rosemond Wesley married Ezachary Wesley Jr, and they have three children, Carolyn, Veronica, and Zachary III. They returned to Branchville, Texas, after retiring from the US Air Force. Carolyn married Adelius Stithe and they have five children: Adelius Jr., Kiana, Treavon, Michalia and Kjia. Adelius Wesley Jr., married Anna Belga, and they have one child, Adrien Joshua. Kiana Wesley married Adam Schroder, and they have two children, Charlemagne and Azzi. Veronica Wesley married Ansel Bingham and they have one daughter, Victoria. Zachary Wesley III married Michelle Montoya and they, and their three children, LaShae, Devon and Zackiaes, live in Albuquerque, New Mexico.

Joyce Elaine Rosemond Agers lives in Dallas, Texas, and has two children; CasSandra Agers and Ethan Wade Agers. CasSandra lives in Dallas, Texas, and has two children, Craig Ware, and Kennedy Ware. Ethan Wade Agers lives in Dallas, Texas, and has one son, TreVon.

John L. Rosemond served in the US Army during the Vietnam War and was killed in combat in 1969. He married Dorothy Douglas (both deceased), and had one daughter, Rhonda LaShaun Rosemond., who Rhonda LaShaun Rosemond lives in Houston, Texas, and has two children, Gabriel and Christian.

James Henry Rosemond of Branchville, Texas, is an Army Veteran who served his country in the Vietnam War. James Henry has two daughters, La Donna and Constance Rosemond of Dallas Texas.

Marion Louise Rosemond (Tump) married David Steamer of Houston, Texas, have five children, Chrystal Renee, La Keshia Denice, Joanie, David Nathan, and Maya Steamer. Chrystal Steamer Davis married Donnell Davis, and they have four children; Christian,

Corian, Trey, and Desmond, who all reside in Houston, Texas. La Keshia Steamer lives in Porter, Texas, and has two children: Trinity and Cree. Daughters, Joanie and Maya, and son, David Streamer all live in Houston, Texas.

Dennis Harold Rosemond lives in Dallas, Texas, and has three sons, Dennis Jr., Jarin, and Johnathan Rosemond. Lucene Rosemond lives in Houston, Texas, and has three daughters, Leeza, ShaRhonda, and Kerria Rosemond. Cheryl Rosemond lives in Houston, Texas, and has two sons, Erroll Dewayne Rosemond (deceased), and Emiel Jamahl Winfree.

Timothy Rosemond (Tim) (deceased) has three children, Shundria Finley, Timothy Adrean Rosemond, and Timia Malone. Shundria Finley has three children, Jayden, Cameron, and Carter.

Victoria Rosemond married Terence Blackshure and they have five children, Addie Renice, Tia, Trencia, Arial and Terence Blackshure Jr. The Blackshure family lives in Houston, Texas. Addie Renice Blackshure has one child, Josiah Yuri Blackshure.

Esther Mae Rosemond Price Wells' family recalled that her "egg pies" were a must have at all family and church gatherings. Esther married Charlie (CJ) Price Sr. and Forris (Griss) Wells (all deceased). Esther and CJ had four children: James Wilbert Price (JW), Ellen Marie Price, Charles Price Jr. (Jr.) Charlie P. (deceased), and Rose Mary Price. Esther and Griss had no children together, but he raised Esther's four as his own. He was truly a father to them. The grand-children lovingly called him "Big Papa!" Esther and Griss lived in Branchville doing domestic work and sharecropping.

James Wilbert (JW/W) Price Sr. married Doris Marie Green (both retired) on June 26, 1962. They have seven children, James Jr. (Buggy); Carolyn; Trent (Cupcake) (deceased); Melanie, Paula; Forrest; and Chris. JW and Doris live in Amherst, Texas.

Rev. James W. Price Jr. (Buggy) married LaWanda Lockridge and they have three children, Anthony, Christa Shay; and Britney Price. Anthony has a son and a daughter. Britney, who has a son. James W. Price Jr. (Buggy,) who lives in Amherst, Texas, is a mechanic, and served on the Amherst School Board. He is currently married to Tosha Johnson and they have no children together.

Carolyn Price, the second child, lives in Amherst, Texas, and is single and has no children. Trent Price (Cupcake) is deceased. Melanie Price For, who lives in Clovis, New Mexico, is married to Joshua Ford and has one son, Jaden Ford. Paula Price Scott married Dale Scott, who live in Lubbock, Texas, had two daughters, Danielle Scott (deceased), and Kendra Scott. Forrest Price, who is single, has three children, Kyla, Trey, and Caden Price. Chris Price is single with no children.

Ellen Marie (Marie) Price Whitfield married Rev. Willie Whitfield on December 23, 1966. They have five children, LaTresia, William, Willis (Anthony), Warrick and LaMeika Whitfield. Marie and Willie who lived in San Francisco, California. After retiring, Marie and Willie moved back to Branchville, Texas. LaTresia Lynette Whitfield who lives in San Francisco, has one child, LaCresha Shanise Whitfield. LaCresha, of San Francisco, has two daughters, Mackenzie Elise Brown, and Madison Denise Esquivel.

William Randolph Whitfield and Warrick Carnell Whitfield, both live in San Francisco. Anthony has two children, Raja Anthony and Rani Kiara Whitfield. Anthony, of Sacramento, California, is married to LaTisha Lewis Whitfield and she has three children: Artimus, TaNisha and TaShay Holmes. LaMeika Marie Whitfield Davenport married Booker T. Davenport II, (deceased) of Branchville, Texas, and they had children, Brooklynn, Marie, and Booker T. Davenport III.

Charles Price Jr., (Jr./Charlie P.), now deceased, served his country in the US Army in the Vietnam War and received several medals, including The Purple Heart. He married Grace Helen Lenued, and had four children, Iperia; Charles III, (deceased), Eric; and Roshunda Price. Grace lives in Cameron, Texas. Iperia Price married Shawn Flatt and they have two children, Netanya Marie and Keenan Flatt. Iperia lives in Fort Wayne, Indiana. Charlie P. had fourteen grandchildren and ten great grands.

One family member has the distinction of being given special recognition in the naming of a highway in his honor, The Charles L. Price Memorial Highway. Distinctively, the highway-naming honor is the first of its kind for an individual in Milam County.

Army Master Sergeant Charles Levan Price III (Popa), (deceased) was killed in Afghanistan in 2011. He married Helen Marie Clark Price, and they had a girl and a boy, Shameka Xscvay Price, who has a baby, Charleesa; and Rashawn Price. Their blended family includes Charles' daughters, Lakriesha (son Kendall), Joshlynn Price, whose children are Darrick; Domineck, who has Timothy Washington; along with Marie's three children, Donovan Clark, Michael Clark (daughter Gabriella); and She'niya Clark.

Also known as the "Army Master Sgt. Charles L. Price III Memorial Highway, the sign is on US 77 at north Rockdale city limits and the Y-intersection US 77/190 Texas 36, southeast of Cameron, Texas. Distinctively, the highway-naming honor is the first of its kind for an individual in Milam County. Popa's family resides in Killeen, Texas.

Eric Price married Diahnna Mims and they have three children, Denecia Jelise Price, who has two sons, Micahi and Rhesia Sample, and Nevaeh Goldsby, and Dequondrius Price. Eric and Diahnna are raising Diahnna's niece, Arion. Eric lives in Austin, Texas. Roshunda Price and partner Antonio Jenkins, together have one daughter, Kyndal Grace Jenkins, and a step daughter, Jada Jenkins. Roshunda lives in Shreveport, Los Angeles.

Rose Mary Price Freeman (Mary) has faithfully has served as chairperson of the Green/McGill Reunions for the past few years. Rose Mary married Donald Ray Freeman (Don, deceased) of Hewitt, Texas. Don died on December 13, 2016. They had four children, Kymla; Josalynn; Dakena; and Kamarya Freeman. Don was a retired superintendent of a state school. They have ten grandchildren and one great grandchild.

Kymla Mashall Freeman Young Meeks married LaMont Young and James Meeks, and had children, Tyrell and Tyreon Young, who has a son, Tyreon II, Tymia, and Tyler Meeks. Josalynn Renea Freeman Harris' children are Jaiden Harris and Ethan Harris. Dakena Odunayo Freeman has a daughter, Chaniya Imani Freeman. Kamarya Donielle Freeman Busby of Woodway, Texas married Tyrun Busby, and has three children together, Kamari Javaar, and twins, Kayla Dominique and Kamrun Dominic Busby.

SEARETHA SMITH-COLLINS

Aunt Ruthie's Family

In the absence of our grandparents, Aunt Ruthie was the historian and matriarch of the Green family. She was known for her cooking; not one special dish, but everything that she prepared. Ruth Lee Green (Ruthie; deceased) was born in Milam County, Texas, on May 20, 1910, and died in Maysfield, Texas, in 1977. She married Andrew Pittman, and they had eight children: three sons, Andrew Jr. (Son) (deceased), Isaiah (deceased), and Cecil; and five daughters, Reddie Mae, Elnora, Flora Mae (deceased), Ruthie Mae, and Nettie Teresa (deceased).

Andrew Pittman Jr. (son), (deceased) had three children, Bennie Lee, Andrew III, and Teresa Jewel Pittman.

Isaiah Pittman (deceased) had two sons, Isaiah Jr. and John Elbert, and a daughter, Bettie Pittman, who died as a young adult.

Reddie Mae Pittman Rosemond King, is known for her devotion to ensuring the Green-Family Reunion tradition was sustained for many years. She married Willie Rosemond (Buck) and Louis King. Reddie and Willie Rosemond had three children: daughters, Charlotte; Minnie; and a son, Reginald (Reggie). Reddie and Louis had a daughter, Erica King, of Illinois, with whom Reddie now lives.

Charlotte married Charles Wyatt and has two children, Va-Shalla Easton and Clifford. Va-Shalla has three children, K'Vante' Aveyah, and Rodney, and one grandson, Prince. Clifford has four children, Va-Shalla, Jalil, Jalila, and Jystic; and two grandsons, Brian and Jarmarcus. Minnie Breaux has two daughters, Kyndra and Sherrita, and one grandson, David. Reginald has two daughters, Crystal and Veronica, and one grandson, Liam. Erica has a son, Tristan, two daughters, Jessica and Jasmine; and one granddaughter, Ariana.

Elnora Pittman Sullivan of Dallas Texas, married Arthur Sullivan and had three daughters, Barbara Jean, Jeanette, and Jeannie; and son, Authur Ray Sullivan. Barbara Diane Cottingham has three children, Cory, Ellis, and Katrina Cottingham Young. Cory has three daughters, Kourtni, Chyna, and Morgan. Ellis has two boys, Silas and Collin, and a daughter, Jordan; and an adopted daughter, Zarania. Katrina has three children, Kaden, McKenzie, and McKoy

102

Young. Daughter Jeanette is married and has no children, and daughter Jeannie is married and has no children; and son, Arthur Ray has no children.

Flora Mae Pittman Johnson (deceased) lived in Springfield, Illinois, where she died in 2012. After graduating from high school, she lived with her Uncle Elbert in Seattle, Washington. There she met and married Gerald (Gerry) Johnson, and they had one son, Lyle, who has three children, Tiffany, Warren, and Nicholas Johnson. Tiffany has one child.

Ruthie Mae Pittman Benavides has two sons, Dean Frederick and Billy Joe Pittman. Dean has four daughters, Juandalyn, DeAndra, Roslyn and Dominic; and four grandchildren, Madison, Maddie and LaAnna Woodfield and Haylee Scott. Billy has two children, Billy Joe Junior and LaTonya Pittman, as well as grandchildren. Ruthie Mae married Mike Delarosa Benavides and they have five children, Sharron, Carlotta, Emmanual, Job and Jonathon Benavides. Sharron has one daughter, Miranda Mose, and Miranda has two children, Tatyana and Anthonie. Carlotta, Emmanuel, and Job have no children. Jonathon has one child, Jaliyah.

Cecil Gene Pittman lives in Cameron, Texas and has one child, Cecil Jr.

Nettie Teresa Pittman, Ruth Green's youngest daughter, had one son, Carlo Andre Pittman (Andre'). Nettie died in Dallas, Texas in 2006.

Aunt Juanita's Family

Juanita Green was born in 1914 in Milam County Texas. Also known as the family historian, Juanita Martin (Aunt Juanita) was an accomplished black woman who was very sophisticated for her time (the 1930–1960s era). She served gourmet food on silver serving dishes and trays, and wore pearls, furs, hats, and the latest fashions. Whenever one thinks of Aunt Juanita, usually there is a little chuckle, because they recall that she was outspoken and really spoke her mind, and she did not care who heard her. Juanita Green Martin (deceased) was born in Cameron, Texas, on January 26, 1914, and died in

Houston, Texas, on January 13, 1988. She attended Franklin Beauty School in Houston, Texas. Aunt Juanita married Charlie Martin (deceased) in Branchville, Texas, on May 6, 1935. They had no children. Aunt Juanita and Uncle Charlie migrated to Seattle where they lived for many years. Later she returned to Houston, where she married Fitz Flemming in 1980 and settled there until her death in 1988.

Aunt Charlie Mae's Family

When I think of Aunt Charlie Mae, I recall that she was stern when it came to discipline, but she had a strong sense of family, and gave handmade quilts to all of her nieces. Charlie Mae Green Parhms Moten Matthews was born on October 16, 1919, in Milam County, Texas, and died in Bryan, Texas in October 2013. Aunt Charlie Mae married Roosevelt Pharms, and they had one son, Lawrence (Charles) Pharms, who died in Seattle, Washington. Charles did not have children. Later, Aunt Charlie Mae married John Moten (Nubby), deceased. They had three children, daughter Johnnie Mae Moten Cunningham (Sister), and sons, Edward Keith (Bubba), and John III (Dute) (deceased). Aunt Charlie Mae was the last living child of Grandma Jim and Grandma Sirlina.

Daughter Johnnie, lived in Garland, Texas, and moved to Houston in 2016. Johnnie married Iney Cunningham (deceased), and they had one daughter, Ina Carmece (Meci), who lives in Houston. Carmece is married to Tino McBayne, and has a son, Trenden Omari McBayne, who was born in 2016. Edward Keith Moten (Bubba) of Houston, Texas, is married to Louise Williams, and they have sons, Randolph (Randy), Gregory, and Edward Moten II. John (Dute) Moten III (deceased) had three children, Renee, John, and Roland Williams of Bryan, Texas.

James Green Jr. Family

My father had a picture of James (Jim) Green, Jr. (Uncle Buddy), and my most vivid recollection was that he was a very good-looking man. I was told he was fun-loving and loved good-looking women, who in turn loved him. James (Jim) Green Jr. (Uncle Buddy; deceased) was born in Milam County, Texas, around 1911. Based on US Federal Census records (Ancestry.com), he was nineteen years of age in 1930. James Jr. died in Houston, Texas, on September 5, 1951. He married Olivia Pittman (Aunt Lump) in 1932 (deceased), and they had one daughter, Leana Jewel Green Taylor (Precious), of Houston, Texas. Uncle Buddy had three older children, Willie Mae Carter Petty of California, Jewel Lee, and son, Tommy Lee who died in Odessa, Texas.

Leana married Byron Craig Taylor (deceased, April 2017). Byron was the author of three children's books, *Tipping Tip Tom, The Fat Girl Bus,* and *Munchy Mollie Mullins.* Leana has one son, Kenneth James Green, who has two children, Cory and Kenneth (Little Ken). Little Ken has two children who all live in Texas. Leana raised Byron's children, Byron Jr., Christopher, and Lori, along with their children as her own.

Aunt Dorothy's Family

Dorothy Higgins, Lyons, Lacy (Aunt Dorothy) was a sweet lady with a great heart. The youngest daughter of James and Sirlina Green, Dorothy Green Higgins Lyons Lacy (deceased) was born in Branchville, Texas, on March 6, 1921. She married Willie Higgins, Christopher Lyons, and William Lacy Jr. They had no children. Aunt Dorothy moved to Seattle for a few years, returning to Houston where she died in 1981. She was buried in the Providence Cemetery in Branchville, Texas.

Uncle Elbert's Family

My father, Elbert Lee Green, a.k.a. Uncle Elbert—loved to take a spin on the dance floor with everyone at the annual O.J. Thomas High School Reunion Dance. He was somewhat quiet, but as the baby brother, he was willing to show his love to his family in any way possible.

Elbert (deceased), the youngest child of Jim and Sirlina Green, was born in Branchville, Texas, in 1923. He married Oleatha Green, and they had three daughters, Virgie Lee Green Harris Haley, Searetha

Green Smith-Collins, and Patricia Ann (Pat) Green Curvey. Elbert also had an older daughter, Melloniece Green Fuller, who was born in 1941, and was raised in Hearn, Texas. Her mother was Ocielee Walker (deceased).

Melloniece married Marvin Fuller of Fort Worth, Texas, and they had four daughters, Cheryl Fuller-Smith, Sandra, Vicki Fuller Brumfield, and Marva Fuller. Cheryl has two boys, Ja-Brian Graham and Cory DeShawn Fuller. Ja-Brian has no children. Cory has one daughter, Brook Lauryn Fuller. Sandra has no children. Vicki married Leon Brunfield and they have one daughter, Hilary Moriah Brumfield. Marva has no children.

Virgie Lee Green Harris Haley of Seattle, Washington, married Leon Harris and Harold Haley, and she and Leon had two children, LeOndre' Lechelle Harris and Teriauna (Teri) Vivienne Harris Duran. LeOndre married Morris E. Miller, and they live in Atlanta, Georgia with her daughter, Giauna Williamson. Teriauna (Teri) is married to Michael Duran and lives in Hyattsville, Maryland. They have a daughter, Micah Tatum Duran, who was born on August 20, 2014; and son, Mykel Alexander Duran, born on March 29, 2016.

Searetha Green Smith-Collins married A. Leonard Smith and Jacob (Jake) E. Collins. She and Leonard have two children: son DaShaun Archie Smith, who lives in Seattle, Washington; and daughter Michelle Tomiko Smith, who lives in Baltimore, Maryland. Searetha has a stepdaughter, Ginger Collins, who lives in Fountain Valley, California. DaShaun has one daughter, Katanna Nichelle Smith, who has a daughter, Lily Ann Winter, born on January 8, 2016, and a son, Linken Patrick Cheney, born in March 2018. He married Teresa Williams, and they have a son, Qualin Caleb Smith, who lives in Seattle. Michelle has no children.

Patricia Ann Green Curvey (Pat) lives in Seattle, Washington, and has one son, Kevin Preston of Seattle, Washington. Kevin's father, Ronald (Ron) Preston died in 2017. Patricia married Byron Curvey, and they have two children, Lesa Nichelle Curvey and Shannon V. Curvey. Kevin has no children. Lesa lives in Las Vegas, Nevada, and has a son, Xavior Ellington Harris. Shannon lives in Chantilly, Virginia, and has stepchildren.

Chapter 11
The McGills[4]

The McGill family lived and worked as sharecroppers and farmers in Grimes County. They were very close friends and neighbors of the DuBoses, Bradleys, Gordons, Praters, Pratts, McClendons, Gardous, and so many more whose names cannot be remembered. According to US Census records, the McGills moved to Milam County at the same time as the Greens around 1935.

Louis and Martha Bradley McGill were Grandma Sirlina's parents. According to 1910 US Federal Census data, Martha McGill was full Cherokee Indian. Louis McGill and Martha Bradley McGill were born in Texas. According to ancestral records, Great Grandfather Louis died in Cameron, Milam County, Texas, date unknown. No information was located on the date of Great Grandmother Martha's death. Louis and Martha married and had two sons and eight daughters—Benjamin (Uncle Ben) and Alfred (Uncle Bud); and Mary, Georgia, Carrie Sylvia, Violet, Laura, Eliza, and Grandma Sirlina, the youngest child.

Aunt Mary's Family

The oldest child of the McGill family was Mary Jane McGill Pharms, who was born on March 4, 1865. She married Alonzo Lawrence, and they had five children, Tobe Parhms, Ira Lawrence, Beatrice (Mama Bea), and Georgia Lawrence (cousin Dilly).

---

[4]   Narrative by Reddie Mae Pittman; Edited by Searetha Smith-Collins

Tobe Parhms and his children lived in Baytown, Texas. John Lawrence had two daughters, Annie Love (Sugar) and Ruby Lee Lawrence. His olderst daughter, Annie, had two children, Ruby Jewel Mason Brown and Collie Williams Jr. Ruby Lee had five sons, Shelton, Walter, Gerald, Lionel, and Albert. Ruby died at an early age. Collie Jr. had seven children: four sons, Collie III, Ronald E., Eric, and Lawrence; and three daughters, Brenda, Angela and Andrea. Albert Collie Jr. and Ira Lawrence had two children, Ora and Buddy.

Beatrice Lawrence (Mama Bea) had three children, daughter Emma Lane Jackson, and sons, John T. Lane (Buster) and Marvin Lane (Cecil). Emma had and two daughters, Beatrice (Bebe) and Mary Jane Earl Jackson Moore. Beatrice Jackson (Bebe) married Lane Greer and had son, Lawrence, and grandchildren. Mary Earl had four children, Melba, Madison, Margaret Ann, and George Maurice. John T. (Uncle Buster) had one son, Romalus Lane, and daughter, Doris. Marvin Cecil had three daughters, Constance, Jean, and April Faye.

Georgia Lawrence (cousin Dilly) Chachere married James Chachere. James had one daughter, Shirley Mae Chachere Bisor, and James Chachere Jr. Georgia and James had no children together, but she raised Shirley Mae and James as her own. Shirley Mae Chachere Bisor had three sons, Lucious (Jerry), Hubert LeAndre' (baby brother), and Michael Bisor. Michael James Jr. (brother) had one daughter, Jennifer Joyce, and two sons, James III and Sidney.

Alfred McGills (Uncle Bud's) Family

Most proper at Grandma's suggestion, Uncle Ben (Benjamin) and Uncle Bud (Alfred) married two sisters. Uncle Ben married Andora Gordon (Aunt Fesse) and Uncle Bud married Laura Rooney.

Alfred Lawrence McGill and Aunt Laura Rooney lived in Porter, Oklahoma. They had one son, John McGill, who worked as a porter on the train years ago. Later, John worked at the US Postal Service in Tulsa, Oklahoma. John McGill married a beautiful lady, Susan (Sue) McGill, but they did not have children together. John had a daughter from another relationship by the name of Rita McGill, who reportedly lived in Chicago, Illinois. After retiring from the postal service, John moved back to the farm his father left him in Porter, Oklahoma. He came to the Green-McGill family reunions until his health failed. You will hear more about John McGill in Chapter 13.

Uncle Ben's Family

Benjamin (Ben) McGill served in World War I. He married Andora Gordon (Aunt Fessie) who was Aunt Laura's sister. He and Aunt Fesse bought a small house in Cameron across the railroad track in an area called Dutch Town. Uncle Ben did not earn much money while in the war, but he and Aunt Fesse saved every penny by placing it in a boot, and throwing the boot under the barn (they did not like banks.) They also operated a small neighborhood store before they died.

Uncle Ben was a carpenter, and had a reputation for helping people in need. He and cousin Silas Woodard had a successful business building houses for people in Cameron and the surrounding area. Some of the houses they built are still standing in Branchville, Texas. He and Aunt Fessie had four children: two boys, Louis McGill Jr. and Benjamin (Ben) Jr. and two daughters, Gladys and Dora B., all deceased.

Louis McGill Jr. was named after Uncle Ben's and Grandma Sirlina's father. Louis moved from Texas to Oakland, California. He had an adopted daughter, Anaka Lewis, who died on February 2, 1993.

Gladys McGill Homer married Lem Homer and lived in San Mateo, California. They had two daughters, Roxie and Gail. Gladys died on April 8, 1990. Roxie had three children, Sharon, Stacey, and Mathew Jr. Roxie died on April 12, 1989. Gail had a daughter, Naya, and they live San Mateo, California.

Dora B. McGill moved to California and lived with her sister, Gladys. After marriage she had three children, Carolyn, Sue, and Sandra Jean. Dora had four grandchildren, and eight great-grandchildren. The joy of her life was a great-great-grandchild whom she spoke about often. She loved all of her grandchildren and often said, "Thank God for letting me see them and love them." Dora often visited her cousins, Juanita Green Martin and Elbert Green, in Seattle. She died on May 9, 2001.

Benjamin (Ben Jr.) married Claradine (Clara) Moore on January 7, 1948. They moved to California where they had three children, Marie Katherine, Steven, and Robert Gordon. Clara is deceased, and Ben died in San Francisco in the 2000s. Ben Jr. was a devoted grandfather and great-grandfather who enjoyed taking his grandsons fishing, and playing computer games with them. Marie Katherine had two daughters, Dana and Denise Sampreth. Dana had two children, Anthony and Kyanna. Denise had one son, Aaron. Steven had two sons, Kwame and Najee. Robert Gordon lived in Dickerson, Texas, and had three children, Robert (Bobby) Gordon Jr., Anthony Benjamin and Angeleina Claradine, who were twins. Evalena had a daughter, Tommie Lee Johnson, who lives in Tulsa, Oklahoma. Tommie Lee raised two brothers, and a young man by the name of Lemuel.

Aunt Georgia's Family

Georgia McGill Bradley, Lawrence, Roney, Albert (Aunt Georgia) was born in 1875 in Grimes County, Navasota, Texas. She lived in the same home for seventy-five years. Aunt Georgia had one daughter, Martha Eliza Lawrence. She married George Elbert and they had no children together. Aunt Georgi died at the age of one hundred (100) years old.[5] She had lived in Fort Worth, Texas in the same house for seventy-three years.

Aunt Georgia's daughter, Martha, had five children: two sons, Milton Young and General Rooney; and three daughters, Mildred, Jimmie Mae Seallst'sll, and Georgianna. Milton Young had an adopted son. General Rooney had two daughters and a son; Mildred had a son and daughter; Jimmie Mae had a son and daughter; and Georgianna had two stepsons.

---

[5] Author's Note: While interviewing relatives about the McGill family, I discovered that my father, Elbert Green, was the namesake of Aunt Georgia's husband, George Elbert.

Aunt Carrie's Family

Carrie McGill Reed (Aunt Carrie), Grandma Sirlina, and Aunt Carrie's daughter, Roxie McGill-Reed, all had the same nickname; they were called "cousin Sug" by everyone. At one time, Aunt Carrie owned a lot of land in Cameron, Texas, on Madison Avenue, where cousin Rebecca's (Beck's) mother, and cousin Anna Jane (Beck's sister) lived for many years. Maggie James (Aunt Koosie), who was Grandma Sirlina's oldest daughter, lived with Aunt Carrie for a while also when she was young and attended the O.J. Thomas Elementary School.

Carrie's daughter, Roxie, married Silas Woodard, who along with Uncle Benjamin (Ben Sr.) had a successful business building houses for people in the Cameron vicinity. Roxie lived in Fort Worth, and later married a county agent by the name of Mr. Phillips, who was from Waco, Texas. She had a stepson, Lawrence Phillips, who lived in Little Rock, Arkansas. Roxie was president of the Old Land Mark Baptist District Association for twenty-one years, and a member of the Lights Chapel Baptist Church.

Reddie Mae Pittman recalled that cousin Roxie always encouraged her to do well and study hard when I attended O.J. Thomas Elementary School. Roxie was a beautician when she was younger. She attended Central Texas College in Waco, and Guadalupe College in Seguin, Texas. Reddie remembered Roxie as being "a very sweet lady." She died on October 23, 1971.

Aunt Sylvia's Family

Sylvia Bradley Steele McGill (Aunt Tip) lived in Cameron, Texas, for many years. She had twin daughters, Alice Reid and Dora Brown. Alice had no children. Dora (cousin Dora) had two daughters, Willie Lee (Totice) Calhoun and Harleam Whitehead. Sylvia graduated from O.J. Thomas High School and attended Prairie View A&M University. She taught school at O.J. Thomas for many years until she moved to Arizona. Harleam Whitehead finished school at O.J. Thomas and married L.C. Moore, who was a Sergeant Major in the US Army. They traveled to places like Belgium, France, Turkey, and Germany. They had six children, three sons and three daughters, Douglass, Marilyn, Wanda, Janice, John T. (Buster), and Marvin Cecil. Their first son died as an infant while they were in Germany.

Douglas, the oldest child, died in February 2004. Douglass and his wife Linda had a daughter, Ashlee Moore, and son, Jermony. Ashley has one son, Doug, and one grandson. Marilyn Moore Smith married Archie and they had a son, Archie Terrell Smith, and daughters, Latasha Smith and Tara Smith. Wanda Moore married James Crane, and they had two children, Nicole Crane and Louis Crane. Janice Moore married Mr. Grant and they had two daughters, Chaisse McAfee and Cameron Grant. John T. (Buster) had a son, Romulus, and daughter, Doris. Marvin (Cecil) had three daughters, Constance, Jean, and April Faye.

Aunt Violet's Family

Violet McGill Bradley, who lived in Ardmore, Oklahoma, had one son, Roscoe Bradley, and one daughter, Vera. Her son, Roscoe, was a Pullman Porter on the railroad along with cousin John McGill (Uncle Alfred's son). You will read more about Roscoe and John in Chapter 14.

Aunt Laura's Family

Laura McGill lived in Oklahoma. She often visited the family in Cameron, Maysfield, and Branchville, Texas. Aunt Laura did not have children.

Aunt Eliza's Family

Eliza McGill, who lived in Brackenridge near Austin, Texas, frequently visited her sister, Georgia, and family in Fort Worth. There are no known children; however, Henry and Lemonel McGill were mentioned as possibly Aunt Eliza's children.

Grandma Sirlina's Family

Sirlina A. McGill Green (Cousin Sug) was the youngest child of Louis and Martha McGill. She was born in Navasota, Texas, on November 23, 1895, and died in Maysfield, Texas, on January 29, 1941. Sirlina married James Henry, who was her daughter, Maggie James' father. According to the 1880 US Census, James Henry was born in Sumter, South Carolina. As you may recall, Grandma Sirlina and Grandpa James Green (Jim) had six children together, four daughters and two sons—Ruth Lee, Juanita, Charlie Mae, and Dorothy, James Jr. (Buddy); and, my father, Elbert Lee Green. Grandpa Jim raised Maggie James (Aunt Koosie), Grandma Sirlina's oldest daughter, as his own.

As mentioned, the Sixteenth Census of the United States (1940) provided more information about the early life of Sirlina A. McGill Green. According to the census, in 1940, her husband Jim was sixty-seven years of age, and they lived in rural Milam County, Texas. Grandma Sirlina was listed as fifty-six years of age, with one child, Elbert (age sixteen), living in the home.

According to her death certificate, Sirlina McGill Green died of a heart attack in 1941 at the age of forty-five (as you can see, there were many discrepancies reported in U.S Census and other historical sources). Grandma Sirlina was buried alongside her husband, James Green Sr. in the Providence Cemetery in Branchville, Texas. As indicated on her death certificate, Grandma Sirlina lived in Maysfield, Texas, for forty-five years, which would have placed Grandpa Jim's and her arrival there in 1915.

As for the accuracy of information found on Grandma Sirlina, as noted, there is a great deal of variation in historical documents, so it was difficult to confirm Grandma Sirlina's family history with accuracy. A case in point was Grandma Sirlina McGill Green's recorded dates and ages:

1. The 1910 US Federal Census (Ancestry.com) reported that Sirlina Green was twenty-seven years old, married for a year, and living in Milam County, Texas. At that time (1910),

a six-year-old daughter, Maggie Samantha Green, lived in the home with Sirlina and her husband, Jim Green Sr. The census data was collected during the early part of the year; therefore, an unborn child was listed as Baby Green (0), who later became Ruth Green, who was born in May 1910.

2. The Thirteenth US Federal Census Population (Ancestry. com), Texas: Milam County (1920); the Fourteenth US Census (1930); and the Fifteenth Census (1940) all documented conflicting data about "Salina" (Sirlina) Green.

3. Records in Ancestry.com reported the following:

- 1910—Age twenty-seven. Sirlina Green lived in Milam, Texas. She was married for one year and had one child, Maggie (age six). She was expecting a baby at that time. If this data is accurate, Sirlina's birth year would have been 1883.

- 1920—Age thirty-eight. Sirlina Green lived in Milam, Texas. She was married and had children in the household: Ruth Green (age ten), James Jr. Green (eight), Susie Green (seven), Charlie Green (Aunt Charlie Mae) (0), born later that year. Jim Green, her husband, was listed as fifty years of age.

- 1930—Age forty-seven. Sirlina Green lived in Milam, Texas. Census data indicated that Sirlina was twenty-three years of age at the time of marriage. Jim Green Sr. was listed as fifty-six years of age. It was noted that she had completed the fourth grade in school.

- The following children were living in the home: James Green Jr. (age nineteen), Juanita (age sixteen), and Charlie May (Mae) (age ten), Dorothy (age nine), and Elbert (age six).

- 1940—Sirlina (Celina) was listed as age fifty-six, with no school or college attended. She and Grandpa Jim had been residents in rural Milam County, Texas, since 1935. One child, a son, Elbert, age sixteen, was listed as living in the home. Jim Green, was listed as sixty-seven years of age. Sirlina Green's official Texas Death Certificate (1903–1982, Ancestry.com) indicated that she was a widow who died of a heart attack on June 29, 1941, in Maysfield, Milam County, Texas.

Chapter 12
The Union[6]

The McGills and Greens united when James (Jim) Green. Sr. met and married Sirlina A. McGill on December 13, 1908 in Milam County, Texas, according to the Texas Select County Marriage Index, 1873-1965, Ancestry.com. According to best guesses from census data, Grandpa was around twenty-nine years old—however, he may have been quite a bit older—and Grandma was around twenty-seven years of age. In 2005, Reddie Mae Pittman King wrote a narrative about her memories growing up around our grandparents as a small child.

Reddie's Narrative

Grandpa Jim and Grandma Sirlina

Grandpa James (Jim) Green was a sharecropper and horse breeder. He would take his stallions and go breed horses for many people in Milam County. He always had beautiful horses. I can remember one special, very smart beautiful horse with red and white stocking feet. He was very gentle.

I stayed around my grandparents a lot. On one special morning, I remember Grandma got up to fix breakfast. They had to draw drinking water from a well, so she always kept a wooden bucket of water on the front porch. That morning, she went to get a drink of water from the bucket. They had a red horse, named Old Rheon, who ran up on the porch and knocked that dipper out of her hand

---

6   Narrative by Reddie Mae Pittman King

with his front hoof! Afterward, my father (Andrew Pittman) took the water and had it tested. They found out the water had poison in it.

After that, Grandma Sirlina started keeping the water in a large crock in the hallway (of the house). As children, we had to draw the water from the well and pack (it back to the house) to fill the big crock. One morning, I saw a small gray checkered snake in the (water) dipper. They said that it was a rattle snake. I sure did scream! Aunt Dorothy ran to get me, (and) we got out of that house!

(There were times) we would go with Grandpa when he would take bales of cotton to be ginned. This (was) where the cotton (went) through a process (of cleaning) to take out all the seeds, trash, leaves, cotton stalks, and whatever else (was in the cotton). Then the cotton (was) pressed in large bales, and wrapped and sent to the factories to make materials (for) clothes. Grandpa would get a sample from each bale to keep. I don't know if they had to send them (the samples) to the government or to the person they sharecropped for.

After all the cotton was picked from the field, we would go back and pick what was left, which they called scrapping. Grandma and Mama (Ruth) would take the seeds from the scrapping, and beat it with switches to fluff it up. This was what they used to put in quilts and pillows, and if they got enough, they would make mattresses too. They used many things to make the family comfortable on the farm. They raised chickens, turkeys, guineas, ducks, and geese. They would kill them to eat, and would take the feathers to make pillows and feather mattresses.

They made their own corn meal from the corn they raised. The cows were milked, and we strained the milk, put it in containers, and kept it in a safe wooden cabinet with screen doors on it. The milk was kept in a cool place with no ice. When the milk was a few days old, the cream would (rise) to the top. They would skim the cream off, and take it and put it with a small amount of milk that was a few days old. Grandma or Moma put it (the cream) in a churn with a dasher. We churned the milk, pushing the dasher up and down until we made butter. We drank the buttermilk, (but) most of the time they used it to cook with.

Grandma Sirlina was a good cook. I used to just sit and watch her make the meals. She loved to cook. She was a short, plump, soft-spoken sweet little lady. She didn't have many friends, (but) she had one very good one (who) was like a sister to her. Her name was Lucy Wimaby, and she lived on the same place our grandparents lived. I found out in 2003 (that) Aunt Lucy was Charles Wyatt's grandma. Charles is a friend of my daughter, Charlotte. Aunt Lucy may have been a bit older than Grandma Sirlina, but they grew up together when they were slaves. They had to hide behind cotton stalks in the field to read; otherwise, they would have been discovered, beaten or even killed if the slave owners knew they could read.

Grandma Sirlina had another friend, Winnie Livingston, who came to visit mostly after church on Sundays. Winnie married Willie Rush Rosemond, (Reddie's) first husband's grandfather, so I called her Grandma Winnie. Aunt Lucy and Winnie Livingston were always a part of the Green family. When I (Reddie) married my second husband, Louis King, he was told by "Grandma" Winnie that he was her grandson.

Aunt Lucy always wore nice long, small flowered dresses with a gingham, and a long white apron that did not ever have a spot on it. She wore a white bonnet on her head, and high-top shoes all the time. No one ever remembers seeing her barefoot. Aunt Lucy had one son whose name was Henry Hunter. She lived with him sometimes, but mostly she stayed at Grandma Sirlina's or our house. My brother, Cecil, who was considerably younger, recalled Aunt Lucy as the only grandma he knew.

Author's Post Note

As a small child, I (Searetha) had the opportunity to see Aunt Lucy when my father, Elbert Green, took our family on vacations to Cameron, Texas. When our family visited Aunt Ruthie's farm, our cousins, Flora and Ruthie Mae Pittman, took my sister, Virgie, and I down a long dirt road and up a hill to visit Aunt Lucy. She usually sat in a rocking chair in the yard while someone braided her hair or she sat in the rocking chair on the porch, usually wearing a long gingham dress, apron, high top shoes, and bonnet.

It occurred to me while writing this family history that Aunt Lucy was a representation of the last of the ancestors who were direct slaves. For those of us who were raised during the 1950s through the Civil Rights Era, we were fortunate enough to witness those who passed through the period of slavery in America. Aunt Lucy lived a long time after Grandpa Jim and Grandma Sirlina died. It took decades for me to realize the treasure of the image of Aunt Lucy. The scene illustrated how the past intersected with my generational childhood. The authentic image of Aunt Lucy dressed in her "old fashioned" attire became the link to those who had lived before.

History has a way of opening doors to understanding situations across time. Not only had I read about the American slave period and seen pictures of those enslaved in textbooks in school, I have a living mental model etched in my mind of a person who had experienced and survived those times. This was a powerful connection to hundreds and hundreds of years of existence, bringing relevance to memories that bookmarked the last of a long line of past generations. I realized that we were the last offspring to see remnants of the most overt, legal subjugation against black people in America---the enslavement of Africans and African-Americans.

Chapter 13
The Gathering[7]

Imagine traveling in a buggy to the family reunion in the early 1900s. Visualize journeying to Calvert, Texas by train in the1920 or 1930s. People came from Cameron, Brackenridge, Navasota, Calvert, Anderson, Dallas, Fort Worth, and Waxahachie, Texas. Initially, the get-togethers started out as funerals, weddings, and other family events. After some discussion, the family decided they needed to gather for reasons other than funerals, so, the Thanksgiving Holiday was set aside as the new time for annual the Green/McGill Family Reunion.

In the beginning, the family reunions took place in Cameron, Texas, also known as "in the country," (the opposite of the city). Each year relatives came from far and near to attend the event in Cameron. They brought cakes, pies, peas, potato salad, and turkey, dressing and many other treats. Jim Green and Riley Green provided fresh hog meat, 'chittlins' (chitterlings), fresh greens and sweet potatoes from the garden.

The family showed love for one another—when one was in need, the others helped with travel and other needs. Papa (Jim Green) and Uncle Son (Riley) were adults at the time. They picked up everyone in wagons. If it was cold and rainy, they put covers over the wagons and placed an old tub with coal in them to keep everyone warm. They took the beds down at the house and put them in the smoke house or barn so there would be room for everyone. They sang and prayed together. The reunion was a time when every-

---

[7] Reddie Mae Pittman King, Co-author

one anxiously looked forward to joining in the family bond. Family members were sure to attend, even if it meant attending the reunion instead of going to church on Thanksgiving.

Earlier, I shared memories of warm family times that were reported by Aunt Charlie Mae as far back as she could remember. She was a little girl at the time, but some or her fondest memories were times when the Green/McGill family gathered together at the Family Reunion, which has been in force for over eighty years. As times passed, the gathering was changed from the Thanksgiving season to being scheduled annually on the second Saturday in August in Cameron, Texas.

Family and friends now travel from Washington State, California, Indiana, Missouri, Illinois, Washington, DC, Texas, Maryland, Oklahoma, and other parts of the country; as well as Cameron, Brackenridge, Navasota, Fort Worth, Anderson, Waxachie, and Dallas. Reddie Mae Pittman King, with the help of Aunt Charlie Mae and others, organized the annual event for many years. The family reunion is traditionally held at the same time as the O.J. Thomas High School Reunion and Parade, because so many family and friends graduated from O.J. High School.

The High School Reunion Dance usually takes place on the Saturday night before the family reunion, and a parade is held prior to the family reunion. After the parade, family and friends of the Greens and McGills used to gather for the family reunion at the West Twelfth Street Park in Cameron. During the family reunion, children played games in the park while adults played dominoes, cards, and other games. Some just sat under trees or in the gazebo, talking and enjoying the company of family.

The Green-McGill Family Reunion has always been a significant event in our family. My father, Elbert Green, always looked forward to attending the reunion every year until his health failed. After I became an adult, I realized why the event had such significance to him, so I decided to support and attend the family reunions with him as much as possible. They were always enjoyable; but since they were held in August, the summer heat made for a very warm (sizzling) day of fanning and swatting mosquitos that seemed to love the "fresh meat" in town.

There were undocumented rituals that took place also. For instance, recall in the introduction of the book, I mentioned that I am a collector, and one of my favorite pastimes is visiting antique and thrift shops. While some of our relatives participated in the O.J. Thomas High School parade and festivities, it was almost a "ritual" for a few cousins, mainly Leana Jewel Green (Precious) and Ruby Adams, and me, to sneak away to nearby historic Calvert, Texas.

Usually we drove together from Houston to Cameron for the reunion, so the trip to Calvert (which is about twenty-seven miles) was a regular part of our itinerary. Antique shops were a part of the original attraction of historic Calvert in the 1970s and 1980s. We got a feel for what it must have been like when our ancestors lived there. Calvert has probably been revived today, but it almost seemed like a ghost town then, because much of the younger population had started to move away. The streets and buildings were original with no modern-day alterations. One of the main attractions was the antique shops that were filled with reasonably priced antiques, artifacts, and other treasures.

We looked forward to the excursion to Calvert, not only because there were unique things to see and buy, but because it was an opportunity to reconnect and enjoy one another also. While wandering and shopping, we were careful to watch the time, because we had to scurry back to the family reunion in the park in time, at least before the business meeting and time to eat. When we returned, we quickly put away our wares in the trunk of the car, then slipped back into the fold, hoping to not have been noticed as missing in action.

Personally, another highlight of attending the Green-McGill Family Reunion during those times was the anticipation of eating the special dinner that was prepared by Reddie and others. It was a treat to feast on barbequed brisket that was catered and prepared by cousin Russell Voss. It was almost torture to wait for the family dinner to take place, with the smell and thought of the tender, delicious brisket and meal that was to come! The menu included baked chicken, lasagna, salad, oven roasted neck bones, greens, sweet potatoes, squash, corn, beans, and plenty of ice cold drinks and desserts, including Aunt Koosie's—then later Van's—famous teacakes.

The day concluded with a family meeting in the gazebo of the park, where family plans, ideas, and issues were discussed. For a while, there was a family church service on the following Sunday morning, but that event was discontinued in consideration for those who had to travel a long distance. It was decided that people could get a head start home on Sunday instead of staying for a family service; therefore, family prayer and songs of praise were a part of the Saturday program.

Several years ago, there was a change in the location from the park to an indoors recreation center in Cameron. The best news was that the building was air conditioned as opposed to having to sit outdoors in the steaming sun in the gazebo in the park. The facility was equipped with a restaurant-style kitchen, serving area, game rooms and clean restrooms. Family members served as caterers, disk jockeys, talent coordinators, and the like.

Now the family reunion committee is headed by Rosemary Freeman, granddaughter of Aunt Koosie. Some of the activities include raffles and auctions for a college scholarship, family recognition events, talent shows; and for the first time, a Lifetime Family Award was bestowed upon a deserving family member, and it was Reddie Mae King in 2016.

The Green/McGill Family gathering and tradition lives on with a modern-day theme: "A celebration of the mind, body and soul." The purpose is "to remember, embrace, and restore the pride of the family, past and present, who have contributed to the Green-McGill communities, with the total focus being family, youth, and the development of the community."

Family gatherings are about celebrating the roads traveled, the mountains climbed, and the opportunity to bring together laughter, inspiration, and family love. Reddie Pittman King wrote and shared a poem entitled *Family* that captured the essence of the Green-McGill Family Reunion.

Family

We have gathered to unite our hearts in love,
To share our daily blessings from the Father up above,
To remember our ancestors,
Their plight from slavery, and
How they endured tremendous suffering, so
future generations would be free.
They made many, many sacrifices, and
Yet this opened up the door, for equal opportunities,
That we never experienced before.
So we are all here to uplift one another,
And understand how our lives are intertwined,
For we are all a part of this family
That has existed over time.
Although we live so far apart, and
Don't see each other much anymore,
Through letters, telephone calls, and visits,
we can keep in touch,
So, we can keep alive our family folklore.

—Reddie Mae Pittman King

Chapter 14
Cousins John McGill and Roscoe Bradley

"All aboard! The Pullman Train is now boarding!"

But not so fast—there was just one problem. It was the 1800s, and if you were black, you were not allowed to ride as a passenger on the elegant Pullman Train, with its new luxurious rail sleeping cars. The founder, George Pullman, had something else in mind for "Negroes," specifically men.

Kinsella (2013) explained that George Pullman revolutionized rail travel in the 1800s by starting the Pullman Car Company in Chicago. He thought it would be great appeal for wealthy and middle-class whites to be waited on and pampered during train rides. Taking advantage of the large numbers of slaves who had been emancipated after the Civil War, Pullman hired black men as porters, waiters, cooks, and "red caps (baggage carriers)."

The Pullman Car Corporation became the employer of the largest number of blacks in the country for the next hundred years. Being a Pullman Porter was considered a prestigious job for the newly freed slaves. They were hired, highly trained, dressed in uniforms, and offered a steady income and chance to travel across America (most had never traveled outside of plantation life). Working for the Pullman Car Corporation was a welcome opportunity, because it provided a chance to be free from hard, heavy, physical labor, which was quite a different role for black men of that era (Kinsella, 2013).

The job of Pullman Porters was held in great distinction in the African-American community, because they were known as handsome, immaculately dressed, uniformed, well-mannered, well-spoken, intelligent black men. That profile was quite different from that of plantation life and labor. Not only were they masculine and held in great esteem, they were role models for young black boys and men who aspired to seek greater life goals. However, in reality, the job was just a step up above being enslaved.

Racial attitudes of most whites had not changed, so Pullman Porters were subjected to the same degrading racial insults, discriminatory treatment, and other indignities that were practiced by white passengers. They were mistreated, overworked, and not paid a livable wage. They did not receive an allowance for expenses or job-related equipment and needs. Even when they traveled overnight and over the course of days at a time, as "Negroes," they were not permitted to sleep in the sleeping cars or eat meals in dining cars. They had to pay for the upkeep of their uniforms, meals, lodging, and all expenses out of their own meager wages.

They had to pay for much of everything at the mercy of tips on the job (Kinsella 2013); consequently, work conditions were not commensurate with the prestige of the job. Around 1925, Pullman Porters finally found some solace for better working conditions through union activism in the form of Brotherhood of Sleeping Car Porters. For several years, they struggled to gain some degree of dignity for better work conditions and fair pay.

Even though it was during a time of great prejudice, racial strife, and discrimination in America, after twelve years, the Pullman Porter Sleeping Car Brotherhood, led by A. Phillip Randolph, achieved what was considered a remarkable first step forward toward improved work conditions for black people (Kinsella 2013). They organized, united, negotiated, persevered, provoked, and influenced change in what was considered a first in the world of large, powerful companies like The Pullman Rail Corporation.

Lucy Kinsella (2013) explained that some of the techniques used by the Brotherhood of Sleeping Car Porters were later applied to strategies used during the 1960s Civil Rights Movement. It was under these conditions that cousins John McGill (Uncle Alfred and Aunt Laura McGill's son), Roscoe McGill (Aunt Violet McGill

Bradley's son), and others worked as Pullman Porters. Since there were no company arrangements for travel and lodging during scheduled trips, layovers were problematic.

As mentioned, legal segregation and inequitable laws barred blacks from traveling in the main rail cars, sleeping in the berths, eating in the meal cars, staying in hotels, having meals in restaurants or hotels or staying in boarding houses during stops and layovers. There were certain places designated for "negro porters to stay for lodging in some black communities, but often it was difficult to afford the cost of rooming houses or hotels." Like many, John and Roscoe often stayed overnight with relatives while traveling for the job. Whenever the train traveled through Cameron, Texas, they stayed with Ruth Green Pittman's family.

As reported by Reddie King, it was during one of occasions that John McGill and Roscoe Bradley knocked on the door of a house, and announced that they were looking for Ruth Green. Reddie Mae and her siblings peeked out of the window and saw what looked like two white men standing outside of the door. It was not customary to have visits from white people, so not recognizing the men, the children decided to not open the door to let them in. They called out to their mother and said, "There are two old white men at the door looking for you!"

Mama Ruth looked out of the window, chuckled, and said, "Oh, they are my cousins, John and Roscoe!"

They stayed with Ruth's family until the train returned to Cameron. When it was time for them to return to work from their layover, Ruth's family always took them back to the train station. On one special day, to the children's surprise, John and Roscoe treated them to a tour of the train, which generated quite a deal of excitement for the children. After a while, they did not see John and Roscoe for a long time. The next time John surfaced for a visit, he no longer worked as a Pullman Porter. He worked for the US Postal Service in Tulsa, Oklahoma, for many years until he retired.

Later, John McGill went back to live on a farm in Porter, Oklahoma, that was left to him by his father, Louis McGill Sr. John married Susan (Sue). Reddie recalled that Sue was a very nice beautiful woman who loved to cook. John and Sue did not have children together, but as mentioned, John had a daughter from another relationship, by the name of Rita McGill.

Before becoming ill, John often rode the bus from Porter to Killen, Texas, to Cameron to attend the Green/McGill Family Reunion. On one occasion, John joined Reddie, Willie Mae Petty (Uncle Buddy's—James Green Jr.—daughter), and my father, Elbert, on a trip to attend an annual O.J. Thomas High School Reunion Dance, and the Green/McGill Family Reunion. It was always quite a sight to watch my father, Elbert, who enjoyed providing a chance for everyone "to take a spin" on the dance floor at high school reunion dances. Sometimes, it seemed he was not aware that he could not stay on beat. In any event, he and they enjoyed his good-humored entertainment.

In August 1983, John planned to go to Cameron to attend an O.J. Thomas High School Dance and the Family Reunion again. He took the bus to Killeen, Texas; however, unaware that he was going to Killeen, Reddie drove to Temple, Texas, to meet him at the bus station. To her surprise, he was not there! The confusion turned out to be a great opportunity for a family intergenerational bond. John was surprised to find Reddie's youngest daughter, Erica, waiting to pick him up in Killeen. It was the first time John and Erica had the chance to meet as first and second cousins.

Even more special, John was thrilled to have a chance to hold Erica's son, Tristan, which was the first time he had a chance to hold a small baby. Afterward, Erica, Tristan, and John developed a special relationship until John died sometime in 1988 or 1989. Tristan had a strong generational tie with his Great Uncle Elbert also. Erica loved visiting John and Sue McGill at their farm in Porter, Oklahoma, which was a beautiful place with a big house, fruit trees, and blackberry vines, which was a perfect setting for developing memories and fellowship between the old and the young.

Chapter 15
The Aunts

The Green sisters were symbolic of close-knit communal strength that built kinship between children and family.

Generally, there were certain characteristics that contributed to family success, such as:

1) Usually children were surrounded by people who provided positive attention, mentorship, care, love, concern, and role modelling;

2) Successful people were provided with coping mechanisms despite challenges;

3) People realized they were armed with a history of survival that started far back in time, and they realized value, strength, and perseverance linked to those who came before them;

4) There was a powerful emphasis on supportive interdependent families and communities.

5) Most maintained relationships and connections to their family, regardless of their location; and,

6) Relatives such as grandparents, aunts, uncles, and cousins bridged family ties and connections between older and younger generations.

There were positive family members and practices that boosted and connected us, as children, to our self-esteem, security, success, and well-being. People like our aunts and uncles brought forth the true meaning of close-knit families during our childhood. The following memories of our aunts illustrate the epitome of extended family who influenced our lives through family support, strength, simple love, protection, care, and nurture.

Aunt Juanita

Juanita Green was known to her nieces and nephews as Aunt Juanita. One of her nieces, Elnora Pittman Sullivan, had great memories spending time with Aunt Juanita as she grew up in Cameron, Texas. Elnora recalled that Aunt Juanita was a pretty, fair-skinned young lady who was easily mistaken as being a white person. With a chuckle, Elnora recalled the many times she and Aunt Juanita went to the store on errands in the mid-1930s. When she was a small child, she remembered they frequently went to the store, holding hands together as they walked along the road.

Upon arrival, most often, they were the subject of stares from white people who assumed Aunt Juanita was a white person. On one occasion, after arriving at the store, they observed stares and whispers as they went about their shopping. Finally, a man approached Aunt Juanita and said, "What are you doing walking along, holding hands with that little black girl?" Known as a feisty, outspoken young woman, Aunt Juanita looked at the man, and sharply and indignantly answered, "White men shouldn't have been 'fooling around' in slave quarters!" At that point, there was no further conversation on the matter!

With a stern look, Aunt Juanita finished her business, grabbed Elnora's hand again, and irately stormed out of the store, swinging hands as they walked along. The threat of the segregated South and all its "Jim Crow" attitudes and terrorist actions were in full force then. I recall hearing that perhaps Aunt Juanita's feisty, fearless attitude and sharp tongue may have motivated her to leave the South. It was safer to live in a place where black people could dare to speak out more freely.

Eventually she landed in Seattle, Washington, where she worked as a beautician and was active in the Seattle African-American business and social community. During the 1940s and 1950s, Aunt

Juanita and Uncle Charlie, her husband at the time, participated in what was considered the "black society" in Seattle. As "Negroes," they were restricted from mainstream social events, activities, and organizations even in the northwest. Regardless, they led a glamorous, fun-filled, purposeful life through involvement in African-American hair shows, social activities and parties, ladies and gentlemen clubs, golf and Bridge tournaments, social and community clubs, and the like.

When my family first moved to Seattle in 1950, we lived with Aunt Juanita and Uncle Charlie. He was an avid golfer, and it seemed he always left home with a golf bag full of golf clubs. Thinking in the mind of a child, I assumed that golfing was his work. Of course, that was not the case, but it seemed he spent a great deal of time on the golf course, especially when cousin Gladys and her husband, Homer, and her sister, Dora, came to visit from California.

Even though this story brought back memories of the times, I am not able to ask my mother about Uncle Charlie, because now her memory has faded. Perhaps he worked at some golf course for whites, and somehow had access to the course as well (I do not think there were golf courses for black people at that time). Aunt Juanita had a beauty shop in the back of her house where she had a regular stream of customers. I recall that she and Uncle Charlie often dressed up in the evening to go to play Bridge or go to parties and other social events. She was quite a fancy dresser, and of course, her hair was always coifed.

Later, after we moved to our own home, I remember that Aunt Juanita and Uncle Charlie got a divorce, and eventually, after several years, she sold her home and moved back to Houston. Even though she did not have children, she made it her business to ensure that her sister's and brother's children were cared for with the best she could offer.

Aunt Charlie Mae

Charlie Mae Green Moten Matthews (Aunt Charlie Mae) was quite active in her family, church, and community. As noted in her obituary, she was a faithful member of the Pleasant Grove Baptist

Church, where she served as Chairman of the Deaconess, and participated in the Gospel and Senior Choirs. She was a member of the Usher Board and culinary committee until her health failed. For many years, she represented her church as a member of the Old Land Mark District Association, and on a citizen committee to install lights at the Eastside Park which later was named the Sadie Thomas Park in Bryan, Texas.

Aunt Charlie Mae always worked on behalf of children. She especially enjoyed helping children learn the books of the Bible, as well as working with youth in Sunday school, girls' and boys' leagues, church outings, and Baptist Training Union (BTU) meetings. Also, she was very active in her children's (Charles, Johnnie Mae, Edward (Bubba), and John (Dute)) school activities. Aunt Charlie Mae served as president of the Parent Teacher Association (PTA) and was a member of the "Have a Dream" Garden Club.

Known to her nieces and nephews as Aunt Charlie Mae, she enjoyed baking, fishing, sewing, and making quilts for family and friends. Quite active in planning and participating in the annual Green/McGill Family Reunion, she enjoyed the distinction of being the last living matriarch until her death in October 2013. Whenever my family traveled on vacation to Texas, the first stop after visiting relatives in Houston was Aunt Charlie Mae's House in Bryan. Before leaving Houston, usually we stopped to pick up my cousin, Leana Green Taylor (Precious). Her father, Jim Green Jr. had died in a car accident by then, so my father was sure to include her in our endeavors whenever we visited Texas.

Once we arrived at Aunt Charlie Mae's house, we were met with great meals and good times playing with our cousins. We sometimes got into mischief, but it did not last long. We knew Aunt Charlie Mae always meant business! All she had to do was just look at us with that very stern stare, and it did not take long for us to get back on the right footing! When one got in trouble, it seemed we all got in trouble, so we were careful to scrutinize each other when necessary!

It seemed that we did everything together during our visits— slept, played, ate, walked to the neighborhood store on errands, completed chores, etc. At the end of the day, Aunt Charlie Mae boiled water on the stove and poured it into a large, round, tin tub of cold water in preparation for our nightly bath. It was amazing how two or three of us could fit in those large metal bath tubs that were usually placed in the center of a room. After our baths, we got ready for bed. There was no watching television before bedtime (they did not exist at that time); in fact, I do not recall hearing bedtime stories, either.

In any event, after a great day of excursions, active play, and a lot of giggling, we heard Aunt Charlie Mae's warning, "You kids had better settle down in there and go to sleep!" After hearing that warning and taking her seriously, we went right to sleep! Perhaps it was the togetherness that was the "secret sauce" of growing up during the 1950s and 1960s. Children had one another, and were supervised and raised as close family under the watchful eye of a nearby adult.

It seemed that our aunts had the same "adult" power as our mother, so there was little room to decide who was in charge. Even though we lived in different parts of the country, we had close relationships with our aunts and cousins. We looked forward to being together during the summer of each year. We were fortunate to have grown up with the structure, stability, and communal support of trusted relatives like Aunt Charlie Mae.

Aunt Koosie

The next stop was Aunt Koosie's (Maggie James Holloway) house in Cameron, Texas. Our car would pull up in the long dirt driveway, and Aunt Koosie would come running out of the house with a big smile and open arms. As soon as we got out of the car, she just scooped us up in her arms and hugged us as tightly as she could. Aunt Koosie had a huge family, and I did not always know my cousins in her family as intimately as I knew Aunt Charlie Mae's and Aunt Ruthie's children, but I remember they were usually standing nearby with big smiles on their faces.

Aunt Koosie was always happy to see my father, her baby brother. After visiting for a short while, we were off to the next stop, which was Aunt Ruthie's farm, which did not seem too far away. I remember watching Aunt Koosie from the back window of the car as she stood standing and waving goodbye until she could no longer be seen in the distance. My dad always fondly reminded us that Aunt Koosie was his oldest sister.

It was not until writing this family history that I found out from her grandchildren and my sister that Aunt Koosie had a talent for making her famous teacakes! I am sure that we had a chance to taste them on some of those visits, because we often left with a bag of cookies that must have been some of those teacakes. What I remember most is the visual image of Aunt Koosie and her warm smile.

Aunt Ruthie

Visiting Aunt Ruthie (Ruth L. Green Pittman) was quite different from all the others, because she lived on a farm. During the late 1950s and early 1960s, the rural south was called "the country" (the opposite of city living). There were wide open spaces (acreage) between houses, farm animals such as cows, pigs, and horses; and crops, wagons, water wells, and acres and acres of land and vegetation. There was another major difference in that there were no indoor bathrooms, because plumbing and certain utilities had not been extended to the rural areas at that time.

There was an "outhouse" (a small wooden building like a Porta Potty or portable toilet), and a sewer tank located a short distance from the main house. For those who are unaware, inside the "outhouse" was a wooden toilet seat (bench) that had a hole in the middle. Underneath the wooden toilet bench was a hole in the ground where the waste was collected, and later treated as sewerage. So, in short, the outhouse was where everyone went to relieve themselves as in a bathroom. It was common for our cousins, Ruthie Mae, and Flora Pittman to tell us tall tales about going to the "outhouse" at night.

As they giggled, they told stories about snakes, monsters, and other creatures that lived in, around, and under the outhouse. As children, our imagination was very active and creative, so we took them at their word, and tried not to have to visit the "outhouse," especially after dark. Of course, there were no such creatures or monsters living in the outhouse, but there were lightening bugs (fireflies) that could be seen on a clear, hot summer night. Lightning bugs flashed patterns of light as they flew at night, which was an uncommon sight in Seattle.

Also, there were a multitude of beautiful stars in the sky that had a clearness and sharpness as never seen in the city. These were beautiful, environmental sights that seemed unique, quiet, and unobstructed. Sometimes, we came across a few small creatures while walking outdoors or going to the outhouse. There were small harmless garter snakes that scurried in the grassy areas as we carefully crept to the outhouse after dark. That did not help matters a bit! Since we did not know the difference, a snake was a snake, so it did not matter if they were big or small!

Our cousins were accustomed to farm life, so they had great fun teasing us as we quickly took care of business and speedily ran back to the main house. It was intriguing to experience farm versus city life. As children, my cousins seemed to know how to do a lot more things, like how to ride horses, attend to the various animals and crops, tend to the land, draw water from a well, and help with farm life. They often teased us about being "city kids." I do not think they meant it as a compliment.

As adults, we talked about our childhood experiences, and acknowledged that there were advantages that we admired, and we had advantages that they admired. Although I thoroughly enjoyed going to "the country," it was always a welcome treat to get back to Bryan, especially when it came to biological matters and tall tales! We loved visiting Aunt Ruthie and our cousins, and we always had a great time, but we looked forward to returning to Aunt Charlie Mae house with the stern rules and all! The big bonus was she had an indoor bathroom with no thoughts of "creatures" nearby. That was always a relief in many ways!

Additional memories of Aunt Ruthie were shared by our sister, Melloniece Fuller, who grew up in Hearn, Texas. She spent time with Aunt Charlie Mae and our cousins in Bryan, Texas, and shared that Aunt Ruthie often picked her up to visit the family in Cameron. She stayed overnight for weeks and weekends, and recalled that she went to church and spent a lot of time with our cousins Elnora, Reddie, Flora, Andrew (Son), and Isaiah.

Melloniece remembered Aunt Ruthie as a kind, sweet person who always shared whatever she had, including fresh vegetables from her garden. Whenever she stayed at Aunt Ruthie's house, she recalled that she always could be found cooking something in the kitchen. Even though times were hard, she always managed to give Melloniece a little spending change, which was a welcome gift for a high school teenager.

Aunt Dorothy

Dorothy Green Higgins Lyons Lacy (Aunt Dorothy) was the baby girl of our grandparents, Jim and Sirlina Green. Aunt Dorothy was a short, plump, kind woman who usually had a smile on her face. She married several times, but did not have children. She lived in Cameron and Houston, Texas, after divorcing her last husband, William Lacy. After moving to Seattle, she lived with my family for a while.

For most of my early childhood, I remembered Aunt Dorothy as Dorothy Higgins, because as a small child, I remember that she was married to Willie Higgins during the few years we lived in or visited Houston. While living in Seattle, Aunt Dorothy was like a second mother, big sister, and special friend. Great fun always was in store when she was around. She told humorous stories and jokes, organized family games, and played board and card games, such as Monopoly, Chess, Spades, Scrabble, and Checkers.

Frequently, we gathered around the dining room table in Seattle to listen to her favorite gospel and comedy albums and records. Aunt Dorothy introduced us to some of her favorite popular comedians of the time, such as Redd Foxx, Moms Mabley, and Richard Pryor. For instance, during the 1960s, Moms Jackie Mabley was a standup comedian who depicted the image of a toothless, old black woman who dressed in a frazzled old dress with a floppy hat on her head. Moms Mabley told hilarious jokes about her preference for handsome young men.

One of Aunt Dorothy's favorite Moms Mabley's jokes was, "There ain't nothing an ol' man can do but bring me a message from a young one!" Aunt Dorothy's hearty laughter could be heard all over the house as she explained that she agreed with Moms Mabley's choice! Also, it was Aunt Dorothy who taught us the meaning of the old African-American proverb, "Men are like buses. Miss the first one, it won't be fifteen minutes 'til the next one comes by."

Our immediate family gatherings were even more special with the addition of Aunt Dorothy. While living in Seattle, she accompanied us to church and on social outings, and could be counted on to provide a listening ear when asked or needed. She loved telling humorous stories about courting and marrying her many husbands. Her energetic laugh often generated the response of contagious, uncontrollable laughter by others.

It was never clear whether she was serious, but with a great smile on her face, and a wink of the eye when she saw a "good-looking" man, she often declared she was looking at her next husband! I recall thinking as a child that it seemed she had quite a few husbands for one person, but she always said her real love was her first husband, Willie Higgins. While living in Seattle, Aunt Dorothy worked as a live-in nanny and housekeeper for a prominent white family. She took care of two young boys whose mother had died while the children were young.

Each weekend, her employer brought her to our house where she spent weekends. On Sunday nights, my father drove her back or her employer picked her up to return for the next week of work. Aunt Dorothy loved children, so it was fitting that her work involved being a nanny and taking care of children who were without their mother. They cared a great deal for Aunt Dorothy also. There are many stories that could be relayed about Aunt Dorothy. I do not recall a time when she had to discipline us. We respected her, and she kept us engaged in ways that involved playing, learning, and enjoying each other's company.

Now that I think of it, spending "time" with us was a precious parenting resource that she provided. She spent plenty of quality time showing us how to entertain ourselves and develop as happy people. Aunt Dorothy knew that fun and laughter were keys to a happy childhood, so she supplied enough for all her nieces and nephews. She will be forever remembered for her happy nature, hearty laugh, good jokes, and a heartfelt love for children. She later returned to Houston where she remarried again, and died in 1981.

Bringing these memories forward shed a headlight on the fact that now there are different challenges and even more complexities—socially, economically, globally, racially, and technologically. The prevalent norm is no longer reliance on an extended or traditional family as it was in the past. We knew our aunts and cousins, and had strong relationships with them because our parents brought us together so we could know our family members. Now we have various new structures, values, and definitions of family and parents—one parent, same-sex parents, adoptive parents, dual parents, bad parents, intact parents, guardians, grandparents, no parent, etc. It is not uncommon for children in a family to have never met their cousins or their aunts or uncles who live in various parts of the country and abroad.

The longstanding family model that provided the wherewithal to adequately educate and prepare children for life, and ground them in rootedness of family, is now diluted; in fact, it seems that many things that were good for families and children have slipped away. Confronting new conditions and times are necessary requirements, but the challenge is to take advantage of change without forfeiting important people, traditions, virtues, institutions, influential legacies, and family practices that served our common well-being.

It is unfortunate that so many children today do not have the benefit of family in their lives like we had Aunt Dorothy, Aunt Juanita, Aunt Charlie Mae, Aunt Koosie, Aunt Ruthie, and the many others. They took responsibility for all of us in one way or another. They valued and helped develop us so we could know and experience their influence as our foundation-builders, protectors, and connectors to our roots. Also, it was not only the Green sisters, there were many others who helped to shape our being. In the next chapter, I would like to introduce you to Aunt Lump.

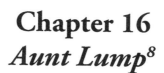

Chapter 16
Aunt Lump[8]

So many of us who are over forty to fifty years of age cherished our ancestors and relatives, who symbolized the fond and cherish memories that are often referred to as the "good old days." Despite all the difficulty, there was something very special about being raised during a time when children were children, parents were parents (and often strict ones at best), and adults were adults. You see, children had to stay in their place, and negotiation was not an option as it is in many families today.

Black folks have always had their own way of raising children and doing things, like coming up with creative names; so growing up, there were family members who fondly had various nicknames. In our family, there was Aunt Sis, Uncle Nubby, Aunt Tillie, Dute, Little Dorothy, Aunt Koosie, Uncle Dude, Aunt Ping, and Aunt Babe. We had cousins who were called Bubba, Candy Boy, and two or three cousins simply were known as Brother or Sister. We did not learn some of their real names until later in life.

Dorothea Carter (one of Leana's cousins) and I would like to introduce you to one of our relatives who had a special nickname— Aunt Lump. We can't forget Aunt Lump's only daughter, Leana's nickname, which was simply, Precious. Aunt Lump was married to our uncle, James Green Jr., so she was an aunt to the Green family through marriage. Her real name was Olivia Pittman Green, born January 24, 1934 in Milam County Texas, but all the children called her "Aunt Lump." Speaking of nicknames, we could never figure out

---

[8] Written by Dorothea Carter and Searetha Smith Collins (2009)

why Aunt Lump's grandchildren called her Mrs. Green. We guess it was some type of endearment and respect for elders.

You see, when we grew up—and it's probably still true today—there was one unique experience that was common to little Black girls, which is the memory of getting our "hair done." As black girls, the task of getting our hair done required a bit more than most others because of the unique texture and nature of our hair. The following is an edited narrative written jointly by Dorothea that describes how special Aunt Lump was to all her nieces.

Narrative by Dorothea Carter

You see, Aunt Lump was a hairdresser, and I think she did everyone's hair at some time or another. As little girls, every week, Dorothea and many of Aunt Lump's nieces went to her beauty shop to get their hair done, but the weekly visit was much more than that. Aunt Lump's place was a beauty shop/daycare center/ corner store/advice health clinic. Each Saturday, mothers dropped their kids off in the morning to get a "press and comb," and then returned around evening time to pick up the children. Dorothea was one of those kids.

Aunt Lump didn't have a telephone (cellphones were not even thought of at the time), so Olivia Green (Aunt Lump) was everybody's mother while they were at the beauty shop. She didn't have much trouble when the other mothers were away, however. There was always a belt nearby for bad behavior, and Aunt Lump was never afraid to use it. In those days, Child Protective Service rules must have been a little different. You see, Aunt Lump and most parents had not heard of things like "time-outs" or discussions about options and alternatives for misbehavior. We knew that when the broad smile that was always on her face disappeared, we had better "straighten up" fast.

We knew Aunt Lump loved us and wanted us to be our best selves. What we learned at home and away from home was called "good home training," and Aunt Lump certainly reinforced all of what was expected. I am amazed at how some people interpret the spankings today. We know that spankings overdone can become abusive or be received as "beatings," but that is not what most of us experienced. The "love taps" that we received taught some serious lessons that many still remember today about appropriate behavior. Enough said about different cultural practices and how the dominant or contemporary culture interprets it.

Auntie always made sure that the kids ate lunch. If you didn't want her corner store items, such as candy, bubble gum, sour pickles with the peppermint in the middle or chips or soda, you could opt to have a "nutritious" meal at the ice cream truck (we all know that ice cream is a good source of milk). As mentioned, Aunt Lump loved doing hair! In fact, she stopped working only a year before she passed on. We loved how Aunt Lump praised her own work. She would say, "Oooh, Dorothea, I really made your hair straight this time. It is sooo pretty! I ordered that conditioner from California." Every product Aunt Lump ordered seemed to come from California. A local Sally's Beauty Supply did not exist then, so we guess whatever was available in Houston just wasn't good enough for Auntie.

Aunt Lump had such a good heart. She never charged much for her services. A "wet set" was about $6.00. If you splurged and got color and a perm, you might have spent a good $20.00. Even with those prices, Aunt Lump still allowed some customers to be on a payment plan. Dorothea remembered one lady who came to pay on her services every week. She later discovered that the lady had four girls, so Aunt Lump decided to let her pay in installments.

Would you like health advice anyone? Aunt Lump could give it. You see, her day job was in the nursing profession. She loved nursing almost as much as doing hair. If anyone had some type of health question, Aunt Lump always had an answer, and usually, our auntie was right. After Aunt Lump closed her shop, she started doing hair for her special people in the evenings in her shop at home. You see, back then, single mothers like Aunt Lump always had to work two or three jobs to keep the family going. James Green Jr., her husband, died in a car accident, so she was left to take care of Precious and all the extended nephews, neighbors, and foster children whom she often took in and cared for throughout the years.

We guess African-American mothers and others just did what they had to do back in those days, and they did not have or need help from the government. People just took care of and shared with one another. It was just being "family" and neighborly friendly, especially when it came to taking care and nurturing children.

Aunt Lump was a wonderful woman with a beautiful spirit of giving and living. Back then, there were many Aunties like Aunt Lump who took care of and watched over us when our mothers were busy, working or just away. We knew what was expected of us, and Aunt Lump made sure we were safe, happy, fed, well-behaved, and lived up to the expectations of our parents and family. Our mothers left us in the safe care of Aunt Lump's beauty shop. We guess that's what's called having our extended family as part of our circle of love and influence. We just remember that we were always welcome at Aunt Lump's beauty shop and house. She "did hair" up until the end. As we told you, our Aunt Lump loved "doing hair," and some of her customers just wouldn't let her stop, especially at those prices!

Author's Notes

Although this story is about Aunt Lump, it is characteristic of many elders and relatives who served as mothers, fathers, advisors, caretakers, friends, disciplinarians, religious leaders, guardians, teachers, counselors, cooks, aunties, uncles, cousins, play-cousins, godparents, grandparents, and extended family to so many of us. They provided historical, religious, and cultural foundations, disciplined us, shared their homes with us, and instilled work ethics and character.

They modeled values of hard work, helped us to understand right from wrong, and provided a sense of belonging and conscience, all of which seem missing as current childhood tenets. Today's children and parents are paying a high price for what was considered progress in this regard. On the other hand, it is very important that this point be emphasized. The past was hard times for Black people in America; there were times of belittlement, lack of respect, and exclusion of people simply based on race, gender, and color.

There were fewer opportunities to spread wings, but there was inspiration and wisdom for self-development, spiritual and moral fiber, family norms and values, and purpose in life. We respected our elders (we had no choice), and we looked up to them for guidance and direction. These were experiences that helped us cross the bridge of life. There is a saying, "The root has to be fed to sweeten the fruit" (Unknown). We were truly sweetened by those who strengthened our roots. We think we turned out just fine. Aunt Lump has passed on now, and we surely miss her.

Chapter 17
Elbert Lee Green
(aka Uncle Elbert)

A recurring theme that runs through the stories of the Greens and McGills is that family establishes our life experiences—past and present. It is befitting that I dedicate the next few chapters to explaining how my father, Elbert Green, provided the glue for carrying on the legacy of family during a time when family experiences had a very different meaning and impact.

The level of gift a person leaves involves helping the youth understand universal truths for achieving levels of success. The story of my father illustrates how the continuum of efforts and dreams were fulfilled. He and other African-Americans managed to keep afloat, enough to create a strong sense of pride, identity, heritage, and family. *Pride* was ignited in the unity and courage to survive. *Identity* evolved through the strength of knowing that somehow families "raised (reared)" generations of children who achieved, thrived, and succeeded from enslavement to prosperity in the contemporary world. *Heritage* stemmed from understanding the legacy of conditions and experiences that were acquired from being born in one of the most crucial associations—*family*.

As mentioned, Elbert Lee Green, the baby son of James (Jim) Sr. and Sirlina McGill Green, was the last patriarch of the Jim Green family until his death in 2002. Fondly known as "Uncle Elbert" to his nephews and nieces, my father was born on September 6, 1923, in Branchville, Texas. He was part of the generation commonly known as the World War II/G.I./Veterans/Builders (born 1900–1924). My

144

father grew up during the transitional period after WWI, the Great Depression, and the Prohibition Era of the 1920s. The general objective in life for this generation was to buy a house, payoff the mortgage, send several children to college, to handle their affairs and save enough money to retire and be somewhat secure in old age.

Life in America at that time was hard and overcast by poverty that stemmed from injustices and virtually impossible opportunities that were unequal and abridged by legal separate, unequal, and unjust laws, policies, practices, and conditions. Despite those conditions, Elbert grew up as a normal, mischievous boy on a farm in Branchville. He loved to swim, hunt, and fish; and even as a young child, he helped his family work as sharecroppers in the cotton fields.

Life dealt my father a grave blow when he lost not one, but both of his parents at the age of seventeen, when his mother (Sirlina) died a few months after his father in 1941. After his mother's death, he lived with his sister, Ruthie, and other relatives before moving to Houston around the age of eighteen or nineteen. My father, and his childhood friend, Clarence Harlan, found themselves in Houston with the intent of exploring life beyond their conditions. They went to school together, always did everything together as children and adults, and were close throughout childhood and adulthood until my father died.

My father set out against the odds without the benefit of resources and support from his parents. He dreamed big, and despite obstacles and hardships, he carved out a quality life that turned into a very different pathway. One of mother's brothers shared that when my father moved to Houston, most employers felt that people from "the country" had a stronger work ethic than people raised in the city. When it came to employment, "country boys" had the advantage with urban employers, because it was believed that they were used to working hard on farms and in fields, so they would not object to hard work or working long hours in the city.

This was true in my dad's case. At the young age of nineteen, he worked at a service station on Wheeler and Alameda Street in Houston. He pumped gas, washed, and oiled cars with a grease guns that lubricated grease fittings under cars. In 1943, he was hired to work in the automotive shop at the Raymond Pearson Car Dealership in Houston. There, he did carpentry work and delivered cars and transported customers to and from the automotive shop in a three-wheeled motorcycle carrier.

Even as a teenager, my father was known to work two to three jobs simultaneously. He was a carpenter-builder by vocation. He loved to work with his hands, and had a talent and passion for designing, building, and making something from nothing. Most people remember him as a family man and worker, with a strong drive and work ethic. While in Houston, he met and married my mother, Oleatha Green. They settled in a small one-bedroom apartment that became a popular rest-stop or live-in place for many families, relatives, and friends who periodically stayed with them or stopped by for a good meal.

As indicated earlier, my parents had three daughters, Virgie Lee, Searetha, and Patricia Ann Green. My dad had another daughter, Melloniece, who was born in Hearne, Texas, before my oldest sister was born. My dad was not a selfish man; in fact, he was generous to a fault. He reached out to help everyone who needed assistance. He had an open-door policy where everyone was always welcome. Many relatives lived with my parents at some point.

I was told that Aunt Dorothy Green and Willie Higgins (her husband at the time) lived with my mother and father for a while in Houston. My father and Uncle Willie both received military draft notices on the same day, so they enlisted in the US Army at the same time during World War II, in January 1943. Uncle Clarence had already volunteered to serve in the army, so he left earlier. My father served in World War II, and was honorably discharged in 1945. As a WWII veteran, he had the chance to further his education using the GI Bill, which financially allowed him to attend Texas Southern University in Houston where he studied carpentry.

Fortunately, during World War II, employers had to hold jobs for war veterans, so after my father returned from the army, he continued to work at Raymond Pearson until he moved with our family to Seattle in 1950. Before leaving Houston, he built a house in the Sunnyside area where he had planned to settle with his family. The house was eventually sold to my mother's sister before my parents embarked on their adventure to Seattle, Washington.

Negotiating the Cards Dealt

My parents, Elbert and Oleatha Green, were a part of the generation that grew up under the legal "separate but unequal" society during the nation's long history of racial discrimination and segregation. As African-American youth and young adults, it seemed they were in a sea of survival, in a little boat, afraid, nervous, and did not know what was on the other side of life. My parents did not let those conditions deter their dreams, however.

They dreamt big, and prepared for what was to become the new American landscape with new horizons for black people. The significance of obtaining a good education as a way to advance in society was the emphasis of their motivation; consequently, they realized it was important to prepare their children to ensure a place in mainstream society. Even though my parents were educated in segregated southern black schools that reportedly had inferior facilities and resources, the schools produced quality teachers and quality students. Since the importance of school was central to black communities, they benefitted from collective efforts that emphasized the importance of high academic achievement, personal pride, respect for God, self, family, and others. Determination, effort, and the necessity to do better than the best to compete in society was their inspiration.

They were taught by family and teachers alike to know how to cope and be prepared for living in the unfriendly society. My parent's generation navigated and negotiated around poor economic times, as well as overt conditions of humiliation. As optimistic young adults, they and others hurdled over injustices and racism that came in such forms as racial name-calling, unjust employment opportunities and practices, low-paying menial jobs, not being respected, and the continuous humiliation of being second-guessed by incessant questioning of qualifications, abilities, and skills.

They overcame the "putdowns" and worked harder and smarter for less pay to find ways to engage in a continuous ascent. Their journey taught them about endurance and overcoming obstacles to find ways to move forward. The legacy of the black church was strong, and their faith provided security during uncertain times. Religious faith, hard work, hope, and a strong belief in a greater power were natural parts of growing up as blacks. The black church was the single place where black people experienced their religious convictions, as well as unity, pride, hope, strength, and the quest for liberty, recognition, community, and leadership. It was a place of refuge, power, protection, support, and relief from burdens and feelings of rejection from the hostile outer society.

One of the most unique observations of my father's and mother's generation is that they had values of the proceeding generation—hard work, independence, care, respect for family, love, religious faith, and togetherness, which stemmed from the heart of a legacy of perseverance and fortitude. Understandably, there were times of frustration and disappointment because of the social, economic, historical, and political realities of the time. Still, they persisted and were optimistic about the potential for a different time to come.

My father's personal story is one of persistence, optimism, and fulfillment of that potential. The legacy of the black family, the legacy of ancestors, and the legacy of the black church were some of the ingredients that contributed to individual and collective progress, survival, and uplifting that was acquired by my parents and previous generations. Their religious foundations, and collective and personal convictions, inspired them to "step out on faith" to further their dreams and opportunities, and to provide a different future for themselves and their children. In the next chapter, you will experience their personal pilgrimage after World War II in the late 1940s, which was part of the Black Migration from the South to the North in our country.

Chapter 18
The Promise

A few years after the end of WWI and WWII, there were reports from black newspapers, friends, and relatives who had moved to northern and mid-western cities that there was more hope for jobs and better things in the western, eastern, and northern parts of the country. During what was coined the "Great African-American Migration (1920s–1940s), most people traveled by train, bus or car to reach what seemed like "The Promise Land." They were on the move, looking for a job—any job in mid-western, eastern or northern cities where they would be paid higher wages offering greater economic opportunities; where there were better schooling and training opportunities, and where there were more chances and advantages versus the hardships of living in the poverty of the South.

For my father, encouragement came from his sister, Juanita Green Martin who lived in Seattle, Washington. He wanted to explore life beyond his present conditions, so my parents decided to take Aunt Juanita's suggestion to move our family to Seattle where job opportunities were more plentiful. The idea was a troubling concept for my mother's parents, who strongly believed in unity and keeping family in proximity as close as possible. In fact, my mother's father, the strong patriarch of her family, insisted that my parents leave us, the children, behind in the safe care of grandparents while they roamed to unknown places.

My parents respectfully declined the offer/mandate and followed the plan with more determination. After loading their 1940s Ford to the brim with clothes, small appliances, and food for the trip, they started on their adventure. There was a contingent of extended family who drove in caravan style to accompany us to the Houston City limits to reluctantly wave us goodbye. As our parents drove off, my mother's father's stern words could be heard. "Don't forget where home is, and don't be afraid to come back if you need to!"

Not to be deterred by fear and words of caution from well-meaning relatives and friends, my parents courageously left Houston, Texas, with a year-old baby girl, a five-year-old, and a seven-year-old daughter. They started on their journey across country, driving to unfamiliar territory and a very different cultural reality that awaited them in Seattle, Washington. Embarking on such a journey had its obstacles, however. If African-Americans traveled by bus or car, they had to stop en route for food and rest reluctantly and timidly or wait to use public accommodations such as restrooms, hotels or restaurants.

Often, they were denied public services and facilities. Legalized segregation policies and laws disallowed access based on race alone, which made travel stops a very selective venture. My parents carried along what was known as 'The Negro Travelers' Green Book', which was a guide created sometime around the mid-1930s to help keep black people from harm during travel across the United States and North America. Motels, gas stations, restaurants, public bathrooms and other facilities were segregated and off-limits, so the 'Green Book' was used especially during road trips until the Civil Rights Act was passed in 1964. My mother and father kept driving until it was safe to make a stop for needs. There were no freeways or intestates as there are today, so distance driving and looking for safe places to stop we quite an uncharted, risky, undertaking.

Traveling through mountain ranges, deserts, and sometimes inhospitable territory was challenging, especially with three small children in the backseat of the car. While traveling up the high mountainous elevations of Utah, the old Ford automobile started to smoke and steam, indicating carburetor trouble. That was a great concern because my parents had limited travel funds, and no financial back up for this trip.

They found a town in Utah, where my father stopped and found a shop to repair the car. The shop owner was so impressed with my father's work that he offered him a job if he chose to remain in Utah. Grateful for the offer, he declined because they had a clear plan, destination, and mission in mind. Most important, our parents were looking forward to settling in a place where there was family, so they continued the journey to Seattle. More trouble surfaced as the car twisted and turned up and around the sharp curves of the giant mountains.

Later during the trip through the mountain, the rear door of the old Ford suddenly flew open! My older sister screamed, "The baby is sliding out of the car!" Extremely calm, my father looked in the rearview mirror and saw that baby Patricia, who was sleeping on a pillow on the backseat, was teetering on the edge of the seat near the opened door. He carefully reached back across the front seat to catch and pull the sliding pillow safely away from the opened door (car seats, baby seats or seat belts were not required or even thought of in those days).

With the baby safely rescued, my parents reflected on the fact that this was going to be quite a story to tell when they reported back to the family in Houston. Indeed, everyone was stunned to hear that we almost lost our baby sister in the mountains of Utah.

Are We There Yet?

It was a welcome sight when we arrived at our destination in Seattle! It had been the longest trip we had ever taken—about five days and nights. As mentioned, we lived with Aunt Juanita and Uncle Charlie Martin for a few months. While living there, my mother made sure we were careful to "mind our manners," and not disturb anyone or anything that was breakable. You see, parents of that generation had a good, firm handle on managing and disciplining their children. Most children had good home training and a good handle on the fact that they were not in charge—they were to obey their parents always.

Even as small children, the last thing we wanted to do was embarrass our parents, and they certainly did not intend to have their children embarrass them in any event. If someone failed to remember the rules or instructions, there were serious consequences to pay. Parents were aware of the dangers, pitfalls, obstacles, attitudes, and issues around being black in America. So much of what was taught was for the safety purposes of learning how to navigate a hostile environment or helping children learn how to manage themselves in various situations, especially in other people's homes.

A few months after moving to Seattle in 1950, the news came that my mother's father had died. She traveled ahead with our baby sister, and my father got the old Ford ready again, and drove my sister and me to Houston for the funeral, and then again back to Seattle. It was on this trip that my father drove through Fort Worth, Texas, and stopped at Aunt Georgia McGill's house to visit.

On this trip, as small children the significance and necessity of the 'Green Book' that was mentioned earlier became front and center. As we traveled somewhere near Dallas, my father found himself compelled to stop to buy something for us to eat. As you recall, 'The Green Book' was used to specify places of safety, but we were nowhere near places listed where African American travelers could stop and not be discriminated against. My sister and I clearly made it known to him that we could not wait to eat, so he reluctantly stopped at a small eating place on the side of the road.

He went inside and told the waitress that he wanted to order hamburgers for his children. The white customers stopped and glared at him as the owner asked him if he was a "Mexican?" He said "No, that he was not." The owner responded, "Well, 'Nigga', you know you are supposed to go to the back door to the kitchen, so get out of here!" Not wanting to comply to the indignant demand, he realized that he needed to get food for us, so he went to the back door to the kitchen. Noticeably, the kitchen had a dirt floor where a few black people were working.

The black workers fussed at our dad as they gave him the hamburgers and told him, "Now, get out of here before you get us all killed!" Not only was this a personal experience of being subjected to denial of services, racism, and an inequitable life-threatening undertaking, most vividly we remembered the expression on our dad's face. This was an impressionable, direct example of seeing the look of insult, humiliation, and degradation. Also, it clearly provided an understanding of the degree to which many of our parents and ancestors had to carefully negotiate the societal landscape to survive and provide for their family.

Our trip back from Seattle was a bit easier since the ends and outs of the journey were fresh in our dad's mind.

Despite stunning setbacks along the way, my father continued to persevere all his life. A short time after returning to Seattle, we moved to our first family home. A short time later in 1951, my father got the news that his brother, James Green Jr., had died in a car accident. This time, he traveled back to Houston alone, while we stayed with my mother and remained in school.

Chapter 19
Greener Pastures

I am sure you have heard of the concept "growing up green," which involves preserving the environment. In the context of this chapter, the term is more about growing up as a part of the Green family in the Evergreen State of Washington. Living in Seattle offered new and different opportunities for our family. There were environmental and cultural similarities, and differences that were outstanding. Although we had moved to a new geographic region, we took our historical, cultural, and family roots with us as we settled into the new environment.

During the 1950s, in most parts of the county, regardless of socioeconomic status and location, black families generally lived in similar close-knit, working-class neighborhoods and communities. There was a mixture of people in our environment and neighborhoods that reinforced positive group identity, support, and modeling, including doctors, lawyers, plumbers, teachers, business owners, auto mechanics, ministers, leaders, postal workers, bankers, etc. The difference in Seattle was that there were fewer blacks than in the east, mid-west or southern part of the country.

After a few years, a few more blacks began to move into our neighborhood. One or two white families stayed, but as time passed, the neighborhood became increasingly segregated. Although the dynamic of racial segregation was apparent, we were by no means wealthy; but as black people, we thrived in those communal, family-oriented settings. For instance, our childhood was filled with play, school, church, friends, birthday parties, picnics, and spending holidays together. We participated in Camp Fire Girls, piano lessons, bicycle riding, and roller-skating (without helmets and knee protection gear), bowling, playing Jacks and "Hide and Seek," and using our imagination to make toys such as bottle dolls (using a coke bottle with straw stuffed in the top as hair).

Some of our family activities and celebrations included drive-in movies, family road trips and summer vacations, going to the beach and mountains, visiting the public library, and playing croquet as a family (the outdoor game where each person uses a wooden mallet to hit balls through an obstacle course, like golf). Much of our time was spent playing in the neighborhood or in the backyard on the swings and slide that my dad set up for us. Often, the neighborhood children came to our house to play on the swings and slide.

Along with play equipment, there were blackberry vines and fresh delicious peaches that hung from a peach tree that was perched over the roof of our garage. Each season, fresh fruit was available for the picking, which turned into fresh jam, jelly, and peach cobbler that came from the natural trees in our backyard. Childhood involved free, creative, healthy, child-focused activities, including being allowed to play outside unsupervised, without fear of harm, but an adult was always somewhere nearby if needed.

Although we were free to play unsupervised, there was one caveat for most children in the neighborhood. We had to adhere to strict rules and deadlines, such as, we could play in the neighborhood and nearby, but we had to be back in the house before the streetlights were on (which meant before dark). Gunshots, gang violence, and decay did not exist in our neighborhoods, nor did we have to negotiate around threats, such as drug dealings and brutality on our streets.

Seeking greener pastures involved reaching for dreams and advances, but the road traveled was not without potholes and challenges. Most likely, there were clandestine occurrences that occurred, but fortunately, most people in our families and communities adhered to strict, expected roles, and codes of morals and ethics; however, we could stay only in the care of trusted parents, teachers, family, friends, relatives, or neighbors.

Family Rituals and Routines

There were rituals and routines that fortified and provided structure for families. For instance, in African-American religious tradition, faith, hope, and unity was connected to participation in the black church, so Sunday was a special family day that was spent in church. Afterward, we visited relatives and ate Sunday dinner together as a family. Not only did we eat meals as a family throughout the week, as in the popular movie and television program *Soul Food*, there was a traditional Sunday dinner that was reminiscent of many black families each Sunday.

My mother was an excellent cook, so we always looked forward to homemade meals in general; but Sunday dinner was extra special, because we knew that an even greater treat was in store. The dinner table was filled with fried chicken, baked ham or tender roast beef, mashed or candied sweet potatoes, mustard greens, macaroni and cheese, potato salad, banana pudding or peach cobbler, etc. Sunday and holiday dinners were often topped off with one of my mother's specialties—fresh, fluffy, golden brown yeast rolls, all homemade, of course. Friends, relatives, neighbors, and others often joined us for dinner, especially when they knew my mother was cooking her famous rolls and lemon pound cakes!

If we were poor, we certainly did not know it, because there was always plenty of food, and always enough for anyone and everyone who came to visit and eat. Sunday dinner and weekly meals at the dinner table was not just about eating; it was a ritual for coming together or bringing the family or clan together to bond, debrief, talk, share, discuss problems or issues, and engender peace, stability, and enjoyment as family and friends.

Parents and community paid a great deal of attention to developing moral and ethical intelligence. We were not raised to be perfect, but we were expected to be responsible and accountable for the consequences of our behavior. We learned about values and character building, such as respect, determining and differentiating right from wrong, developing love for self and others, and realizing that there were consequences for every action. Activities were designed to build and develop racial, social, moral, emotional, and religious conscious-ness, as well as cultivate feelings of concern, care, sympathy, trust, kindness, compassion, empathy, etc.

We were members of the New Hope Baptist Church in Seattle, and as children, going to church was not a choice, it was a family event. As a family, we participated in children and youth choirs, Sunday School, and related programs and activities, including a youth program called Baptist Youth Training Union (BYTU). Years later, after we moved to a new neighborhood, my father and younger sister joined the First African Methodist Episcopal Church (FAME) where they attended religiously. My father proudly served as an usher there until he became ill. Spending family time together, worship-ping together, eating together, and being a part of family and com-munity where rituals reinforced the importance of being a part of a communal unit were some of the memories that became etched in our mind.

Making a Way

My father worked as a supervisor/superintendent for the US Postal Service in Seattle for thirty-four years. As mentioned, he believed in working and providing for his family, which oftentimes meant working multiple jobs at the same time. In addition to the post office, he was a carpenter, so he moonlighted and worked, repaired, remodeled, and built things for others on the side. After retiring from the post office, he worked as a freelance carpenter. He understood that it took both parents to provide for a family, so my dad shared in securing and steadying the home by providing and taking care of us as well.

Although my dad worked hard, he understood that life required a balance, so periodically, he went to Moses Lake, Washington, for hunting and fishing trips to get a break from the hassles of work and life. He brought home trophy "catches" and took great pride in skin-ning, cleaning, and preparing a meal of fish or deer meat. Speaking of cooking good food, his specialty was preparing breakfast. When the aroma of his fried bacon circulated through the house in the mornings or when he cooked fried green tomatoes or smoked barbeque ribs in the backyard on his homemade barrel smoker during holidays and cookouts, everyone knew they were in for a delicious feast.

After retiring, he worked as a school crossing guard, and as a bus driver for a senior citizen center. Also, he worked part time as an usher at the Seattle Center Arena, which was the athletic center for the Seattle Super Sonics basketball team where he enjoyed watching his favorite team play. My mother stayed home while we were young. As we became older, she worked as a maid at the Waldorf Hotel in downtown Seattle. Next, she was a food service supervisor in the cafeteria of the hospital at the University of Washington. Later, she worked at the Boeing Aircraft Manufacturing Center as a silk screener until she retired. My parents were beneficiaries of the period of post-World War II prosperity in the country. The economic boom of the 1950s, 1960s, and 1970s allowed many of the WWII generation (such as my parents) to move firmly into the black middle-class.

Like most men and women of their generation, after World War II, they took advantage of job opportunities that opened to black people in civil service and factory work. Such jobs offered good wages and benefits that propelled them into a better lifestyle. This in turn allowed them to acquire comforts for their family, as well as necessities, including disposable cash to finance our college education. After graduating from high school, there was an indisputable, automatic expectation that we were to attend college. For many families, money was the question, but for Elbert and Oleatha, college was a premium advantage, so it was a non-negotiable career option.

Somehow, they figured out how to make sure money was available to pay for college for all three of us; in fact, at one time, they paid college tuition for both my older sister and me at the same time. Like most youth at that time, we were expected to commit to graduating from college on time within four years, with no excuses. There were no student loans, no time-outs or time off to "dilly-dally around" or "find ourselves," which often happens with second or third plus generation college-going students today. Our job was to not waste the opportunity or time to gain the advantage of an education. The longstanding vision and goal was to attain a better place in society than was available to our parents as well as to be put in a position to serve and uplift others. That was our imperative.

New Rules, New Roles

Can you imagine being a woman and not being able to wear pants in public? Although that seems to be something that was required hundreds of years ago, when I was a teen and young adult, women wore dresses or skirts and never wore pants to certain venues such as work, school, church or most affairs (that was only a few decades ago). The exception was only if it was very cold could you wear pants under a skirt or dress. I recall when I went to college in Central Washington, during my freshman year, it was extremely cold that winter, so a formal request was made by the residents of the women's dormitories to wear pants instead of skirts (there were men and women dormitories).

Finally, due to inclement weather reaching far below freezing, the college administration granted permission for us to wear pants during the emergency situation only. Women's rights have come a long way during my lifetime. There were many such gender-based rules and taboos in those days, and the decorum did not change until after the Women's Movement of the 1970s. The old gender-biased ways that dictated past practice is one of those areas that dictated necessary change. The following are other situations that centered on gender bias and discrimination during my assent from childhood to adulthood. Keep in mind that the examples illustrate gender practices during a generation that dictated different needs and conditions.

My mother was raised in true African-American tradition. In the book *African-American Wisdom* (McKnight 2002, Gerda Lerner 1972), it is explained that some of the motives behind the values and perspectives of women of my mother's generation followed a traditional cultural model:

> (Black) women ... (were) trained from childhood to become workers, and expected to be financially self-supporting for most of their lives. They

> know (knew) they will (would) have (had) to
> work, whether married or single; work to them,
> unlike to white women, is (was) not a liberating
> goal, but rather an imposed lifelong necessity.
> (African-American Wisdom, p. 47)

Black women pretty much passed on the culture, and generally taught what was right and wrong. Most African-American girls were raised and taught to be responsible, to be achievement and goal-oriented, and fully prepared for whatever circumstances life offered. Of course, everyone could not afford to send their children to college, but it was the goal of most parents to seek such a future if possible.

As mentioned, many parents sacrificed and worked multiple jobs to provide the opportunity for their children to have access to college, so it was not taken for granted by most. If you were from a middle to low-income family, and if you were one of the lucky ones, higher education was the pathway to future success. Other people took other routes to developing a livelihood, so they went into the armed forces or gained job training or a technical skill that often-times was developed in high school and translated into productive lifework.

In any event, the goal was to become independent adults who could "stand on their own feet." For the most part, children gained a strong basic education that translated into fruitful lives, jobs, and careers. Our post-secondary opportunities came in the form of life skills training and preparation. For instance, my mother felt it was important for girls to have a college education and a backup plan for future financial security. She always preached, "As girls, you never know if something is going to happen, and you might have to take care of yourself and your children alone."

Black women such as my mother knew that black men and women alike were marginalized in society; and as blacks and women, the future was always uncertain. Most black girls were taught a similar lesson. My mother's antidote was to acquire a good education, so we could get a good, secure job or career. She guided us to always save money for an emergency, and understand if we had a husband who couldn't or wouldn't provide for the family, we had to always be prepared to do so. There was more advice that most black mothers advised: "Always keep a secret stash of money someplace for a rainy day. Keep it in a shoe, can, box, under the mattress or wherever you can hide it so you will always be prepared for an emergency or exit plan."

Married women could not have separate bank or credit accounts or acquire credit in their name in those days (this was only about fifty years ago or so). Further, after marriage, all legal papers were in the husband's or man's name as the head of the household. This became very problematic for women if they wanted to become independent; thus, there was a need for progressive change in that matter as well.

Before the Women's Rights Movement of the 1970s, there were gender practices and rules based on a white woman's standard. For most blacks, living life was a mutual condition and endeavor. The main point is that many black mothers taught lessons about how to be a strong woman, which served as a safety net or contingency plan for unforeseen turbulence and family survival. In the best of situations, beginning in the home, the family taught principles of belief and worship. The family taught concepts and ideas about receiving, giving, and sharing love.

In most circumstances, the family goal was to have someone available to care for children. That might have meant making sacrifices and not having luxuries or wants. Rightly or wrongly, women were the child bearers; therefore, childrearing practices dictated that mothers were expected to be the major nurturers of children. As was seen in slave quarters, if both parents were not available, women shared responsibilities and took care of one another's children. Fathers were expected to be responsible for providing for the family, but some, like my father, shared in securing and steadying family and children by providing and taking care of us in the home as well.

Family Partnerships

Progressiveness always has been the goal; yet, it was contingent upon timing and circumstances. My father's story illustrates that hunger, tenacity, sheer will, desire, dedication, hard work, and being a family man who provided a secure home for his family was an important aspect of his character. He was not complacent, nor did the past deter him from being energetic, self-motivated, transformative, and full of life. In fact, part of his consciousness spurred him to ensure that his children and those around him had a life that was better than the one he had.

Although differences in cultural and gender roles changed, the need for a partnership in the home worked best for most families. For instance, my father understood that life required a balance in drive, work, responsibility, and joy.

It might have been more financially productive for both parents to work to "make ends meet," but rightfully or wrongly, as mentioned, our parents followed the ancestral/generational model that children were taken care of by women as their priority (daycare or childcare centers were not existent as they are today, and most people believed in taking care of their own within the vicinity of close relatives and extended family). There was no plan to depend on others or on welfare or other government assistance during those days.

In fact, during that time and before, most girls were considered "an old maid" if they had not married by the ripe old age of twenty-one. The goal was to find a man who was "good marriage material" before turning twenty-one. African-American boys had a similar menu. They were expected to "get a good job (any legal job)" much earlier, and to "find a girl" who could be a good wife and mother of their children.

Life was somewhat homogeneous in values and views during my generation, so most people shared similar goals based on Christian, American, and African-American principles. Of course, the Women's Rights Movement took place during the maturation or my generation (the Boomers), so thankfully, many things changed. There were many taboos in those days, and the biased practices did not change until after the late 1970s and 1980s. For the most part, up until then, the atmosphere and environment for raising children generally provided a predictable, self-shielding structure; however, all was not well.

Women generally were compelled to sacrifice their potential, and career aspirations, in exchange for placing more emphasis on family and children. Of course, this was not true for everyone, but for those who were fortunate enough to have positive, caring family environments, and caring, devoted parents during this period of our journey, the promise of childhood was fulfilled. I have said several times, however, that the past in its entirety was not good, and some past practices did not need to continue. Gender and racial bias are prime examples of practices that needed to be reexamined during the modern-age.

Knowing about this history in contemporary times is important as a reminder of how far we have come in just a short period of time. Understanding the context of this part of our journey reminds us that we cannot fall prey to an agenda that might require abdication of our survival. Family and the power of family are principles that we cannot afford to abandon on behalf of contemporary trends and popular culture. In any event, parents generally placed more importance on family and children. Perhaps that was one of the ingredients for the success of many families and children, especially African-Americans prior to the 1990s.

Chapter 20
Anchors and Cocoons

It must be acknowledged that the traditional family as an anchor was not in place for all children. Some were abandoned and suffered mistreatment, lack of attention, and others were exposed to violence, physical, sexual or other abuse. Such treatment did not seem as widespread then; or perhaps it was more a matter of people just did not talk about such issues during those times. For the most part, parents seemed to have had similar core values and understandings about family roles and responsibilities.

In the best situations, it seemed that family, neighborhood, church, school, and community provided the glue that held generations together. All in all, past family-life represented a time when parents were parents and children were children, and roles were not violated, mixed or confused. I mention African-American parents, because that was my experience up close and personal. In retrospect, there was value in family life that provided successful transitions from childhood to adulthood.

Parents sounded the message loud and clear that it was their responsibility to prepare children for dispositions of learning and living. It was the schools' responsibility to guide and help children attain educational and citizenship skills and knowledge necessary for attaining a productive life; and it was the church's responsibility to help parents impart a moral center, character, and spiritual guidance. Such understandings created a "village" or "cocoon" type approach to creating conditions and environments for children's development and success.

Such a pattern was seen throughout the Green/McGill family stories. For instance, if a young girl had a child out of wedlock, and later married, the spouse raised the children, without reservation, as his or her very own. Or if parents went away for whatever reason, children stayed with grandparents or other family members, and were raised by them without reservation. In any event, for the most part, children were usually entrusted with someone with the responsibility of taking care of them, as opposed to being left abandoned or unattended.

This appeared to be a significant cultural theme and general feeling in the past. For the most part, there was someone, most of the time someone in the family, who took the responsibility for their own and other people's children, even if they were not the biological parents. Out of necessity, Black life pretty much existed where everyone depended on and supported one another for existence, healing, and help. There were other sacrifices made on behalf of children as well. For instance, some parents married and stayed together for the sake of children or some kept the family unit together at the expense of personal happiness.

Mothers and fathers represented most parents living in the home. Broken families existed, but they were not as prevalent then. Other than a rare divorced family, the traditional family structure was the rule rather than the exception. Also, normally, children were encouraged and permitted to be children, as opposed to living in an adult world inundated with sex, violence, adult predatory attacks, exposure to adult stress and pressures as seen today. The idea of family was anchored in a family environment that steadied life conditions and circumstances.

Four-Pronged Approach

The idea of family as an anchor or cocoon was explained by a wise friend, Joseph Nickens, who allowed me to share his story. Joe had a very simple theory that characterized how families raised what he called "pretty decent kids" up until the 1970s or 1980s. Black people, in general, tried to safeguard and rescue children from the throes of life. Joe compared the ingredients and experiences of growing up in the past, to a four-pronged stool as communities that consisted of the same people across the village. He described the village as being a "decent community" that had a "decent" school, a "decent" church, and "decent" parents in a home who took an interest in their children's development and education. The four-pronged approach—the family/parents, church, community, and school reinforced one another.

Joe's Story

Although everything was not flawless, the environment was created to raise, not perfect, but "decent" children. Joseph Nickens' family story is an example of how the four-pronged environment worked. The norm was for everyone to have respect for adults and elders. Joe mentioned that no matter how they were "cutting up" as teens, children knew to "straighten-up" and show their best behavior when among adults. It was unheard of to curse or be disrespectful, especially to grandmothers and mothers who were held in high esteem.

Joe was raised in a rural community in Virginia where, despite the era of racial segregation, people got along across racial lines. Before going to Virginia, Joe was raised in a large, east coast city; but as a young teen, his parents decided to send him to live with his grandfather on his farm in Virginia. Joe's parents provided the following shrewd explanation for his departure. They told him his move to live with his grandfather on the farm was carrying on the family tradition. They explained it was customary for the youngest son to go live on the grandfather's farm to help maintain the land and family inheritance. Joe felt very special, but later, while living on the farm, his cousins told him he was sent there to be raised by his grandfather to get him away from the throes and threats of living in a large east coast city.

In reality, the peer influences that were pulling him away from the cocoon were removed so that Joe's talents would not be negated or wasted. When his parents and teachers saw the potential for him to stray, as a part of the anchor and cocoon, along with his parents and grandparents they steadied the environment of peer pressure and influenced Joe's chances and options to become the man he was intended to be. He chuckled and reflected on the real reason he was sent to the farm.

He explained that his parent's decision probably made the difference in the outcome of his life. Instead of becoming a victim of the city streets, he thrived in the haven of the farm. He learned a great deal about farming; in fact, he loved living on the farm, having the responsibility to do such chores as feeding chickens and milking cows each morning before and after school until he was eighteen years old.

Although schools in the rural town of Virginia were segregated, black and white children played and got along well together. Being an African-American, Joe attended the "colored school" where he was a very bright student. He spoke of how teachers saw his potential, and mentored and watched over him. For instance, when he signed up to take basic coursework, they placed him in advanced courses, which challenged him to learn more. Joe finished high school as class valedictorian, and with the help of his teachers, they facilitated and anchored his matriculation in a historically black college and university.

He attended and graduated from Hampton University in Virginia. It was almost as if the educators took control of his choices, and helped his grandparents and parents ensure that he was guided in a pathway that allowed him to become the successful person he became. As a part of the four-pronged approach, his teachers became extended parents and family who influenced Joe's chances to become the man he was intended to be. Joe expressed the attitudes, aspirations, and game plan that was perpetuated as a part of the anchor and cocoon of black life during the 1950s and 1960s.

As high school and college graduates, it was a given that they were to get a good job and acquire a home in the nicest neighborhood possible. Then they were to marry and raise children who could attend a nice school and church in a nice neighborhood where children could grow up and associate with known friends. Parents covertly controlled the sphere of friends, and limited (at least tried to limit) locations where children could go. Peers were chosen from families in the local community, neighborhood, school, and church.

The prevailing attitude for developing children was like spinning a cocoon or tapestry of silk. Communal upbringing was likened to being raised in the cocoon that was spun around children as a protective casing. Like the cycle of a caterpillar in a cocoon, parents covertly, and sometimes overtly, protected children from the harsh, unfriendly, hostile, segregated society, and world. Friends, relatives, educators, church, other community members, and significant others who lived in and around the cocoon (environment), stuck together and nurtured the babies and youth until they emerged like butterflies, as functioning adults.

Children remained inside the cocoon through adolescence until adulthood structures, expectations, and foundations were formed. Like the baby caterpillar, this was the lifecycle of black children, and perhaps others, growing up. In short, the cocoon was in the form of family, neighborhood, school, church, and close-knit communities that created the village in which children developed, grew, and matured. Many youth and young adults benefitted from such a communal environment, despite circumstances and social class conditions of family life.

Such powerful environments still exist in some rural and small communities and cultures; however, the cocoons no longer exist for those who live in large and urban cities. Consequently, now many children are left without an anchor or cocoon consisting of an adult to provide guidance, supervision or life support for options and chances as was experienced by Joe. Without reliable and secure attachments (anchors) or shelters and protectors (cocoons), childhood involves fear, stress, frustration, instability, and/or an unbalanced existence that often shatters a spiritual, psychological, intellectual, and emotional center.

The four-pronged approach expressly underlines the need for common sense parenting, and a balanced support system for nurturing and developing the well-being of families and children. As seen in the experiences of Joe and others, no matter where the family resided, there were common or similar experiences, motives, and powers that families, especially parents, exerted over their child's environments.

While it is difficult to separate attributes of successful families from other dynamics, there are timeless elements or attributes that proved valuable over the generations, and still loom large for family success today:

1. Tight-knit, family-focused environments that shape purposeful commitments to the well-being of children;
2. Dependable parents and others who provide structure, security, stability, safety, love, and warm adult/child relationships; and
3. Investment and strategic devotion to using whatever resources available, including time and experiences that promote spiritual, emotional, intellectual, physical, health, family/child growth, development and well-being.

Many parents and grandparents fulfilled those roles and prepared their children for a great liftoff! They, and the ancestors before, provided so much with few opportunities, resources, and assets. We were the benefactors of a combination of opportunities that were carved out by parents and grandparents as well as others who made an imprint on the next phase of the journey from adolescence to adulthood. As you will see in the next chapters, the ancestors could not have imagined what was in store for their children's children.

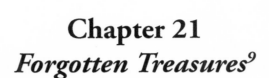

Chapter 21
Forgotten Treasures[9]

Many discussions were generated with others while writing this family history. One such conversation took place at my fiftieth high school reunion with a former classmate, James Bell.

We talked about our life's journey after high school, and shared information about our progression from our family's migration from the South to growing up with the anchors and cocoons of our homes and community in Seattle.

James shared an article he wrote about our fiftieth high school reunion, and he and the publishers graciously allowed me to adapt it for this chapter. Living in Seattle during the 1950s and 1960s did not fully shield people from the realities of the segregated South. It was common for African-American parents to prepare their children for the awareness of racism, segregation, and prejudice that inevitably would be faced wherever they lived.

Our childhood experiences were somewhat different, especially when it came to matters of schooling, but there was one thing that we held in common, no matter where we lived. African-Americans and other youth from all income levels achieved in significant numbers. Parents expected them to achieve. Grandparents expected them to achieve. Teachers and school principals expected and saw to it that they achieved, and life and cultural experiences supported their efforts to achieve. Before sharing my personal story, as a disclaimer, it

---

[9] Written by James Bell and Searetha Smith-Collins (2012). Adapted, reprinted, and expanded from an original article with permission: Bell, James. (2012, September). Madrona to Garfield's 50th Reunion. Seattle, WA; (Madrona News); 245, 1, 2.

is important to note that some of the names of people in the stories were changed, but the truthfulness remained intact.

Having moved so far away from our roots, we did not experience the same effects of segregation. There were no recycled textbooks, inadequate, neglected facilities, lack of funding and resources, and other poor conditions that were characteristic of the "separate but equal" laws and policies that were inflicted upon "colored schools" in the South. The major difference was that schools in Seattle were not segregated, and they were not populated by a predominantly black student population as was in the South. In fact, there were only three other children of African-American families who attended my first elementary school, totaling five black students in the entire school.

There was one circumstance that existed in most schools in the country. Even under segregated, inadequate circumstances in the South, there were good schools, good teachers, and support from close-knit family and neighbors in most communities. I started school in Houston at the age of four. When we moved to Seattle, our mother enrolled my sister, Virgie, and I in the neighborhood school, Harrison Elementary, which was near Aunt Juanita's house. I completed kindergarten, and Virgie completed third grade, which was the final school level offered at our first elementary school.

Soon after, we moved and attended Madrona Elementary School. There were a few more African-American students than in the first school. Although schools in Seattle were integrated, there were only a small number of African-American families in the city, so the school population reflected the demographics of the city, state, and neighborhoods at that time.

Interestingly as an aside, in comparison to others, Seattle was and still is the largest city in the Pacific Northwest; but the current numbers of African-American students have not changed dramatically in proportion to the past. Tonya Mosley (2013), a broadcast journalist in Seattle, noted that according to US State Census Data in 1940, the black population in Seattle was a mere 1.0 percent. In 1950, when my family moved there, the black population was approximately 3.4 percent. By 1960, it was 4.8 percent, and in 2014, the African-American population in Seattle had risen to only approximately 8.4 percent, consisting of approximately 47,000 people categorized as either Black or African-American.

According to the Seattle Area Population (Seattlearea.com, Suburban Stats 2016) and the US Census bureau, the current total population in Seattle is approximately 659,000 residents. While there was a slight rise in the population over the years, as of 2016, approximately 45,000 of those residents are Black or African-Americans, representing approximately eight percent (Seattlearea.com 2014). To say the least, we had migrated to an area of the country that did not have many African-American people; therefore, by the very fact of geographic, regional, and demographic factors, our experiences were very different from our relatives in the South.

A white society surrounded us, including teachers, but our cultural heritage and continuity were provided in the cocoon of family and community that supported and influenced group identity, values, self-confidence, and self-worth. It was during the elementary school years that I met classmate and co-author, James Bell, who is African-American also. Not only were there a few black students in school, there were fewer black teachers, which was another difference between northern and southern school experiences.

There was only one black teacher at Madrona Elementary School, Mrs. Lewis, who taught the sixth grade. In those days, we didn't choose our class or teacher; simply, we were placed in a class without fanfare or choice. My older sister, Virgie, had been in Mrs. Lewis' class two years earlier, so I had heard quite a bit about her. When it was our turn as sixth graders, everyone was on "pins and needles" wondering which teacher they would be assigned, and who their classmates would be. James was elated when he found himself with Mrs. Lewis. In the fifth and previous grades, his teachers tried to induce him to write with his right hand instead of his left, using a ruler tap on the left hand as a reminder to use the right one—but delightfully, he found this to not be true of Mrs. Lewis.

I was assigned to Mr. Jones' (not his real name) sixth grade class, which was disappointing at first, because I had hoped I would be assigned to Mrs. Lewis also. Mr. Jones was a tall, young, white man who had a very pleasant demeanor. Very soon after the start of the school year, I was elated with my new teacher also. We had a great, stimulating sixth grade experience with Mr. Jones. I especially remember learning about the history and culture of Native Americans who were indigenous to Seattle. As a culminating activity in the sixth grade, we converted our classroom into a tribal Native American village.

Our parents were invited to come to our classroom for a pow-wow (a Native American celebration of singing, dancing, and honoring native culture). During that time, parental involvement at school had a different meaning. It was not common for parents to come to school unless there was a problem. In fact, it was common for parents, especially those who were African-American, to warn us by saying, "Don't make me have to come up to that school to see about you!" No, that was not what any black child of my generation or previous wanted to have a parent do when that declaration was made!

Usually, teachers took care of school, and parents took care of the home. An invitation to a program or school event was a special occasion for parents. My mother's presence at this school even stands out, because it was this study that initiated my sensitivity to other cultures—especially those that struggled, lost human and land rights, and had plights to struggle for justice, and human and civil rights.

There was another powerful sixth grade memory—studying poetry. Mr. Jones assigned the task of selecting a poem from a poetry study list. After identifying a favorite poem, we studied and wrote about the poet, the historical context of the poem, and the motives and interpretation of the message that was conveyed in the historical versus the contemporary context at that time. We had been studying figures of speech, using similes (comparisons of like or similar things) and metaphors (comparisons of different things).

Our task was to memorize and recite the poem, citing examples of symbolic descriptions and images (similes and metaphors) in the poem. After reciting and explaining the poem to the class, we had to be prepared to answer questions asked by class members. This seemed a tall order for a sixth grader, especially the part about standing in front of peers reciting a poem! I recalled several thoughts that flowed through my mind. *What if I cannot remember the poem? What if I forget certain parts of it? Maybe I should have selected a shorter poem!*

I was relieved to find that the task was not as frightening as I had initially anticipated. In fact, I was fascinated to learn new vocabulary words that I shared with my parents, all of which turned out to be the initiation of my interest in the beauty and power of words. To my delight, I successfully remembered and recited the poem *The Daffodils* by William Wordsworth. Still today, I remember and can envision the scene that was painted by the poet with his use of smiles and metaphors.

Another example of the influence of growing up in the cocoon was my third-grade teacher, Mrs. Smith, who made a strong impression on me at an early age. I distinctly remember one special day in class when Mrs. Smith (no relation) leaned over my shoulder while I was working at my desk and whispered, "You are so smart, and such a great speller!" As it turned out, that was the conscious beginning of my spiral to achieve in school with pride and confidence, and later with my interest in writing.

I mentioned all of this as a part of family history, and perhaps reminiscent of "the good old days," because they illustrate the spirit, legacy, and support of a communal experience that existed during our upbringing. In the name of progress during changing times as African-Americans, we set out looking for something better; but we did not realize that through the process of change, we would lose those who knew how to touch the gems buried inside of us as children or the "jewels" that were buried in our existing cocoons (homes, schools, communities, and church environments).

Transitions

There was respect for certain values, norms, and constants that produced experiences of acculturation and continuity. There were certain predictabilities that centered on family and cultural expectations. For the most part, quality schooling was a process that was value-added, regardless of race, region, class or circumstance. As mentioned, in our case, there were great teachers who were and were not

African-American, who provided the best care and education they could be give us as children, regardless of who we were.

There was something inspirational and motivational about seeing African-American teachers, which, unfortunately, is becoming less of an occurrence today. Being a teacher or educator was a highly respected profession at that time. They, along with our families and community, instilled self-esteem and expectations that prepared us to navigate society inside and outside of our community. They were role models of achievement, pride, and respect. Their presence, professionalism, dress, modeling, interest, care, and abilities inspired us to see and climb to be something better.

After elementary school, we moved on to Meany Junior High school for the typical seventh, eighth, and ninth grades. During my discussion about writing this book with James Bell, he shared that before we even started junior high school, the older neighborhood kids who preceded us told him about a swimming pool on the third floor of the school. If they were paid a nickel or dime, they would let the new seventh graders use their swim passes. I did not personally have the pleasure of hearing that proposition, and the truth was there was no swimming pool in the school. In fact, there was no second or third floor at Meany Junior High!

This urban tale led to a lot of disappointed youngsters who made the investment and transition from elementary to junior high school. More discoveries were in store as we entered junior high school. There was no school busing at the time for those of us who lived in "The Valley" of the Central District in Seattle. The area was called "The Valley" because it was at the bottom of the big hill. Since my family lived at the very bottom of the hill, exercise was not something we lacked as children.

We walked to junior high school up a steep incline that was called "John Hill" (named after John Street). We walked about a mile to and from school each way, but it seemed that we climbed up and down John Street Mountain every day! Once we reached the top of the hill, after a few more blocks on flat ground, there sat the wonderful sight of Meany Junior High School. When it snowed, John Street (the hill) was closed and cordoned off, because it was too steep and dangerous to walk or drive. We were happy when the hill was closed, because it meant we had the treat of my father driving us to and from school, which did not happen often enough.

On the first day of attending junior high school, I arrived at my seventh grade Social Studies class, only to find that my teacher was none other than Mrs. Smith—yes, the same one who had been my third-grade teacher at Madrona Elementary School. She was our seventh, eighth, and ninth grade class advisor, and I think she had an underlying motive of watching over and guiding our peer group through the early adolescent years.

School extracurricular activities provided the glue that created cohesion and continuity between family and school. Many of the males joined organized sports teams. In the case of Meany Junior High students, the team was known as "The Fighting Irish." The team met and played football and baseball at the Garfield High School playfield during the seventh and eighth grades. In the eighth and ninth grades, the boys at Meany Junior High continued playing organized football coached by Booth Gardner—the same man who later became Governor of Washington State.

For the first time in our schooling experience, we found more than one African-American teacher at Meany Junior High School. I was assigned to Mrs. Roberts, a black woman who taught the seventh grade girl's gym (physical education which was separated by classes for boys or girls). The other African-American teachers were Mr. Parker and Ms. Woods, who lived in our neighborhood. Having teachers who lived in the neighborhood brought true meaning to the African proverb, "The eyes of my mother are in my neighbor." They knew our older brothers and sisters, and if necessary, it was not unusual for them to report necessary information to our parents to help keep us moving in the right direction.

Junior high/middle school normally is an awkward time for most children. Out of necessity, there was an alliance between parents, teachers, friends, and community that provided clear boundaries, planned structured activities, and adult attention and supervision that assisted with the adjustments and emotional difficulties of adolescence. As students and friends, we met up after school and walked home together, trailing off as each person reached his or her neighborhood.

Before trekking down John Hill after school, it was common to meet and stop at Mr. Gideon's Drug Store where we talked, sipped on ice cream sodas, and listened to our favorite songs on the miniature jukeboxes. We were convinced that Mr. Gideon, the owner, was wealthy, because he was distinguished, and we did not know any other black person who owned a fancy drugstore in the Central Area of Seattle during that time. He always had a smile on his face, and greeted us as we arrived and sat at the soda fountain counter, giggling, talking, and drinking our sodas before starting our group walk home.

Our parents did not have to worry about our safety after school, because Mr. Gideon had a laser eye on us. Not only Mr. Gideon, but so did one of my best friend's mother, who worked as a part-time worker at the drugstore after school. It seemed that she was there to watch everything we did, and she did not hesitate to give us that stern look that most African-American mothers would when they thought we needed a behavior intervention. There was not much to worry about, however. We knew the rules, we knew right from wrong, and we knew that our parents were serious!

We did not venture too far from what was expected. The family infrastructure and backings were in place, and children knew the limits and boundaries from home to school and back again. All in all, we were fortunate to grow up in an environment where, and when, education and family mattered most. We were raised during an era that has been called "a time of innocence." Fortunately, children were positively influenced by the three most influential environments: (1) home/family, (2) school, and (3) the neighborhoods/community. We were the beneficiaries of critical lessons that surpass time:

- If children experience safety, structure, discipline, guidance, security, and feel loved and connected to parents, family, schools, and community, most likely they will develop positive, trusting bonds and relationships.

- If the right resources are applied, and time is carefully designed to channel energy and development, most likely, children will have a chance in life.
- If parents provide foundations upon which to build progress and success, and if the right people and environments are in place, then most likely, children will learn, grow, and feel worthy of a place and purpose in the universe.

Stay tuned as even more adventures and greater experiences are shared.

Chapter 22
Days of Wine and Roses

The generational time was the 1960s and 1970s. In case you were not born yet or you experienced childhood during a later generation, the following is a glimpse of what it was like to grow up during times when family was foundational. For those who experienced growing up as a teenager during that time, I am sure these memories will revive themselves.

During my teenage generation (the 1960s and 1970s), we had a great deal in common as teens. We were coming of age, raised during the days of Elvis Presley's "All Shook Up," Aretha Franklin's "Respect," and Frankie Lyman and the Teenagers' "Why Do Fools Fall in Love." We did not have tape recorders, CDs, DVDs, mp3 players, iPads, iPods, or playlists at the time. We listened to music on the radio, record players/phonographs or jukeboxes.

Instead of downloading from iTunes, music was recorded on vinyl 45 RPM records that had a doughnut-type hole in the middle or it was recorded on large 33 ½ RPM (rotations per minute) albums. As children, we listened to our parents' music that was recorded on 78 RPM vinyl records, which was the size of a dinner plate with a small hole in the middle. We could hear songs and musicians from our parent's collections, such as Fats Waller, the Delta Rhythm Boys, Earl Father Hines, Jimmy Witherspoon, Lionel Hampton, Count Basie, Jimmy Rushing, Ella Fitzgerald, Josephine Baker, Pearl Bailey, Billie Holiday, Nat King Cole, and the like.

Later, we experienced what seemed like the most forward-thinking device—the tape recorder. We could record albums and records on tapes, and share them with friends. Like every new generation, music is the lifeblood of most teenagers. It seemed that on most talent shows and city neighborhood corners, girl and boy singing groups could be found emulating popular songs and musical groups. Motown, the historic black-owned music production company that originated in Detroit Michigan, exploded on the scene in the early 1960s. We experienced some of the most definitive rhythm and blues and "soul" music that was characteristic of a musical renaissance.

Some of the popular music that we listened and danced to was performed by the Temptations, Marvin Gaye, Stevie Wonder, Diana Ross and the Supremes, Smokey Robinson and the Miracles, and the Jackson Five starring little Michael Jackson. Other music of the time was performed by the Beatles, Tom Jones, James Brown, the Bee Gees, and many who you can still hear today on "old school" radio stations. The Motown golden era of music occurred during this special time of a black cultural renaissance in America. In fact, this was a time when some of the most timeless music was created, and is still popular and enjoyed today.

There were talent competitions, high school dances, skating parties, and get-togethers in basements with blue light bulbs setting the mood for dancing to our favorite slow dance—that is until our parents came down to turn on the lights again. We joined the *"soul train"* line that was an outcome of the popular music television show *Soul Train,* where we showed our special "moves" as we took turns strolling down the dance line doing the Twist, Jerk, Mashed Potato, Cha-Cha or danced with our partner doing the Bop or other Hand Dances.

In addition to listening to music, we gathered around the radio to listen with great anticipation to the next episode of the soap opera *Stella Dallas* or the *Amos and Andy* comedy show featuring Rochester. *The Jack Benny Show* or mystery dramas such as *The Screeching Door* were also favorites. It was a special treat to gather around the record player to listen to favorite gospel choirs belt out popular tunes by James Cleveland (the gospel music genius), the Blind Boys of Mississippi, Clara Ward Singers, Mahalia Jackson, Sam Cooke, etc.

When you hear the saying, "Time brings about a change," it is true as you will see. Imagine having to wait until you got home to make or receive a phone call. Well, that was just what we had to do in the 1950s and 1960s—that was after our chores and homework were completed. Then, maybe, we could spend a few hours on the phone talking with friends. Being teenagers, we did not spend hours and hours on social media networks (they did not exist). Instead, we spent as many hours as possible on the rotary dial telephone talking to our friends. There was just one problem, however.

If we wanted to call to talk about something that just couldn't wait, we could not always make the call, because someone else was using the one phone in the house with the one telephone line. During our pre- and early teen years, we had "party lines," which were shared community telephone lines. If another party from another household was on the line, we had to wait until the line was clear before we could make a call. If someone was already on the receiving end of the call, there was just a busy signal indicating that someone was using the line at the other house that shared the same phone line.

There was no call-forwarding, conference calling, Skyping, voice messaging, redialing, instant messaging or texting! The phone line just buzzed with a busy signal, and our important conversations just had to wait until the line was clear! From a teenager's perspective, another great invention surfaced—the single household telephone line. Instead of sharing a line with another household, it was exciting to have a single private phone line that we could spend hours talking to friends. That was the case, at least, until our parents made us get off the phone so another telephone call could be received (there was no call-waiting also).

After the rotary dial phone, the push button dial phone arrived. There was no cell or smart phones, if you can envision that! If information or directory assistance was needed, a telephone operator (a real person) answered the call, with no pauses or prompts spoken by a recorded message. There were no telephone prompts to "Dial 1, 2, and 3 through 9" to receive assistance or reach the operator. All we had to do was simply dial "0" for the operator to help with a call or an emergency or dial "411" for an operator to assist with information. Later, more innovations evolved.

The Gift of Change

It was Price Pritchett who said, "Change always comes bearing gifts." Can you imagine being en route somewhere and having to stop to use a phone booth to make a call? For those who have never seen one, there were booths that had phones that could be found along roadways, on street corners, in public buildings, in the workplace, at church, in train stations, airports—everywhere. Most of us were pretty much stuck with using phone booths and sharing one telephone in the home.

We used phone booths when we were away from home, which required paying a dime or quarter per call. Our parents always made sure we had a dime or quarter to call the "Operator" from a phone booth, in case of an emergency. Later, huge car phones surfaced as a special feature in some cars. Initially, car and regular cell phones were very large and awkward, and were not accessible to everyone because they were very expensive.

It might seem a bit ancient to newer generations, but prior to car phones and cell phones, another twentieth century invention exploded on the scene—the electronic black and white television. At first, most families did not have televisions in their home, so the radio was the vehicle for entertainment and communication. One of our cousins was fortunate to have an early version of the first television, so after church and dinner each Sunday, our parents loaded us in the car to visit so we could watch shows on the invention. Soon, my parents bought our first television set. Friends and neighbors came to view the black and white images and programs that beamed fuzzily from the small screen in the small wooden frame that sat in our living room.

There was an antenna on top of the television that was called "rabbit ears." We manipulated and moved the "rabbit ears" until the fuzzy lines (snow) and images became clear. Televised programs began at around 6:00 a.m. and signed off around 10:00 p.m. to midnight with a traditional symbol and the sound of "The Star-Spangled Banner." Afterward, there was a humming sound that came from the screen, along with fuzzy snow images that started at midnight until it was time for the one channel to sign on again the next morning.

Special excitement was in store when the *Nat King Cole Show* came on the air. He was the only "colored person" who had a television show, so families gathered around the television screen to proudly watch the program, while others scurried to start a telephone chain to let others know that a colored person was on television! By the 1960s, we began to hear about another invention—the colored television and remote control! We couldn't have imagined such a wonder! It was unbelievable that as children, we no longer had to get up to turn the television on or off or change the channel while our parents sat leisurely and directed us to do so at their convenience! Of course, these were silent or "inside" thoughts or objections that were never revealed to our parents!

Some of the popular family television shows were *Bonanza*, *Twilight Zone* (a science fiction thriller), *Rawhide* (another western), *The Ed Sullivan Show* (an entertainment program), and *The Adventures of Ozzie and Harriet*. By that time, there were three television channels instead of one! As teenagers, we raced home after school each day to see the latest dance or hear our favorite musician featured on *American Bandstand Live from Philadelphia with Dick Clark*! Later, our eyes were glued to the popular television program *Soul Train* (the Black version of American Bandstand).

Home and school activities were designed to consume our out-of-school time. Teenage life was filled with activities, such as participating in sock hops (a dance where we wore socks and no shoes), hayrides, sleepovers (girls only), and family game time, such as playing Monopoly and other games. Each family participated in annual school paper drives during a specific period during the year, where mounds and mounds of newspapers and magazines were collected at school to help raise money for school activities and events.

We organized carwashes and flea markets to raise money for specific teen activities that we initiated. We connected with school through activities and courses such as singing in the school choir, after school sports, participating in pep rallies to build school spirit before attending athletic games, and involvement in art and music classes and school clubs. In junior high and high school, we took mandatory electives that prepared us for home and family life skills, such as home economics (cooking and sewing), industrial arts and woodshop, and consumer math and business. A part of education was learning how to cook, manage finances, repair, and build things, sew, eat nutritious meals, etc.

The High School Years

Our next school stop was James A. Garfield High School, which was, and still is, one of the most noted high schools in Seattle. Garfield High School was a special place where several notable people attended, including Quincy Jones (the great composer, producer, and music arranger), Jimi Hendrix (the pop rock star), and Minoru Yamasaki (architect of the former World Trade Center). We spent the tenth through twelfth grades in what was a potpourri of diversity culturally, racially, and socio-economically. Approximately a third of the students were African-American, a third Asian, a third white, and the others were from other various ethnicities.

We were a mixture of people who studied, grew, and intermingled with one another. We learned to appreciate the benefit of learning about life experiences of various families with different backgrounds. At that time, our high school was a history lesson. We learned about the Chinese ancestors of students who settled and worked on railroads and started businesses in the Pacific Northwest, such as grocery stores, laundry shops, etc.

We learned from the parents of Japanese students who as American citizens living in the Northwest were directly affected by the Japanese Internment that was stimulated when WWII sparked a US Embargo on Japan. This led to the Japanese attack on US soil in Pearl Harbor in December 7, 1941. As a result, WWII commenced, and Japanese families were corralled into concentration camps in Idaho, California, Utah, Arizona, Wyoming, Arkansas, and other places.

We learned about the Holocaust from Jewish classmates and their parents, whose families and descendants were victims of concentration camps in Germany and German occupied countries in

1941–1945. Many Jewish families lived in the same neighborhoods as African-Americans, Asians, and others, mainly because there was overt prejudice against them as well. Jewish families owned delicatessens, grocery stores, and other businesses in our neighborhoods.

Jewish, Chinese, and Japanese families practiced and celebrated their own family, cultural, and religious traditions within their own communities, as well as in the general community. After school hours, the children attended culturally-based schools in their own community to ensure that family and cultural consciousness and continuity were passed on. There were other people from a variety of ethnic and social backgrounds, including Irish, Scottish, Italian, German, Scandinavian, a few Latinos, and those who were working-class, wealthy and poor.

Our high school experiences created a cross pollination of exposure to a strong educational experience, and diverse backgrounds, and perspectives from other people of various races, ethnicities, and social classes—all within one peaceful school environment. We did not realize it at the time, but those experiences prepared us for changes that were to come at the onset of the mid to late twentieth century. Peaceful coexistence and understanding difference were great skills that benefited future demands in an integrated society and workforce.

Earlier, I talked about my third grade and junior high school teacher, Mrs. Smith. To my surprise, she appeared as the new school librarian and our sophomore class advisor at Garfield High School as well. Mrs. Smith was visible every time we went to the school library, and she always seemed to be aware of our routines and moves. As class advisor, she organized and arranged ice cream socials, get-togethers at her home, carwashes, study and practice sessions for the talent show that was popularly called "Garfield's Funfest," and she coached our cheerleading squad practices.

There were only a few African-American teachers at Garfield High School also. One was a social studies teacher who became a noted historian in the city. One taught honors and advanced English courses, and another was a former Garfield student who returned to become a physical education teacher and assistant track coach.

The biggest surprise was the teacher who taught my sophomore gym class. When I reported to the physical education class, there stood Mrs. Roberts—yes, the same one who taught girl's physical education classes at Meany Junior High!

Seeing Mrs. Roberts provided a shortcut to her needing to orient the class. We knew the drill. First, we had to go to the dressing room to change into uniform shorts, blouses or shirts for gym class. After dressing, we reported to the gym where Mrs. Roberts stood waiting with her whistle. With a big smile on her face, she blew her whistle, which we automatically knew what that meant. Instinctively, we knew it was time for order, attention, and readiness for class!

We knew the expectations, so each day we were ready on time, in full uniform, and ready to start the physical warmup exercises. At the end of the period came a shower, redressing into our school clothes, then off to our next class. It was not an amenable idea for a teacher in any of our classes after P.E. to report to Mrs. Roberts that we were late transitioning from gym class. She expected us to be accountable for time management, so we met her expectation without delay!

Later, Ms. Woods, who had been at Meany Junior High, joined the Garfield High School faculty also. It seemed that many teachers, especially the African-Americans, were invested and stayed close to their students. They knew us and seemed to genuinely care about us. They expected—rather, insisted—that we do well. We were very excited to see the other familiar faces in each new school setting. We knew they were people who we could trust and count on if needed. At the same time, we gained new friends and relationships with new teachers and peers.

I failed to mention that Ms. Woods and Mrs. Roberts attended the same church as our family, so I saw them on Sundays as well. Each week, my mother and I were greeted by a warm smile from each of them. In retrospect, all of this might seem nostalgic; but these experiences and sentiments have hidden, instructive messages. There was a partnership between the home, community, and school that sustained the ability of children to experience childhood under the guidance and protection of family (in the cocoon).

There were problems and challenges, but in contrast to the present, we were consumed with a sense of belonging and trust. In turn, we were surrounded by people who provided genuine relationships. Our environment spilled over to our teenage relationships. We "hung out" after the high school football and basketball games at our teenage meeting spot, Dick's Hamburger Drive-In. Everyone parked their cars (their family's car, most families had one car that was shared) and hung out in the parking lot, enjoying twenty-five cent cheeseburgers and ten cent French Fries, which were the best fries you could have ever tasted!

Thorns and Bristles

Usually there are thorns that come with roses. Although Garfield High School seemed like a haven, inequities did exist, and high school was not as pleasant and captivating for everyone. Garfield had the largest diverse school population in the city because most students of color lived in the same school attendance area. During our fiftieth year high school reunion, some of our white classmates revealed that when they participated in the general white society and communities, often they were taunted and targeted by white students from other schools. They were called names and referred to as "the kids who went to school where the colored kids attended."

There were experiences of teacher bias and prejudice also. The most outstanding example happened at the end of my senior year. After taking a career assessment and grade prediction test in preparation for post-high school transition, each student was responsible for making an appointment for an exit interview with a school counselor. During my meeting, the school counselor asked about my post-graduation aspirations. I shared that I planned to pursue a career in journalism as a television news anchor. The counselor, who was a white middle-aged woman, quickly bristled and responded that based on my career assessment profile, I was not suited to be a journalist.

She informed me that my career assessment and grade prediction test indicated that I would best be suited to go into agriculture. In addition, she declared "Negro' television anchors did not exist, and there were no women who worked as television news anchors either. Her statement was true at the time, but my vision and aspirations were ahead of the changes that were yet to come. One way or another, I saw beyond the current condition. The counselor was a product of her acculturated time, and she could not see my vision; but change and possibilities were on the horizon.

The Awakening

My hopes were redirected and discouraged as a fleeting thought. I was puzzled to understand how or why a career assessment could lead to such a conclusion. Although agriculture is a notable and necessary field, it certainly was not compatible with my interests. As mentioned in earlier chapters, my experiences growing up and going to "the country" with my family to visit Aunt Ruthie's farm in Texas had a few drawbacks (recall my cousins' tall tales about creatures crawling in the grass near the outhouse at night).

I did not know much about agriculture, and I could not fathom what created such a prospect for my future. I recalled my introduction and reaction to the world of agriculture, farming, and cultivating and growing crops when Aunt Juanita Green Martin took us berry picking during childhood. Looking back, I quickly reflected on experiences when Aunt Juanita took my sister and I fishing. Also, she took us on a farm with a bus load of people to pick beans and strawberries when we first lived with her in Seattle.

The reflections of those excursions reaped unpopular memories. I remembered the long ride on the rickety bus that took us to the strawberry farm, and I recalled that I ate more strawberries than I picked, resulting in hives. The idea of using worms for fishing bait did not help much either! I recalled seeing worms in the soil and in a can that Aunt Juanita had collected for fishing. Certainly, this was not a good sight for someone whose future would involve an occupation centered on caring for and breeding livestock and creatures who could be gleefully found in the soil.

Certainly, the results of the tests were somehow inaccurate. Agriculture was certainly a mismatch and not the desired destination of my journey. Given this information, I had to figure out something fast! Although somewhat a fanciful story now, it clearly demonstrated the reality that limitations can be placed on one's destination, but that only calls for staying the course. During the summer after high school graduation, I worked as an assistant to a legal secretary in a black lawyer's office in Seattle. I enjoyed working with people, but secretarial work was deskbound, so by the end of the summer, I decided to attend college as my parents had expected. Soon, I was off to college to become a teacher.

My mother was a bit disappointed that I did not attend Texas Southern University (TSU), the same HBCU (Historically Black College and University) that my father had attended. She thought an HBCU would broaden my academic, social, and cultural experiences. To her dismay, TSU seemed a long way from home, so I attended Central Washington Teacher's College (now called Central Washington University), which was a few hundred miles from Seattle. I was one of a very few black students who attended Central Washington College during that time; so once again, I was called upon to adapt to a white homogeneous environment.

The school was excellent and I was treated well, and received a grand education in teacher development and preparation. I felt isolated being in a small town, however, so after two years, I transferred to Seattle University where I graduated. As it turned out, becoming an educator was the best professional choice, because I embarked upon what became a longstanding, exciting, successful career in education and related fields.

The most common marker of transitioning from childhood to adulthood is turning eighteen years of age and graduating from high school. During our fiftieth year high school reunion, I found out that other African-American students had received similar misguided advice from the same high school counselor. Some graduates never sought their optimal options; others simply gave up on their dreams. Still others found pathways to their vision later in life.

Some among our high school graduating class immediately went to work and started families. Some practiced vocations until retirement or a disabling accident or illness ensued. Others attended institutions of higher learning to become teachers, physicians, lawyers, bankers, professors, architects, and, yes, politicians. Far too often, timing, discrimination (intentional and unintentional) or ill-advice from family, friends, educators, counselors, and others discourage possibilities and dreams.

Each generation is a product of their time, and we are the result of support and influence of family, school, and community (or the absence thereof), and such experiences are a part of the journey in life. As for Journalism, the Civil Rights and Women's Rights Movements of the 1960s and 1970s opened more doors into the field as news writers, television anchors, cameramen, etc. As for me, my dream was fulfilled in later life by accessing the best of both worlds as an educator and author.

An anonymous person said, "What a person becomes is developed within them, not defined by others." There are many pathways to "becoming," inclusive of vision, timing, preparation, opportunity, access, willingness to take risks, and getting along with other people.

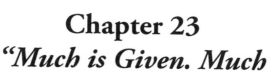

Chapter 23
"Much is Given. Much is Expected"[10]

There is a saying, "To whom much is given, much is expected." During our maturation, the Civil Rights Movement of 1960s built on the progress of the 1920s and pushed the limits of political, social, gender, and racial barriers. There were changes in housing, transportation and other public access, employment, educational practices and opportunities, and general cultural, structural, and societal rights and existence in America.

In addition to the Civil Rights Movement, the Women's Rights Movement started the ongoing push to break the glass ceiling (the invisible structural and organizational barriers to management and workplace equality), and to seek opportunities and access for women and people of color. We were not the first generation, but as change started and spread from the deep South throughout the nation, we were among the activists and anti-traditionalists determined to change existing barriers, conventions, and paradigms through bold action.

Along with other African-American youth, my sister, Virgie, and I found ourselves in the middle of political and civil rights struggles in Seattle in the late 1960s. We were recruited to test the legally mandated integration of hiring practices by seeking employment in

---

[10] James Bell, coauthor. Adapted and reprinted from an original article: Bell, James (2012). From Madrona to Garfield's 50th Reunion. Seattle, WA. Permission from *Madrona News* (September 2012), 245, 1, 2.

one of the larger downtown department stores. Like in most other places in the country, up until that time, black people were barred from working in front-line positions as clerks, managers, elevator operators, buyers, and the like.

After boycotts and other civil rights efforts, a few of us who were young adults were the first African-Americans hired to work in Seattle department stores in sales positions. The job aspiration seems a bit limited now, but the traditional role for "colored people" at that time was to work behind the scenes in most department stores as housekeepers, janitors, seamstresses, etc. We were a part of the efforts of the local chapter of the National Association for the Advancement of Colored People (NAACP) to break the color barrier for equal employment in job opportunities in general.

Little did we know at the time that the actions were yet another milestone in our journey.

At the end of the summer of forced hiring, my sister and I returned to college, while others remained as employees. Eventually, some of the people who remained were promoted to higher positions and made lucrative careers in department stores or other retail businesses. Since this period was a time of war and conflict as well, some of our classmates joined the fight for democracy in other ways. Many of them fought in the Vietnam War and gave the ultimate sacrifice of duty in the defense of their country. Some never returned from Southeast Asia; others came back, needing assistance in readjusting to daily life. Still others returned, much the same as they left, but with a wider perspective than ever before.

Although these were uncertain times, we learned how to work and compete in an integrated society. Some classmates and peers became presidents of various entities, preachers, and students during the period of civil unrest at Jackson State, Kent State, and other universities. Some involved themselves in the Black Panther Party or became students for a Democratic Society (SDS). Several of us were the first teachers to desegregate and integrate schools during the1970s. Others were the first students, university professors, deans, or the first to integrate colleges, universities, law, and medical schools.

Some were the first school superintendents, administrators, supervisors, CEOs or employees to work in newly desegregated corporate, federal, public, and civil service positions. Still others were involved in social action and changes that either supported or opposed positions that dictated their political point of view. As African-Americans, we were part of the great awakening that broke the ideology of racial inferiority that had started generations ago. The goal for unity of African-Americans demonstrated communal action to take power and control over our own lives, educate our own, and reset the language and conditions of society as equal members.

New racial categories were introduced that reflected greater importance and value as black people. Initially, the call for a change in racial preferences was a way to affirm self-acceptance and group identity that had spread from the deep South and throughout the nation. Instead of the historical designation of "colored" or "Negro," most simply preferred to be considered Black. Later, in recognition of the newly found consciousness, our dual African and American roots and heritage was shifted to the racial identity of "Afro-American" and "African-American."

We were a part of the journey to gain positive self-identity, respect, and value in a society that had denigrated our presence in the past. Up to that time, it was a dedicated effort of parents to worry about keeping their children safe from legalized, discriminatory, overt bias and racism. My parents were very nervous about our involvement in change and social action against racial discrimination. Despite misgivings, they understood the significance of what it meant for black people to accomplish the simple task of being able to acquire a basic job if desired.

As part of the new day and a societal order, the fight and unfinished journey had shifted from just liberation to inclusion and access to human and civil rights and equality. Fortunately, our childhood and school experiences had included learning about, and interacting with, people from different races, ethnicities, cultures, backgrounds, and social classes; therefore, we were prepared for the new life experiences and expectations in the new societal and generational landscape.

Chapter 24
A Culture Steeped in Continuity

It has been said by authors unknown that, "We should forget only the things that deserve to be forgotten." Also, it was said that, "Sometimes we hold onto things that should be forgotten or forget some things that deserve to be preserved." Even under horrific conditions of slave ship voyages, and despite cruel and inhumane treatment for hundreds of years, resilient individuals and collective African-Americans influenced identity and evolved into solid families that produced strong offspring.

This occurred despite persistent societal manipulations, distortions, diversions, and confusions that were perpetuated through generations of enslavement, discrimination, and injustice based on race.

Shifts in American families underwent tremendous transformations over the past decades. No longer is there agreement on the definition of a family; and there are different views on what constitutes a conventional family. Formerly, African-American families, in whatever composition, took on responsibilities for raising children, and providing shelter, care, nurturance, and shared moral viewpoints. This was simply their heritage and a fact of their cultural and generational continuity. Through extended families and others (aunts, uncles, friends, etc.), basic needs, skills, and necessities were provided that shaped and reinforced socially expected and accepted ways; as well as maintained common behaviors and expectations in the home, school, community, and in society.

It has been a constant quest and challenge for people from different cultures to gain parity in mainstream American life, yet hold on to their cultural identity and principles. People from different cultures often struggle to maintain mainstream American ideals, and maintain and cultivate norms and influences within their unique cultural ideal. The struggle and conflict can be seen in people from different cultures, such as Asians, Latinos/Hispanics, Jewish, and others who often are viewed as communal cultures. As communal communities and cultures, characteristically, they are perceived as having consciousness, continuity, and strong commitments to social group norms, and family and community connections and bonds.

In contrast, the individualistic mainstream American ideal suggests that the most important focus is on self-achievement, attainment, success, and competition, as opposed to group attainment, success, and collective bonds. The priority for communal societies and groups is to provide and maintain unity, and a communal focus. As a case in point, Asians, Latinos/Hispanics, and Native Americans often feel a pull and tug between operating in an environment where importance is placed on "we, us, our," or togetherness (communal) versus significance placed on "I, me, mine," self-interest and the autonomy of each member (individualistic culture).

The modern-day emphasis has strong implications for families, such as the contemporary shift away from mutually shared goals and norms, to a more detached function and idea. Most people no longer perceive African-Americans as a communal culture, because they have lost the influences of collective, group-orientation, tradition, and continuity over the last few generations. In the past, African-Americans were perceived as belonging to cohesive communities, neighborhoods, and families out of necessity.

As noted in the Green-McGill and other stories, past generations of Africans and African-Americans wove protective family and community environments around their children. Families and communities provided places for children to safely learn, grow, and develop. When families and children are torn away from their anchors, they are no longer centered and protected in a safe environment or community. Shifting from a communal group orientation to a mainstream individualistic-orientation created unexpected consequences. When communal environments and anchors are missing, people who are disadvantaged often lose control over their lives.

This was seen when Africans were torn from their homeland, and again during the 1980s and beyond when integration took hold in this country. Perhaps this occurred because of progress and movement away from sole dependency on African-American communities. Perhaps this occurred because of a lack of understanding of internal consequences of well-intended social policies in mainstream society. Perhaps this occurred because African-Americans moved away from the continuity and consciousness of cultural and generational heritage base as a collective.

Many progressive African-Americans took advantage of new opportunities, and grabbed hold of individualistic norms and expectations that focused on the theme, "It's all about me."

The unintended consequence was relinquishing commitments to unity, togetherness, collective progress, community survival, the health of the group, and upward mobility for all. Cultures that remain communal tend to gain and preserve more generational, family, cultural, and social capital. Past generations demonstrated periods of great collective capital such as uplift and mutually agreed upon needs, goals, values, and efforts. Family and community resources provided for sustaining individual and group needs, especially during adverse times.

Communal families and communities safeguard and strengthen relationships between the young and old. This was illustrated when considering how enslaved Africans survived the early voyages and communal life on plantations and in slave quarters. Loss of a communal and traditional family focus produces generational and family silos, disconnection, isolation, and uncertainties.

Previously, there was constancy and commonly understood components of a family structure, such as a mother, father, and children. Regardless of the situation, each American family generally did the best they could to provide certain elements of a traditional family structure and life. According to the Pew Research Center (2010), the traditional American family as we knew it has been in decline for more than fifty years, and it continues to be redefined more and more. A Pew Research Center Survey (2013) reported critical generational differences. In 2008, about half (fifty-two percent) of all adults in this country were married. In 1960, seven-in-ten (seventy-two percent) were married.

There are race and class differences also. Today, single women head about one in five families. The marriage decline gap is most severe among low-income, non-college educated, and African-Americans (Bouvee, 1993). Despite the weakening of marriage, there seems to be a glimmer of hope. The Pew Center Survey (2013) revealed that despite a proliferation of cohabitation among younger generation parents, and growing uncertainties about the future of marriage and family, at least sixty-seven percent of newer generations of Americans expressed optimism about the future of marriage. This finding has implications for consideration of a future shift toward a more positive state of marriage and family among the newest and future generations.

Relationships: The Family Unit

The institution of family, and the impact of its transformations, resulted in greater numbers of broken families and a variety of new outcomes. The impact is even greater and more compounded for people of different races and socioeconomic classes, especially African-American and low-income people. Outward symptoms and risks of the new shifts have special significance to the well-being of families. The meaning and structure of family varies, and thoughts about family can engender very different ideas for some.

Some family experiences involve missing parents and dysfunction. The idea of a traditional family unit, consisting of both a caring mother and father in the home, is a foreign concept to a greater segment of the population. Rather than thoughts of supportive foundations, nurturance, stability, and balance, the idea of family for some can trigger feelings of bewilderment, abandonment, conflict, fear, disillusionment, vulnerability, loss, disappointment or anger. Such feelings and emotions often cloud clarity of the meaning of a sense of traditional family bond, affiliation, membership or relationships.

Families are rooted in personal experiences, varying by community, region, race, ethnicity, educational level, age, religious affiliation, and the interplay of demographic, social, and economic factors (Wetzel 1990). Although there are different family views, compositions, and cultural aspects, families build capacity for experiencing love, stability, and togetherness. The concept of family in the past served as the anchor for social continuity; the locus and source of strength, motivation, and overall security.

Realizing there is now more cultural and family diversity, it is critical to understand what it means to be family and parents, involving a mother and father. Parents have a strong impact on the development of people, especially children. Well-developed family and home environments teach skills and concepts about community, caring, loving, sharing, anger management, responsibility, and perseverance. Constructive families teach the significance of knowing what it is to have and be a family.

Healthy families teach the significance of a sense of self, an understanding of commonly expected values and character. Healthy families model, and teach, how and when to choose right from wrong. All has special meaning as families struggle to thrive, survive, and provide the sustenance needed for its members, particularly children. All people and families have both good and bad traditions that are passed from generation to generation. Shared experiences often provide applicable comparisons, and offer determinations for why certain traditions or practices were good, not good or should not be repeated.

Seduction by popular culture has resulted in what appears to be a less conscious segment of people, who are fragmented or engaged in detrimental relationships, and/or confused children with feelings of disconnection and loneliness who are continuing throughout life to search for belonging and purpose. The power of identity and self-knowledge are tied to the family unit and relationships.

By now, one might wonder about the relevance of this chapter to the family history of the Greens/McGills. It has a great deal to do with reasons why it is important to preserve and strengthen family and generational consciousness, continuity, strength, and survival as critical to our continued existence. It has something to do with the unfinished journey, and understanding the importance of strengthening the branches and roots of the family tree so that children can stand connected, strong, firm, and fruitful.

Earlier, I stated the intent of this book was to document our heritage and the work of ancestors in shaping our chances. The stories of the Green and McGill family are not unique; they are reminiscent of times when families built foundations that undergirded our development, survival, and welfare. The past explains some of the opportunities, constraints, and injustices that were witnessed and experienced; but it also explains how we became an extension of the symbols of ancestral pride, strife, and dignity.

Younger generations bare the same responsibility and challenge today. They are an extension of the legacy that existed on behalf of the collective.

A Portrait of Collective Strength[11]

Ultimately, our survival depends on individuals who understand shared cultural values, rootedness, and centeredness that translate into families who can produce well-adjusted, self-actualized individuals. Some of the prerequisites that must be passed on to newer generations are embedded in the next family story recounted by Jacob E. Collins (Jake), who lived in the rural south in one of the cocoons of a black rural community in Louisiana during the 1940s and 1950s.

Jake's family story brings together the elements of what comprised the continuity, the "glue" that held families and communal communities together. Also, his story provides a portrait of the conditions and components that allowed people, most specifically black folks, "to have the advantage and experiences of culture, continuity, and consciousness that allowed people to have a chance."

---

[11] Narrative by Jacob E. Collins.

Jakes's Narrative

I, Jacob Collins (Jake), was born during a time when children were not turned over to be raised by others outside of the family. We were taught to protect what we had.

We were influenced by foundational value systems, and family and cultural norms and nuisances that were the basis of our culture in a dual societal system. The 1940s and 1950s, and prior, were times when mothers, fathers, and grandparents had a strong influence on building character and foundations. There were strong families, cohesive neighborhoods, strong schools, and strong male and female influences on black unity, leadership, commitment, and guidance.

Starting at an early age, we were privileged to be raised when there was authentication of self by significant others in one's family and community. We were raised at a time when feelings of inferiority had not set in, so later experiences transitioned into feelings of capability, caring, and commitment to a "calling." Like many others, my family was raised on a farm in the country. As a child, we saw nature in its purest landscape—animals, corn, cotton, peanuts, sugar fields, sickness, death, and learning about life, and the complex ecosystem that maintained survival and integrity.

Poverty was not a focus or barrier. Regardless of living in the rural south, there were feelings of pride, self-assurance, and success, because the generations before had modeled hard work and the fruits of labor. There were things that people who lived in rural areas knew, and learned, that were and were not experienced by people who lived in cities. There were general experiences, such as the man who came by to sell Watkins liniment oil, which was intended to be a cure for all ills. There were the doses of castor oil and "360" medicine that was intended to cure colds and other health-related illnesses, which was purchased at a country store owned by a black man who was a relative.

There were the unique experiences, such as how we learned to milk cows and raise acres of sugarcane that looked like corn. Crops, including acres of peanuts, were raised and harvested by the wagon load so they would last until the next season. Sugarcane was hauled in a wagon to my grandfather's mill, which was located on a little creek on our 160 plus acres, where my grandfather made hundreds of gallons of syrup to last until next season. There was a milling machine that had a gear to make the wheels turn that squeezed the juice into a spout that landed in a fifty-gallon drum.

The wheels of the machine were turned by the force of a mule that tugged at the end of a thirty-foot pole that went around and circled the mill repeatedly. My father, Clyde Collins, lost two of his fingers when they got caught, while putting piles of five to six-foot sugarcanes in the mill. As a five or six-year-old, all I could do was watch in horror as the other men happened to notice and rescued him before his entire body was pulled into the mill. The rescuers had to walk from the mill, up to the house, then drive an hour or more to the hospital for surgery. Those men were my models—real men in action!

After the milling process was finished, the result was dozens and dozens of gallons of sugarcane syrup that were used as one of the staples for family and extended family. In addition, my grandfather packed many gallons of syrup in sparkling new buckets, and sold them to the whites in town. There was the canning of berries, peaches, pears, the slaughtering and curing of meat and sausages made from animals, and the homemade syrup and biscuits were like a delicacy!

All of this was a part of authentication and self-assuredness that helped link us to the values of who we were and where we came from. It was the "stuff" that was subconsciously generated, and helped us grow and develop. We saw how people solved complex problems to meet their needs, and how they improvised to create resources for things they did not have. We did not think of ourselves as "wanting" or lacking or being poor. It was the norm, the standard way black people sustained themselves independently.

On Sundays, our big dinners were a product of the original creation for meeting needs, such as milking the cows. We took the milk to put it in the well so it could cool. Some of the milk would be left out so that it could change into cream and clabber milk, where it becomes sour and forms into buttermilk. The clabber milk was mixed into flour to become bread that turned into wonderful fluffy, delicious biscuits. The cream was churned and turned into butter. We had sweet potatoes that were baked after they were dug up by the dozens of bushels. They knew how to keep them fresh under straw and a tarpaulin until the next planting season.

After church on Sundays, there was anticipation of the joy of eating all the food that came from nature, and the thought of commiserating with family and friends, which was a part of validating the meaning of family and one's humanity. The essence was that we felt whole because we saw the genius, reason, creativity, and intellect all around us. We witnessed things that made us feel valued, capable, and a part of something that we wanted to help perpetuate. We were fortunate to not have lived during the worst of times when Black people covertly and overtly had their community violated, had their purpose for existence violated, and they did not have a feeling that there was a place on earth.

They prayed that there would be a chance for a better life, and they prayed that there would be recognition of their place of value in the universe, eventually. They understood that if they stayed emotionally and spiritually bound, even in difficulty of the destructive effects of being the focus of ridicule (which created many of the problems in their life), and if they could protect what they had, their chances were more endurable. Church was a place—sometimes the only place—where a person could display their abilities and best presentation in suits, hats, and other clothing that was not worn during the work week. We presented ourselves as giving thanks and honor to God in our "Sunday Best."

Black people were "somebody" important in the world on Sunday. The men shared wisdom of how to manage the business of the church. This was a chance for some to fulfil the role of Sunday School superintendent, head of the usher board, missionary, trustee, head of the deacon board, bus driver, church nurse who wore a nurses' cap, and other significant roles of leadership and meaning that were not available in any other forum in their life and time. Some of these roles still hold over today, especially for black church communities where some people do not have as many chances to succeed in other ways.

At church, we experienced fish fries, choirs, preaching, and hymns of praise that inspired hope, possibilities, goodwill, and prospects for a better day. Church gatherings engendered feelings of the soul of a people, because there was an understanding of what it meant to have a day of mental, physical, and spiritual rest from the hard work of living. These experiences helped us understand the interrelationship of people, communities, and families. They were the source of where we got our feelings of worthiness, belonging, and responsibility.

Church was the source of a collective environment that explained mindfulness of our hope, sustenance, place, and role in the ecosystem. Going to church was a chance to get dressed up to demonstrate another dimension of our essence. This was not just a dimension of "old-fashioned" values. It was a part of the rituals and summons to prepare for the opportunity to not miss our chance for the purposeful meaning and intent of life and living. Life was not a matter of dependency on real estate agents, construction companies, architects, funeral homes or outside financial institutions. It was a routine, and a matter of believing in self, and assembling the gifts and talents of self and others. It was a continuation of gifts and abilities to adapt, and continue with a dignified life.

As time moved forward, now we see that life's processes have started to systematically take away and tear down the foundations, which are crumbling piece by piece. There was a need to integrate and open chances in society for everyone on an equal basis; but although the goal was somewhat achieved, it is a long way from being equal. The interrelationship of race and class created subtle, and sometimes not so subtle, actions that emasculated a people. Currently, those actions are more destructive and complex than we now pretend. Through buffoonery, bedazzlement, foolery, greed, and gullibility, we have been pushed into an arena of confusion.

Our present life has been exacerbated by television, social media, and a hip-hop generation that influenced our value system, cultural norms, and inflicted misguided nuisances placed on the younger generation of children. Certain video games, reality television, text messaging, selfies and the like influence subliminal destruction of character, values, emotions, communication, empathy, and connections.

Chances are about the probability of having the openings or likelihood to have opportunities or options. In the past, the focus was to seek more than just fortuitous luck or fate, but to be prepared with the necessary foundations, and to avoid distractions from the prerequisites and summons or "callings." The business of family, work, and life was a serious mission. Life today seems to focus more on "what I want at any expense;" or "I can be anything I want to be," with instant gratification; or "It's all about me," with a lack of a sense of the cost or investment in what it takes to become, and withstand, the issue of the time.

In the contemporary landscape, oftentimes, children and young adults have difficulty separating themselves from adults. They see themselves on the same level as adults; yet they have not had experiences to mature or gain the skills and knowledge or will to live up to responsibilities, commitments, consequences, and obstacles as adults or parents. Feelings of younger generations seem to be that, "My parents must respect me *if* I respect them. This is my room, my privacy, etc." The illusions of life are masqueraded as reality in that they fail to realize that they live in a room in their parent's house, and most parents pay the mortgage, household bills, and expenses for children to have a room.

Author's Summary

Jakes's story sums up the idea that there are destructive forces that continue to obscure and plague our demise as strong committed communities, cultures, people, and families. This is true, certainly not for all, but for far too many; modern-day social turmoil, problems, and complications have created transitional and debilitating conditions, involving the:

- Disintegration of strong families;
- Disintegration of cohesive neighborhoods;

- Disintegration of cohesive communities;
- Disintegration of strong neighborhoods and schools;
- Absence of large numbers of strong black men in families and the community;
- Absence of strong black leadership;
- Loss of fathers and strong, healthy males, and female guidance and influence;
- Feminization of males;
- Loss of childhood, and fantasies and illusions masqueraded as truth;
- Demise and elimination of local schools and educators of color who were dedicated to more than a paycheck and self-aggrandizement; and
- Loss of caring, commitment, and purpose that link to "a calling" or long-term purpose or mission.

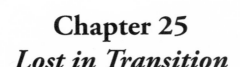

Chapter 25
Lost in Transition

Anthropologist Margaret Mead explained much of what is behind the loss of certain degrees of cultural continuity and consciousness, and many of the important traditions and institutions as we progressed from the past to the present. In a book entitled *Theory of Cultural Continuity and Change* (1997), Mead identified phases of generational and cultural change and transitions, which involved a confluence of social, economic, cultural, political, and technological changes over the course of the Green/McGill family history.

Culture refers to the "complex whole of life, including knowledge, beliefs, art, customs, and any other capabilities and habits acquired (E.B. Taylor)." *Consciousness* refers to the attitude of the mind, a way of life, the awareness and sensitivity to what is going on around you. *Continuity* refers to the glue that holds something together, the uninterrupted, lasting, valued permanence. The three phases of generational and cultural change, consciousness, and continuity identified by Mead are:

1) *Post-figurative Culture*—represents the past, where change is slow, requiring catastrophic intervention, such as wars or natural disasters (i.e., earthquakes, flooding, volcanic eruption, hurricanes, etc.) Children are influenced by and learn from elders, the church, and community.

2) *Co-figurative Culture*—represents the present where experiences are radically different from those of the past. Children are influenced and learn from elders, the church, and com-

munity; but also from peers with influence from parents and elders, to a lesser degree.

3) *Pre-figurative Culture*—represents the future and a new conception of living with alternative lifestyles, and fast-paced, radical change. Elders learn from children; children learn primarily from media and their peers.

Clearly, Mead's three phases of generational and cultural change, continuity, and consciousness reflect transitions over the generations, including the decline of family structure and stress on family life. Reflecting on the transitions observed while writing this family history, Mead's theory—coupled with those of authors Lois Benjamin and Charles Simmons (2000), George Barna (2009), and Rita Soltan (2004)—was adapted to partially explain transitions over the five past generational eras, which are significant to the present and future as family, individuals, and a collective.

Generalities will be used to describe a sampling of the characteristics of each defining generation:

Five Generational Eras
World War I Generation (1900s–1924)
Post Figurative

- Education-Dual system(Builders)
- Socialization-Elders/Church/Family (Prior to 1946 (62+)
- Mostly southern roots/traditions
- God-fearing people
- Foundation builders/Communal Culture
- "Can do, get it done" attitude
- Segregated society

World War II Generation (1925–1949)
Co Figurative

- Segregated Society/Black Migration(Bridges)
- New Technology/Media

SEARETHA SMITH-COLLINS

- Less influence of elders
- God-fearing people
- "Can do, get it done" attitude
- Communal Culture
- Passed the baton to the next generation

Civil Rights Generation (1950–1975)
Co-Figurative

- Shifts in socialization(Boomers)
- Restlessness/change in the status quo (1945, 1946–1965)
- Integrated schools/neighborhoods
- Influenced by elder, parents, church

Pre-Figurative

- Planned actions carefully nurtured and executed
- Emergence of new models that improved/replaced the old
- Divorce/weakened family structure
- Latch-key children left home alone
- Produced pathways for children to follow in steps
- "Me" generation/Lessening of communal culture

Post-Civil Rights Generation (1961–1983)
Pre-Figurative

- Integrated educational system
- Socialization-Peers/Mass Media, Gen X (1961–1981)
- Eclectic roots/traditions, not necessarily southern
- Decline of family structure/Stress in family life, Busters (1964–1983) (Gen Y)
- Collapse of local church as we knew it
- Dependent on parents/adults, Children of Boomers/ Not strategic or poised to lead Grandchildren of Builders
- Lack ferocious work ethic
- Conflict between generations over positions of authority

208

- Text generation, cell phones, play stations, rap, hip-hop
- Broad flight from existing institutions/movements that were labored for in the past
- Toys, amenities, comforts, pleasure options
- Immigration/Globalization/Cultural Discontinuity/ Racial Amnesia
- Dichotomy in religious versus spiritual beliefs

Information Age Generation (ten–twelve-year-olds)
Pre-Figurative

- Collapse of family/parenting in question (Tweens)
- Socialization by media/technology (Text Generation)
- Sophisticated environment through media/parents (Today's Bridges)
- Integrated/re-segregated schools/neighborhoods
- Chat rooms, television commercials, Internet influences
- Break/free from parental controls/distance, supervised freedom
- Cellphones, pagers, latch-key, toys, comforts, fund-based attitudes, security mechanisms
- Personal/social needs contain belonging, power, freedom, fun, feeling of acceptance from peer groups
- Successful parents who provide appropriate motivation, encouragement/feeling of limitless possibilities
- Instant gratification/success expected as a given/liberal social values
- Often have values and viewpoints of the WWII generation
- (Bridges)—Logical thinking/motivated to think about right or wrong
- Entering in to a more responsible state of adolescence
- Childhood innocence is gone/over-exposed to everything

As mentioned, The Civil Rights/Boomer Generation (approximately 1943–1968) were the last to collectively benefit from fundamentals that produced strong family and group power. There were boundaries and limitations; yet, the future hovered over new and uncertain possibilities amid transitions that were destined to come. They understood how progress and success were achieved and inter-woven, so the battles and struggles became a part of our collective memory.

The Boomers understood they were steeped in the continuity of culture and family; and whatever success they had resulted from growing up in a world that depended on cohesion, and the recognition of a common plight and history. As we consider the past few decades of generational transitions, the instability of childhood that followed the Boomer Generation leads us to consider a question about the future of family. Is there a need or can the traditional family survive or be revived in the present and future? It might be beneficial to determine the benefit of hindsight to guide foresight, such as, had we known the present outcome of the state of families beforehand, how could we have yielded a better outcome?

One of the first areas that requires further consideration or examination are the roles of the family unit—the mother, father, and children, which are increasingly shifting. The past cultural family model served as the backbone for disadvantaged people who were in poverty, including African-Americans. Billingsly (1992) described the impact of the destruction of the cultural shift on families: "We now have a two-family nation—one thriving and intact, and the other broken, and far too often, African-American."

Wetzel (1992) explained that when family and community resources are weakened or lost, there are no buffers to help shield the family from adversity. The following portrait illustrates the impact of the disintegration of the traditional, cultural family model, and what the institution of family has become in America now versus fifty years ago:

- In 1980, at least eighty percent of African-American families were headed by two parents (Billingsley 1992). The percentage was even greater for other races and cultures, such as white people. Currently, African-American families are fractured and in great decline more than most others. In fact, the traditional African-American family seems as devastated today as it was when African and African-American families were torn apart and sold during enslavement in this country.

- As early as 2007, most data sources noted that as much as seventy percent of black children were born to single mothers (both educated and uneducated women). This concern is attributed to fatherless homes leaving most households headed by single mothers living in poverty, which often is passed onto children from generation to generation (Bouvee 1993).

There are differences in the institution of family more than ever before. If only a mere twenty-five to thirty percent of African-American children in particular have two parents in the home, a daunting challenge and adjustment lies before us. The looming question is, "Who is providing the strong family models needed for developing children and healthy male/female relationships?" A large percentage of children being raised by single mothers are males, which raises a continuing concern for the future of black males. Also, there is a profound impact on girls as well as the psyche of boys who are trying to develop as young people.

We see the struggles and pressures on mothers and grandmothers who live in poverty, raising children and grandchildren alone. More than ever before, we are faced with troubled youth who have been shaped by upheaval and a lack of nurturing in the home, community, school, and society. Youths have been influenced by television, radio, videos, films, sex, drugs, music, the Internet, varied forms of technology, and real-world experiences that often are well beyond their years.

Understanding these issues in the contemporary context must be front and center in the minds of old and young people alike. The seismic and tumultuous changes that have taken place in society, and in the character of youth—particularly in the last decades—have presented new and bewildering challenges for parents, schools, and the community. In 1980, a friend and pioneer in the field of gifted education, Irving Sato, shared a profound assessment of the state of the young and modern-day societal change on families; and forty years later, his statement holds true for challenges that newer generations are facing today:

> Young people now are confronted with confer-ring and complicated social problems and tur-moil that earlier generations never encountered. These situations have had a profound effect on today's youth, and upon the attitudes and per-formance of young people, in and out of schools.

Chapter 26
Transitioning from Old to New

We have made it, but where.

—Anonymous

Stories about the 1960s and 1970s seem an infinite time ago to most youth and young adults. Thirty or forty years ago seem like an eternity to newer generations, so talking or studying about historic occurrences and people often has little relevance to youth today. Pauline R. Kezer, explained that "Continuity gives us roots; change gives us branches, letting us stretch and grow and reach new heights." Times have changed, but memories bridge the pathway to the present. For example, success among Blacks was traditionally rooted in continuity and kinship, and the common bond was struggle. Segregation reinforced inferiority, but it also galvanized Blacks to thrive, achieve middle-class status, and succeed.

Earlier, I mentioned that our family used to go to Texas to visit friends and relatives. During one of those visits as a child of elementary school age, my mother took us shopping to a popular nickel and dime store in downtown Houston, Texas. I do not think there was much that costs a nickel or dime in the store, but they were very popular shopping places at the time. Nickel and dime stores usually had lunch counters that served hotdogs and soda drinks.

The stores had an aroma of fresh popcorn that was popped in a machine right at the entrance of the store. I recall visiting similar nickel and dime stores in Seattle during the Christmas holidays. They were the best places to take children to shop for Christmas gifts, because an entire family gift list could be covered with no more than ten to twenty dollars. My sister and I usually pooled our money to buy the annual surprise holiday gift for our father, usually a bottle of Old Spice cologne. My mother's customary gift was a little blue bottle of Evening in Paris perfume. As children, we thought we gifted her with the best perfume money could buy, which was true of our available funds!

We were excited to go to the dime store in Houston, especially because of the promise of getting a bag of popcorn, an ice cream cone, or candy treats before returning to our relatives' home. After a while, I decided I wanted a drink of water, so as small children often do. I anxiously ran off from my mother, and started in the direction of the water fountain. Suddenly, my mother called to for me to *stop*! Hearing the tone of her voice, I immediately stopped in my tracks.

She grabbed my arm and told me that I could not drink out of the fountain where I was headed. She pointed to another water fountain that had large printed letters written above: Colored. I gazed at the water fountain, and looked at the sign again that said Colored; then I looked at the fountain underneath the sign. Indignantly I said, "I am not going to drink out of that dirty old fountain!" I insisted that the fountain my mother pointed to looked too dirty and uninviting. She told me to look above the other fountain and read the words. I noticed the large letters printed above that fountain read Whites Only. I looked at the other sign again that said Colored.

This was the first time I had seen such a sight! All I remember after that point was my mother sternly grabbing my hand, and pulling me quickly along as we left that store! We did not have a chance to buy anything. We did not even have a chance to get popcorn, ice cream or candy. The horrified look on my mother's face told me that something was wrong. It was a look of fear for one's young that remains etched in memory. Having been raised in the north, in what seemed to be an integrated society, this was the first time I met overt racism and discrimination smack in the face.

Many young people hear or read about this phase in American history when there were visible signs of racism and separatism, but the White Only and Colored images on the signs were a part of lived history that remain vividly imprinted in my mind even today. Later, my mother shared why we had to abruptly leave the store, and explained the meaning of the unfairness and separate signs. I understood the indignity of such treatment even as a small child; in fact, that is when I first learned that life is not fair, and there are different rules for different people as a matter of fact.

I share this story not only because it is real and very personal; it illustrates that no matter how time progresses, the images and lessons from history have relevance and deep meaning that cannot be easily forgotten. Sometimes, members of newer generations insist that parents and elders should simply get over past experiences, and move on into the new world order. As I grew older, I understood the implications and dangers of past discriminatory practices, and internalized the wise words of the late Coretta Scott King, who said, "Struggle is a never-ending process ... freedom is never really won—you earn it, and win it, in every generation."

Based on personal experiences that revolved around just wanting to get a drink water from a clean water fountain, I realized early on the struggles for civil and human rights—and I would add now, the struggle for a strong, solid family life—are continuous and cannot be easily ignored. Minister and professor Dr. Cornell West, expressed it this way: "Every thirty to thirty-five years or so, we have to be reminded, and we have to remind others about freedom, justice, compassion, service, love, and truth that is at the center of our past collective existence" (Sermon at Rankin Chapel, Howard University in Washington, DC, 2016).

As young people grapple with the issues of this generation, there are wise prescriptions that come before us. It is judicious to understand what was behind the respect for culture, continuity, and consciousness that greatly influenced ancestors and elders, and their spiritual upbringing and belief in something greater than self. Children in the past were taught by parents and elders, and they knew the prescriptions and communal expectations, i.e. drive, hard work, unity, and perseverance to achieve a better future.

The bar and standards were high. Past generations learned they had to compete and perform better than the best, because it was just the way it was. As successors, they represented the progress of their race and heritage, because the struggle of the journey has been incremental, and continues to be a challenge for many. Past generations knew they wanted to change the rules and conditions, but they also knew they had to be prepared, educated, and involved to carry on the banner of uplift, freedom, and change that was yet to come.

Perhaps as a collective, we forgot some of our foundations. Perhaps in the more integrated environments, we became more influenced by others. Perhaps we neglected to teach some of the important fundamentals that were engrained in our being. Perhaps we neglected to transfer some of the collective responsibilities of the cultural model as a part of the progressive movement, including ensuring uplift of the downtrodden and less fortunate.

Possibly, we did not pass on the important spiritual, motivational, traditional, cultural, practical, intergenerational teachings that provided a sense of togetherness, wholesomeness, and continuity. These were some of the qualities that served as our epicenter when it was time to navigate the ups and downs of time. Perhaps in the name of individual uplift and achievement, we abandoned the cultural ship or at least changed the course of the journey.

As successive generations of the pre-figurative cultural modern-age are determined to do things differently, to raise children differently, to live differently, to deliberately move away from the influence of the old to mainstream goals, and to implement new ideas and theories of our contemporary times, an important lesson must be remembered—to consider the tracks of the past as new ones are made. In hindsight, had we known the impact of some of the changes to now, perhaps we would have done some things differently.

As newer generations come to grips with the realities of their generation, both older and younger generations can mutually learn from the wealth of old and new knowledge, experiences, and hopes. We can all learn and grow from our mistakes. An unknown person said, "The beauty of mistakes is they can be corrected." A Swahili proverb said it best. "To lose your way is one way to finding it."

Recapturing Family Strength

While there are various ways families operate, and instill values and life chances, there are universal, timeless roles that have launched functional children over time. Children are lost in a sea of change, crisis, and confusion. Everyone deserves to be cared for by a nurturing, responsible mother and father or someone who fulfills those roles as parents. There are human needs for love, security, and spiritual, moral, and human connectedness and centeredness. There are universal needs for predictable relationships, and connections to a stable home and family that ensure the opportunity to grow successfully into adulthood.

It is important to recapture strength in providing cultural health and resources, and dedicated family growth, and community support. Despite the proliferation of single parents, cohabitation, co-parenting, shared-parenting, no-parenting, nontraditional, and other alternative family structures, we must figure out what we are going to do to sustain our role as fruitful parents and family. It is also important to clarify that I am not saying that children should have their father and mother present at any cost. If there is abuse of any kind—exposure to drugs and violence, neglect or any debilitating circumstance inflicted by parents—a child should be entrusted to another responsible, committed adult.

For those who may not have had the benefit of experiencing a cohesive family or had no family in the traditional sense; or for those who never received nurturing attention, love, concern, emotional security or a close bond with a mother, father, sister, and/or brother, for the last time, let me share, by example, what it means to be cared for in a functional, nurturing family, influenced and guided by a responsible mother and father, in contrast to what is often missing in many families today.

A Father's Hand

Like most, my parents were not perfect or problem-free. We had the usual "growing pains" and disagreements that most children, teens, and parents experience; however, we were blessed to have

217

good, devoted parents. It seemed that parents like my father and mother strengthened and taught life's lessons through natural activities and experiences in the home. Coupled with spending quality time, and showing acceptance and joy, there were strong expectations for behavior and educational attainment, all of which alleviated concerns about motivation and aspirations for learning, achievement, and behavior.

Our parents did not follow a documented child psychology book or prescription from the child expert of the day. They just did the things they felt were forward-thinking during their time.

They did what they knew and had experienced or what they thought they could do to improve upon the traditional cultural model that had been passed on to them. For example, my father made certain we had fundamentals for educational success. He supported and reinforced what we learned in school, thus providing the possibility for more skills and confidence to perform.

When it came to homework, my dad took the time to teach mathematical procedures and shortcuts, insisting that we memorize, learn, and apply math facts in real life, and in ways to solve mathematical problems. He had a strong mathematical background that applied to his work and life, so he knew and emphasized the value of education through direct involvement and examples. For instance, he loved to play card games with friends. As it turned out, that was another tool used to reinforce what we learned at school.

Although he did not call it homework, he used card games to provide practice and application of math in a problem-solving situation. At first, he insisted that we use mental math to compute numbers, tally, and keep score during card games. Later, he taught us how to play Dominoes, and other games, such as Spades, Hearts, and Bid Whist as foundations for learning cooperative team work, social skills, and strategies to think and outwit the thinking of others. For those who do not have a mathematics background, the lesson here is that there are various ways parents can reinforce and help their child learn in ways that are not obviously academic ways.

As mentioned earlier, the shared parenting role and responsibility was a natural way of life in our home. There was not just "man's work" or "woman's work;" there was family and community work in our home. My dad washed, ironed, folded clothes, cooked, vacuumed the floor, washed dishes, repaired things that broke down in the home, and modeled cooperation in home living, and taking care of us as children.

Now that I think about it, his commitment to washing dishes pretty much ended when we became teenagers, and dishwashing became one of our duties on a rotating basis. Our parents believed in communal living, so they assigned weekly chores and assignments, such as taking turns, each week, washing dishes after meals (our baby sister was an exception, however). After we became adults and left home, my father returned to his dishwashing duties.

A disclaimer may be appropriate at this point. The next examples are not intended as recommended techniques or practices for everyone. They are shared only to show how some parents managed, and had control of, their family environment; and how they taught values of responsibility, accountability, and right from wrong. It seemed that our parents naturally understood child psychology in ways that many would be in awe of today. For example, one of my father's vices was smoking cigarettes, and he occasionally smoked a cigar, both of which he finally stopped later in life (unfortunately, this cumulative habit contributed to his death from lung cancer later in life).

One time, when I was about eight or ten years old, I observed him smoking a cigar as he relaxed and visited with a friend. As I watched the adult exchange, it seemed they were enjoying their cigar so much! I was curious to know what it was like to smoke a cigar, so I asked if I could take a puff of his cigar. My dad contemplated my curiosity, looked at me, thought for a minute, and said, "You want to know what it is like to smoke a cigar? Well, go ahead and try it." I couldn't believe my ears! He was letting me smoke a cigar! He gave me the cigar, and I took a big puff and inhaled it as I had seen him do when he smoked. All I remember is that it had an awful taste! He encouraged me to take another puff. I quickly declined and hurriedly handed that cigar back to him! Right at that moment, a lifetime decision was made. Cigar smoking was not for me!

My father was not through with the lesson, however. He then said, "Here, try a cigarette!" With a big smile on my face, my inside thought was, "I was going to have a chance to smoke a cigarette like I had seen in the movies!" I was excited as he gave me the cigarette and lit it. I put it between my lips and inhaled a big puff of air. All I remember is the terrible taste after the puff; then, a horrible feeling of smoke entered my nose, and then fits of coughing followed until I could get my breath again! I guess I must have swallowed or inhaled the smoke, which was not a good idea! I never wanted to smoke another cigar or cigarette again! He had used a deterrent that taught me a great lesson! With a smile on his face, he asked, "Would you like another cigarette or cigar?" My answer was clearly, "*No way!*" That was the beginning and end of trying to smoke cigars or cigarettes!

Because of this experience, by the time I was a teenager, there was no need to experiment with smoking. Of course, as a teenager, I was faced with peer pressure and offered a cigarette on occasion. As you might have guessed, my response was consistently a big, "*No thank you!*"

My dad had taken advantage of a "teachable moment." Under his shrewd supervision, his lesson reaped lifetime results. I had a similar experience with tasting alcohol (I think it was Johnny Walker Red Whisky). In like manner, after allowing me to take a big gulp of his beverage, the taste and my burning tongue took care of that inquisitiveness! To this day, I am not a very fond or frequent partaker of alcohol either! Pass the Kool-Aid, please.

A Mother's Hand

Mothers hold special places in the heart of many families also. Many modern-day mothers have the responsibility of trying to provide the roles of both mothers and fathers. The role of mother has its special requirements that are quite different from fathers, however. Mothers have the responsibility of teaching daughters they are valued, and how to grow into strong, healthy, sensitive women, and potential mothers. Of course, the best example that I know firsthand is that of my mother, Oleatha Green.

Like my father, raising children was central to her family role and life. She was a stay-at-home mother for a great deal of our childhood, not because she could afford to do so, but because it was by choice and a duty to raise her children. It was simply what many women of her generation did as their key role as a mother. Having three girls, my mother taught us how to gain self-respect as girls and women. She stressed the importance of following our faith, knowing right from wrong, and having the discernment to know the difference.

For instance, in the face of peer pressure or desire, if we asked her to do something that other people's children could do, her typical, thought-provoking response was, "If Mary (not a reference to a real person) decided to jump off a bridge, would you do it too?" We knew that, most likely, we were not going to be allowed to do something just because other parents allowed their children to do so. Of course, her response was frustrating at the time, but later we realized that she was teaching us how to develop independent thinking and use good judgment, rather than just going along with the group.

When considering peer pressure and knowing how to think, act, behave, and make decisions and choices, this was a great lesson; especially when it meant maintaining safety, character, strength, and virtues. Having been firmly grounded in the traditional cultural family model, there were lessons of etiquette, responsibility, and respecting self and others. Teaching these lessons were not only a part of our mother's role; she felt it was her duty to pass such knowledge on to her children.

Although there were differences in values and how women operated, the underpinnings were put in place. We were taught how to be productive, caring, ethical people, with high standards and aspirations for family, self, and our children to come. Our mother's guidance and major lessons seemed stern and overprotective at the time, but in later life, we realized she taught life-sustaining lessons of responsibility, kinship, love (sometimes tough love), survival, and the importance of family. It was up to us as adults to carry the lessons forth, and connect those experiences to later life as women and adults.

A Family's Hand

It really took both parents to construct a successful family unit. My father was usually nearby providing care and support to my mother as they guided and reinforced what it meant to build confidence, high self-esteem, concern, and relationships as family. He modeled the value of having a man in the home as a father. He showed strength and demonstrated what it meant to provide a protective, secure environment for a family, which is a characteristic that is missing in many homes today. Although he did not have sons, he taught us useful skills, such as how to paint walls, hammer nails, use screwdrivers and a measuring tape, and other gender-neutral skills that came in handy as we managed our households as adults.

Together, our parents invested a great deal of resources in providing positive family experiences. Consistent, strong expectations for behavior were key factors in the functioning of our family also, no matter where—implementation and enforcement of commonly respected family rules, behavior expectations, and standards simply removed any concerns for serious problems at home, school or in the community. Although our mother did a lot of the daily guiding and monitoring of behavior, our father was the real enforcer in our home!

If something got to a point that my mother lost her patience or when we "got on her last nerve," it was common to see her put her hand on her hip, give us that deep-level stare, and say, "I brought you into this world, and I will take you out!" Or she would declare, "Just wait until your dad gets home!" We knew that she had enough and something good was not in store! We did not have the benefit of having a choice or a "time out" to think about our misbehavior! Most likely, we were in for a spanking!

Perhaps the method seems outdated, old-fashioned or politically incorrect now, and some may disagree with the technique, but selecting one's own consequence was not the order of those days! Parents used methods that were a culmination of years of guiding and caring for children through the cultural model that they inherited. Although some may have taken disciplining through spanking to a different level, that was not what was in store in our household.

I recall one time when my mother declared, "Wait until your dad comes home," which produced a scene that was made for a comedy hour. I do not remember why she was angry with me, but in the naive reasoning of a child, I decided I would proactively prepare for my father's arrival by taking matters into my own hands. I decided to scoot myself under my bed so that my backside was halfway underneath and not visible or reachable. In my child's mind, I reasoned that my father would not be able to spank me if he could not reach my "behind," which was safely tucked under my bed.

I stayed tightly positioned halfway under the bed for a few hours and fell asleep. I sort of put myself into a self-imposed "time out" position as it turned out. When my father came home from work (which was several hours later), my mother showed him where I was sleeping. They proceeded to heartily laugh at the scene of my antics. I guess my creative thinking was successful after all. I was not one who usually needed a spanking, and I did not receive many of them (I was a quick learner). On that day, I was "saved by the bell;" or was it my buttocks that were saved by the bed?

You see, most African-American parents were strict disciplinarians, because they knew that their children had to learn to operate in an unfriendly society. They wanted to protect them from ill-fated decision-making or life-threatening situations that might have been inflicted upon them in a volatile, hostile society. As a life and death survival matter, black people had to obey inequitable rules and conform no matter how unjust the situation. Black parents wanted to protect and teach children how to maneuver in society and avoid dangers and threats to their well-being.

The intent here is not to make judgements or debate the practices. It is more to explain the motives behind family practices and traditions across the generations during different time periods. It was important for children to learn how to follow directions, demonstrate judgment and knowledge of appropriate responses and behavior as well as know what was right and wrong under various situations. For the most part, practices such as those illustrated how and why discipline was practiced.

The operative idea is that parents must guide, teach, model, and structure the home environment as the training ground for children in caring ways, starting at the earliest of ages. If that occurs, children will grow up feeling safe, secure, and cared about with expectations, knowledge, values, and a moral compass that will help determine what is right and wrong in appropriate situations. In today's context, that often means less yelling and hitting, and more talking, explaining, and consistently teaching young children, starting when they are infants. This is a crucial role that new parents (both mothers and fathers) must improve upon if we are to nourish socially and emotionally healthy children.

Although we did not have brothers, my father served as a role model for males who were cousins, play cousins, nephews, and grandsons. When fathers are positive spouses and dads, they serve as role-models for sons who become uncles, brothers, grandfathers, spouses, and fathers. In turn, mothers who are positive role models for girls, teach them how to be women, sisters, aunts, spouses, grandmothers, and mothers. Fathers have a key role in the development of daughters as well. My father was cognizant of the need to show approval and encouragement, so even as adults, he complimented us on our appearance, effort or whatever positives he could find.

I do not know if he knew of the importance of such simple acts as frequently complimenting us; but now it is common knowledge that positive reinforcement by fathers is critical to feelings of value, confidence, and the emotional well-being of daughters. Positive, healthy attention and guidance from a father affects a child's self-worth as well as future relationships and choices of a daughter's male partners.

When children are separated from either parent, a void can be created for the parent, the child, and the child's future children. My father was separated from his oldest daughter, but fortunately, they had a chance to come together and connect as father, daughter, and grandchildren later in life. This is an important connection that needs to be repaired as we live in the modern-world of family division, because far too many fathers are not involved in the family life of their children for various reasons. No matter how well-intended or how hard one tries, fulfilling the entirety of parental roles in the traditional sense is difficult.

Truthfully, women cannot be fathers or men in the traditional sense. In the best family situation, a trusted woman must fulfill the role of teaching a female how to become a mother, sister, aunt, wife, and grandmother. No matter how well-intentioned or hard one tries, a man cannot be a mother or woman in the traditional sense. A trusted man must fulfill the role of teaching a male how to become a father, brother, uncle, husband, and grandfather. Given the universal nature of these needs, it is incumbent upon newer generations to determine what adjustments are needed to strengthen the family roles and responsibilities in this new contemporary landscape.

The reality is that there is a need for both parents—having a devoted mother and father holds true as much today as in the past. Sometimes grandfathers, grandmothers, and others must step in to reinforce family roles and expectations when fathers or mothers are not present; however, accessibility to grandparents has changed also. If each family member fulfills the necessary role, the possibility is stronger that children will cultivate a positive sense of self and belonging. In the absence of a mother or father as parents, someone must stand in as best they can to provide financial and emotional support, guidance, development, and nurturance.

The role of grandparents is significant also. Nowadays, we have grandparents who are mid to late thirty years of age and older Although conditions have changed for many, the need for development of family strength remains a generational effort and responsibility. When considering an understanding and example of how family strength was built, maintained, and transmitted, I had a first-hand view of my father, Elbert, who stood on the shoulders of his father, James (Jim) Green, Sr., as well as his uncles, aunts, and those of all the descendants of the Greens and McGills who preceded him. His nephews, nieces, daughters, and grandchildren now stand on his shoulders.

As mentioned, my father loved and was proud of his family. He especially adored his grandchildren and great-grandchildren to whom he provided both fatherly and grandfatherly roles. During retirement, my parents provided childcare for their grandchildren, especially my grandson and their great-grandson, Qualin, starting when he was only a few months old. A frequent scene was seeing my father drive his black truck to and from the Red Apple store or the once popular Catfish Corner restaurant, which used to be an African American historic site in Seattle. As a baby, Qualin was introduced to Catfish Corner's specifically prepared catfish, which immediately became one of his favorite meals. His great-granddaddy made certain that Qualin had hot, fresh catfish on a regular basis. They enjoyed sitting together at the kitchen table eating, sharing, and enjoying their catfish lunches. To this day, Qualin still loves catfish.

Like many of the Greens and McGills, my father, Elbert loved and had a strong bond with his grandchildren, and they still have fond, loving memories of him. Another grandson, Kevin, who was dear to his heart, was nurtured by his grandparents from an early age also. My father's grands, great-grands, and extended others who lived in Seattle were raised and well-cared for under the communal protection of my parents. Like many families there simply were no others like their Granddaddy and Grand mommy, who were always there, supportive, loving, caring, and always willing to lend support, time, and an affectionate helping hand.

In like manner and in the spirit of passing on what was given to me by my parents through familial and multi-generational support and care, with the support of my husband, I placed my career on somewhat of a partial pause to provide childcare support to another generation of descendants of the Greens and McGills. We have been providing childcare for my great-niece and nephew since both children were two months old. It has been delightful and enlightening to see the growth, development, and prospects of the future generation, such as the three-year old's ability to show me how to recapture or recover an image on an iPad! Just as Granny Fannie could not have imagined, we cannot imagine the possibilities of today's young children! Intergenerational cooperation, sustenance, and investment are needed to shore up newer generations, so they and their parents can gain strength to more aptly feel connected and develop a stronger communal sense of belonging, develop and cultivate a sense of family and self; find ways to embrace personal heritage and relevance, and become armed with real connections, fellowship, and authentic family relationships and experiences.

As we continue the path of the unfinished journey in this modern era, perhaps there are two sets of words of advice that should guide the thinking. L.H. Turk & E.A. Allen (1956), said, "Usually there is much more than meets the eye, and often there are centuries of history and tradition behind (what exists as tradition)." Rich parental and family environments usually produce children who flourish, because they have the underpinnings of family strength and endurance.

For instance, starting from Granny Fannie's submissive and humble beginnings, offspring and descendants evolved to participate and contribute across all aspects of American society. As we gain more privilege in life, we must stay passionate about those who somehow figured out how to influence the choices and decisions that present themselves today. In turn, when life's transitions seem most chaotic, frustrating, challenging, and seemingly hopeless, an African-American saying reminds us of what to do: If you come to the end of your rope, tie a knot and hang on!

Chapter 27
The Last Words

The pilgrimage ends and begins with each new generation.

—Anonymous

Connecting the Dots

There are successful families, but there are more who lack positive family experiences and opportunities. According to the *Raising Him Alone Campaign*, approximately half of the general population, and seventy-seven to eighty percent of today's African-American population are children of divorce, children living with a single parent, children living with those who have never married, and very often they are children living in poverty.

If those statistics are correct, then it is no wonder we are struggling as family and children. Our collective strength has dissolved from approximately eighty-four percent of African-American children who lived in two-parent homes, consisting of a mother, father, and children up to the 1980s. It is difficult to attain and maintain basic needs when foundational systems and institutions, such as family, are drifting or disintegrating. This very fact surfaces several menacing questions that loom large as the uncharted family journey presses on:

(1) Who is providing the healthy models needed for developing children, and who is forming healthy male/female relationships?

(2) Will significant traditions be lost?

(3) Will we regain potential as families?

(4) Will our children maintain potential as torchbearers?

Much will depend on how we choose to understand and protect our heritage, and remain as strong, purposeful families that collectively:

1) Gain clarity of purpose for self and family;

2) Attain pride, love, protection, self-esteem, belief, and encouragement;

3) Acquire broad fulfillment of love and affirmation;

4) Acquire a sense of belonging, acceptance, and execution of provisions for safe, secure home environments and economic well-being;

5) Achieve resolution for finding an emotional and spiritual center;

6) Acknowledge the importance of family life and parenting as an important life task;

7) Achieve broad understandings of issues and needs for equity and peaceful co-existence;

8) Realize the importance of culture and the value of respect for others and self, including heritage, elders, and historical and family knowledge; and

9) Find success in showing love, nurture, and care for children from the moment they are born and throughout their life.

We inherited wisdom and the accumulation of experiences of those who lived before us. True wisdom is timeless, and the beautiful thing about wisdom is that it comes from different people, different places, different times, and different cultures and experiences. Because the final chapter of our journey remains unfinished and unwritten, the last words will come in the form of generational gems and mental games that explain what is probable or possible.

Achievement/Success

- "I have made it, but where?" Anonymous
- "Ability is a poor man's wealth." John Wooden
- "Big ship need deep river." Jamaican Proverb
- "Fishing in deep water requires skill." African Proverb
- "All things are difficult before they are easy." African Proverb
- "The road to success can be a difficult journey." African Proverb
- "God doesn't give you the people you want; he gives you the people you need ... to help you, to hurt you, to leave you, to love you, and to make you into the person you were meant to be." Anonymous
- "Remember life is short, and it's up to you to make it sweet." Anonymous
- "We must teach our children to dream with their eyes open." Henry Edwards 1942

Courage

- "Courage is not the absence of fear. It's the mastery of it." Anonymous
- "A ship is made to sail. It is not safe in the harbor." Anonymous
- "Insecurity exists in the absence of knowledge." Anonymous
- "Don't let discouragement discourage you. Let it encourage you." Anonymous
- "Storms always take out trees with the weakest roots." Wintley Phipps

Cultural History

- "Elders hold the history of our pain and success." Anonymous
- "History has thrust something upon me from which I cannot turn away." African-American Proverb

- "We can transcend the past by learning from our errors." Anonymous
- "To see your history erased before your very eyes—with no concern, no remorse, and no explanation—deserves attention." David Catania, *Washington Post* 2014
- "We must understand that the most important thing (that we can do) is to tell the history of (our) people. Tell the history of (our) time. Tell the truth of the future." Harry Belafonte, in Mayo and Lemieux 2016
- "Yesterday is history. Tomorrow is a mystery. Today is a gift, that's why it's called 'present.' You don't know what's ahead." Anonymous
- "You can judge the comparison of a nation by the way it treats its elderly, the vulnerable, and its children." Anonymous
- "Always keep a little bit of suffering in your mind. Don't let it fade away. Never forget the small things that paved the way to living large." Cyrous, Alexandria, Virginia
- "Ancestors are a point of reference—a gift to you to give vision and voice, and to connect time (past, present, and future). Traditions span far after life." Anonymous
- "There is no agony like learning the untold story inside you." Zora Neale Hurston
- "Our lives begin to end the day we become silent about the things that matter." Dr. Martin Luther King

Education

- "Need an education not just from school, but also from family and community." Anonymous
- "One who does not move about knows very little." Haya
- "Most of us can read the writing on the wall; we just assume it is addressed to someone else." Ivern Bell
- "Without preparation, opportunity is an empty promise." Edenburg North
- "Education without common sense is like a load of books on the back of a jackass." African Proverb

- "Knowledge is knowing a tomato is a fruit; wisdom is not putting it in a fruit salad." Anonymous
- "What good de education if him got no sense?" Jamaican Proverb
- "Wealth, if you use it, comes to an end. Learning, if you use it, increases." Swahili Proverb
- "School achievement has more to do with the types of experiences you've had and what you were able to learn from them." Anonymous
- "Do not confine your children to your own learning, for they were born in another time." Hebrew Proverb

Emotions/Behavior

- "The greatest remedy for anger is delay." Swahili Proverb
- "If you're happy in the Lord, notify your face." Wintley Phipps
- "Over discipline makes a child stunted." African Proverb
- "A child's good manners give credit to the parents." Swahili Proverb
- "An egg cannot fight a stone." African Proverb
- "A child's name influences its behavior." African Proverb
- "Learn how to handle emotions, solve problems, treat and trust others, share, and learn right from wrong, and be responsible for one's actions." Anonymous
- "Negative people need drama like oxygen. Stay positive, it will take their breath away." Anonymous
- "All children come into the world crying. You have the responsibility of putting a smile on their face, and turning the crying into laughter and joy." Cyrous
- "Hunger does not reason." Haitian Proverb
- "Clouds are everywhere. When they come over your life, notice that clouds come and go." Cyrous
- Gray skies are just clouds passing over." Duke Ellington
- "Our slave chains are long gone, but we still bind ourselves with invisible chains. You can't see them; you can't

feel them. You can't hear them clank, but they do a better job of controlling us than the other kind ever could. And why? Because once a person believes he(she) is inferior, you no longer have to chain him(her) down; s(he) will do the job (her)himself." Susan Watson (*American Black Journal* 1987)

- "Don't let your mouth rewrite a check that your butt cannot cash." African-American Proverb

Environment

- "We are all beneficiaries of our heritage." Dorothy Height
- The environment is the beginning of success." Swahili Proverb
- "To bring up a child by spoon-feeding will breed a lazy one." African Proverb
- "No one sends a child on a difficult errand and gets angry if she does not perform well." Ashanti
- "Children have no wisdom, kindness or love. They need to learn these." Swahili Proverb
- "The family's job is to help you find your passion and joy, set you free, then let you fly." Cyrous
- "Examples have children." Tish
- "Every choice you make has a direct connection to your children." Unknown
- "To expect the unexpected shows a thoroughly modern intellect." Oscar Wilde

Excess/Effort

- "Plenty sits still. Hunger is a wanderer." African Proverb
- "A person lays the bait before they pull out the big fish." African Proverb
- "The happiest people don't necessarily have everything; they just make the most of what they have." Anonymous
- "A single spark starts an enormous fire." Anonymous

- "Yes, time flies. And where did it leave you?" Anonymous
- "Children can be pawns in the game of self-aggrandizement." Jacob. E. Collins
- "You are a part of something bigger than self." Jacob E. Collins
- "Nothing comes to a sleeper but a dream." Anonymous
- "Patience, persistence, and perspiration make an unbearable combination of success." Napoleon

Experience

- "If you think you won't have the same problems and ills, keep on living." African-American Proverb
- "Appetite comes by tasting." Igbo
- "Expertise is accepted when it comes from experts." African Proverb
- "Time is a tutor." Swahili Proverb
- "There is no reason to repeat bad history." Eleanor Holmes Norton
- "One single place gives no experience." African Proverb
- "A new broom sweeps clean, but an old brush knows the corners." African Proverb
- "A hard head makes a soft behind." African-American Proverb
- "An archer cannot hit the bull's eye if he (she) doesn't know where the target is." African Proverb

Future

- "It's better to construct the future than to vanish in the past." African Proverb
- "Past is noise, present is a choice, future is your voice." African Proverb
- "Tomorrow is pregnant, who knows what it will deliver?" Igbo
- "Yes, time flies. And where did it leave you? Old too soon, smart too late." Mike Tyson
- "Control future generations and you control the future." Anonymous

- "If the future doesn't come to you, you have to go fetch it." William Gibson
- "Yesterday does not pass away." African Proverb
- "You want to make God laugh? Tell him your plans." Anonymous
- "Do not observe what is before, and forget what is behind." African Proverb
- "Armed with the knowledge of our past, we can charter a course for our future. Only by knowing where we've been can we know where we are and look to where we want to go." El Hajj Malik Shabezz
- "We have a rich heritage, a noble past, untapped potential, and an uncharted future that can, to a large degree, be determined by our efforts here and now. Whether we follow the path of significance and distinction depends on the commitment to bridge the best of the past and the best of the present. The future is yet to come." Dr. Samuel McKinney (1965)

Life

- "You are the sum of your life experiences. The more experience, the more interesting your life story gets." Suman Rai
- "There are three grand essentials to happiness in life: something to do, something to love, something to hope for." Joseph Addison
- "You have to run twice as fast to catch up. You have to be twice the best to beat the rest." African-American Proverb
- "You step in life, through life, then out of life." Anonymous
- "Those who can, can; we hope they will, and they may. Those who can't, can't; if we teach them, they probably will." Anonymous
- "All groups have fools, people in the middle of the road, and geniuses. Teach children to differentiate each." Lew Dickert

235

- "I am not as young as I used to be. I am not as old as I am gonna get." African-American Proverb
- "Blessed is he who expects nothing, for he shall never be disappointed." Alexander Pope
- "Be what you is, because if you ain't what you is, you is what you ain't." African-American Proverb
- "Sometimes life will knock the life out of you." Anonymous
- "You don't get out of life alive." Jacob E. Collins

Purpose

- "Why is their life? Why are we here? What is life all about?" Anonymous
- "A very important part of navigation is knowing that you are lost." Rick Page
- "The prospects of arriving where you want to go are helped immeasurably by defining the destination and travel plans beforehand." Chuck Shelton, Diversity Management
- "Remember life is short and it's up to you to make it sweet." Anonymous
- "Had I known comes too late." Ugandan Proverb

Solutions

- "Trust in God, but tie your camel." Persian Proverb
- "Visits always give pleasure—if not the arrival, the departure." Anonymous
- "You've cracked the egg, but have no idea how to make the omelet." African-American Proverb
- "When the snake is in the house, one need not discuss the matter at length." African Proverb
- "Start by doing what's necessary. Then do what's possible." St. Francis of Assisi
- "For every problem there's a solution, even if it's only learning to live with it." Anonymous

Togetherness

- "A people without the knowledge of their history, origin, and culture is like a tree without roots." Marcus Garvey, Philosopher and Revolutionary
- "When minds are one, what is far comes near." African Proverb
- "Language differs, but coughs are the same." Nigerian Proverb

Tradition

- "Women should be the coffee—black as hell, strong as death, and sweet as love." Turkish Saying
- "The river that forgets its source will dry up." African Proverb
- "If you want your eggs to hatch, sit on them yourself." African Proverb
- "As the family goes, so go the children." Daniel Patrick Moynihan
- "We are the hope we've been looking for; may it begin with us, take the gift of whose shoulders you stand, take it to the light years of time, for hope is the human family." Dr. Alton B. Pollard III, Speech, School of Divinity, Howard University, Washington, DC

Generations

- "A good man leaves an inheritance to his children's children. What will you leave?" African Proverb
- "The family is the present generations' link to the past. The present is tomorrow's history—we are all tomorrow's historians." Anonymous
- "We live in the present, we dream of a future, and we learn external truths from the past." Madame Chiang Kai-Shek

- "Allow newer generations to discover things the older generation already knew. Guide, encourage, and care." Anonymous
- "Generational teachings document the natural experiences of gratifying lives, albeit with some scars." Stephen and Sybil Wolin
- ""We are a part of an ancient chain and the long hand of the past is upon us—for good and for ill-just … our hands will rest on our descendants for years to come." Anonymous

Vision

- "Vision exceeds you." Anonymous
- "Utopia—where is it, what is it? Don't be fooled." Anonymous
- "It's better to look ahead and prepare than to look back and regret." Jackie Joyner-Kersee, American Olympic Athlete
- "I see my not yet. I see what will be." Frederick Hayes III
- "Vision without action is a daydream. Action without vision is a nightmare." Japanese Proverb
- "Put down roots and dig deeper. Tradition was created over time. We have benefitted from a long tradition, one that was personalized, but was bigger than self. Learn from elders who went before. They were right about many things and made mistakes about others. Learn from a tradition that is older than we are … stay on course. Don't settle for a life that passed you by. Nothing comes together in one lifetime. Be a determined spear. Sowing seeds has come to pass." Joel Osteen 2015, *The Generational Blessing: Live a Life of Excellence*

Wisdom

- "And don't you know that common sense ain't common?" Anonymous
- "Blind belief is dangerous." Anonymous

- "Always pray to have eyes that see the best in people, a heart that forgets the worst, a mind that forgets the bad, and a soul that never loses faith in God." Anonymous
- "The old believe everything. The middle age suspects everything. The young know everything." Anonymous

Journey So Far

"It's been a marvelous journey so far!
We've had to kick some large stones from the
road and often maneuver a sharp turn
And even back up to start again when the
pathway has been hard to discern.
Sometimes we've been forced from the
road to let some others pass by
And had to sit on the side with our heads hung
down so folks wouldn't see us cry.
It's been a marvelous journey so far!
Because since you started this life, God has
been traveling with us each day
So we could explore and venture to the edge, yet still find our way
When we've fallen we've gotten up again,
because God has been right above,
Yes, we've had joy in our travels and even found folks we could love
It's been a marvelous journey so far!
Now we've gotten rid of some baggage so we're traveling light
And we've learned to read directions to find the path that is right
Our journey ahead is still considerable, we know
But if we keep God as our compass, we'll know which way to go
It's been a marvelous journey so far!"

—Anonymous

Epilogue

A pilgrimage or journey can be imposed, but at other times it occurs by choice. Along the way are personal insights and lessons that can be uncovered, which can translate into wisdom that brings all issues into focus. Detached from our heritage, our stake in family and community, and from our homes, neighborhoods, churches, and schools, we are likely to suffer from detachment and lack of protection from what is significant to knowing our history and the context of who we are.

When considering the past and wisdom of those who came before us, usually there is much more than meets the eye. Without clear direction, without understanding of one's past, without heroes (including women) and positive role models, without family, without connections to neighbors and a viable community, without social tranquility or firm rootedness, without at least one parent who can be at home to parent, without community control, power, and influence, without a reference group with whom to identify, without stability of one's personal world, without clearly designated leaders, without hope and a clear vision of life's expectancies and survival prospects, without spiritual and moral centeredness, there is chaos. Where there is chaos and lack of vision, the people perish.

How can you promote ways to shape success out of circumstances, so as, to empower current and future generations to come? The expression of music, especially in African American spiritual and gospel tradition provides insight into how we have sustained over the generations. Whether we are talking about our personal storms, or our family, societal, or global threats, trials or traditions, the first stanza of an old gospel hymn, entitled, "In Times Like These," written fifty years ago by Ruth Caye Jone, rings true, inspires, and calls out to each generation still today:

"In times like these, we need a Savior,

> In times like these,
> We need an anchor;
> In times like these,
> We need a friend;
> Be very sure, be very sure,

Your anchor holds and grips a Solid Rock."

As we continue the ongoing journey to help shape and guide the understanding and perspectives that will be needed for current and future generations to thrive, regardless of life's pitfalls and challenges, keep in mind the enduring message of the following pledge that was offered by an unknown person:

Black Family Reunion Pledge
Because we have forgotten our ancestors,
Our children no longer give us honor.
Because we have lost the path our ancestors cleared kneeling in perilous undergrowth,
Our children cannot find their way.
Because we have banished God of our ancestors,
Our children cannot pray.
Because the walls of our ancestors have faded beyond our hearing,
Our children cannot hear.
Because we have abandoned our wisdom of mothering and fathering,
Our children give birth to children they neither want nor understand.
Because we have forgotten to love, the adversary is within our gates,
And holds us up to the mirror of the world, shouting "Regard the Loveless."
Therefore, we pledge to bind ourselves to one another, to embrace our lowest,

To keep company with our loneliness,
To educate our illiterate,
To feed our starving,
To clothe our ragged.
To do all good things, knowing that we are more than keepers
of our brothers and sisters.
In honor of those who toiled and implored God with golden tongues,
And in gratitude to the same God who brought us out of homeless
   desolation,

WE MAKE THIS PLEDGE.

Anonymous

References

Ancestry.com (2014). Texas, Select County Marriage Index, 1837-1977. [database on-line]. Provo, UT, USA: Ancestry.com Operations, Inc.

Ancestry.com. (2013). 1860 United States federal census [database online]. Dr. Tyrone Tilory, and Susan Watson. Host Ed Gordon. Provo, UT, USA. Retrieved from: www.ancestry.com/1860census

Dr. Robert Newby, Dr. Tyrone Tilory, and Susan Watson. Host Ed Gordon. 1987. "American Black Journal: Documenting Detroit & American History from African-American Perspectives"

Dr. Tyrone Tilory, and Susan Watson. Host Ed Gordon. 2013. "1860 United States Federal Census (Database Online)" Provo, UT, USA. Retrieved from: www.ancestry.com/1860census

Augusta County (VA.) Chancery Causes. 1746–1912. (1814-097, 1861-074). "Local Government Records Collection Augusta County Court Records." The Library of Virginia, Richmond, VA. Accession Numbers: 43054, 43167, 43339 and 43608. Retrieved on May 30, 2014 from: ead.lib.virginia.edu/

Archives. 2013. "Census Records" Retrieved from: www.archives.com

Barna, G. 2009. "Gracefully Passing the Baton" Fourpercent.blogspot.com/2009/12/gracefully-passing-the-baton-by-george.html

Benjamin, L. 2000. *Three Black Generations at the Crossroads: Community, Culture, and Consciousness*" Chicago: Burnham Inc., Publishers.

Bettman, R. 2016, April 28. "A Review of Back There Then: A DC Historical Genealogy Memoir" *American Eagle News*; Washington, DC. XXIII; 2.

Billingsley, A. 1992. "Climbing Jacob's Ladder: The Enduring Legacy of African-American Families" New York: Simon and Schuster.

Bruce, Laparte, & Tolbert. 1992. "Americans All. A World of Difference" Anti-Defamation League (ADL), NY. (Out of Print). Printed with permission: hbernstein@adl.org.

Bouvee. 1993. "Educational Testing Service (ETS). (2007). The Family: America's Smallest Schools" Washington, DC.

Devitt, Leanne King. 2016. Leanne King, M.A. Retrieved from: Leanne@SeattleElderConnections.com

Digital Library on American Slavery. 2000–2009. The University of North Carolina at Greensboro. ERIT, University Libraries, UNCG. Retrieved from: http://library.uncg.edu/slavery.about.aspx.

Colson, E. 2007. Family Search (2013). "United States Census Slave Schedule 1850 (Family Search Historical Records)" Retrieved on May 28, 2013, from: http://www.familySearch.org

Farrell, W. C. 2015, Oct. 29. "Our New Public School Students Are We Up to the Challenge? The Farrell Report: Defending Public Education" (2002). Managing Editor: Nancy Littlefield.

BlackCommentator.com October 29, 2015 - Issue 627. Retrieved from: www.blackcommentator.com/627/issue_627.html

Feelings, T. Juneteeth.com. "The Middle Passage–Tom Feelings." The Middle Passage@Tom Feelings. Retrieved on November 22, 2013 from: www.juneteenth.com/middleep.htm

Gates, H.L. 2013. "Did Black People Own Slaves in the Western Culture?" New Century Foundation. American Renaissance, VA. Retrieved on March 8, 2013 from: www.amren.com/news/2013/03.

Georgia County Census. 1830. Ancestry.com, p. 345.

TheUSGenWebProject. 1849–1871. "Grimes County Marriages" Rootsweb/Ancestry.com.

Handbook of Texas Online, Charles Christopher Jackson, "Grimes County," accessed March 11, 2018, http://www.tshaonline.org/handbook/online/articles/hcg11.

Handbook of Texas Online, Charles Christopher Jackson, "Stoneham, George," accessed March 09, 2018, http://www.tshaonline.org/handbook/online/articles/fstaj.

Handbook of Texas Online, Charles Christopher Jackson, "Stoneham, TX," accessed March 29, 2018, http://www.tshaonline.org/handbook/online/articles/hns91.

Harper, A. 2018, May 3. "School Leaders Can Inspire Student Success by Sharing Personal Stories." EducationDive Brief. Retrieved on May 9, 2018 from: https://www.educationdive.com/news/school-leaders-can-inspire-student-success-by-sharing-personal-stories/522634/

Howe, N. & Strauss, W. 1997. "The Fourth Turning: An American Prophecy—What The Cycles of History Tells Us About America's Next Rendezvous with Destiny" New York: Broadway Books (24).

Hymowitz, K.S. 2005, Summer. "The Black Family: 40 Years of Lies" *City Journal*. The Manhattan Institute, NY. Retrieved from: www.city-journal.org.

Ibekwe, P. (Ed.) 1998. "Wit and Wisdom Of Africa" Trenton, New Jersey: African World Press Inc.

Ingraham, C. 2014, Dec. 24. "Fewer Families Match the Old Ideal" *Economy and Business*: *The Washington Post* (AP). Excerpted from: washingtonpost.com/blogs/wonkblog.

Kirby, J. 2011. "Single Parent Families in Poverty" Ohio State University. Retrieved from: http://wwwluakron.edu.

Kierkegaard, S. 2013. "In Quotes, Poems, and Inspiration: A Lifetime of Memories" Retrieved on February 17, 2013. Retrieved from: amemorytree.co.uz.

Kinsella, L. 2013. "Pullman Porters: From Servitude to Civil Rights" Chicago: Windows to the World Communications. Retrieved on May 23, 2013 from: WTTW.pbs

Ball, James. 2013, February. "Newsletter of the Madrona Community Council" *Madrona News*. Seattle, WA. 250, 1, 3. Reprinted with permission in original form. Retrieved from: madronanews@gmail.com

Mayo, K. & Lemieux, J. 2016. "The Amazing Race of People" *Ebony Magazine* (Ebony.com). Chicago: Johnson Publishing Co. LLC. LXXI, 2–3, 136–145. McKinney, S. 1965. 75 Diamond Jubilee. Mt. Zion Baptist Church. Seattle, WA.

McKnight, R. (Ed.). 2000. "African-American Wisdom" Novato, CA: New World Library. p. 47.

McNerthney, C. 2012. "Famous People Who Attended Seattle-Area Schools" Seattle PI. Retrieved on December 30, 2011 from: SeattlePI.com.

McWhorter, J. 2005, August 14. "Burned, Baby Burned: Watts and the Tragedy of Black America" Washington, DC: *The Washington Post*, Outlook. B1, B2.

Mead, M. 1978. "Culture and Commitment: The New Relationships Between the Generations in the 1970s" New York: Columbia University Press.

Meyer and Sargent Notes; Pat West File. 2013. "Notes from Myer & Sargent" Generated by Personal Ancestral File. Ancestry.com. Retrieved on May 19, 2013 from: Freepates.genealogy.roots-web.ancestry.com~meyer465/pafn94.htm

Milam County, Texas. 2013. "WWI Draft Registration" TXGen Project. Milam County, Texas.

Mosley, Tanya. 2013. "Black in Seattle" *KUOW News and Information*. Retrieved from: KUOW.org/topic/black-Seattle

Murphy, S. A. 2007. "Leading a Multi-Generational Workforce" Washington, DC: AARP. Retrieved from: www.aarp.org

Myers, Walter, D. 1991. "Now Is Your Time! The African-American Struggle for Freedom" New York: HarperCollins Children's Books. HarperCollins Publishers.

National Park Service. 2012. "Introduction—Social Aspects of the Civil War" Retrieved from: www.nps.com

Newby, R., Tilory, T., & Watson, S. 2014. "Psychological Slavery: Interview by Ed Gordon" *Detroit Public Television's American Black Journal*; Produced by Tony Mottley. Retrieved on August 17, 2014 from: http://abj.matrix.msu.edu/videlfull. php?id=29-DF-57

Osteen, J. 2015. "Generational Blessing 2015" YouTube. Retrieved from: www.youtube.com/watch?v+=exJknhDN6Qc

Parker, B. (Editor). 2012, September. *Madrona News*. Seattle, WA. 245, 1, 2: Girlie Press.

Bell, James. "Madrona to Garfield's 50th Reunion" Seattle, WA. With permission from: *Madrona News*: madronanews@gmail.com

Passow, H.A. 1980, June. "Education for Gifted Children and Youth: An Old Issue—A New Challenge" Ventura County Superintendent of Schools Office. Ventura, CA. (p.iii)

Perry, E. 2013, June 12–July 3. "Dads Make the Difference" Letter to the Editor: Opinion/Editorial. *The Washington Informer*, 25. www.washingtoninformer.com; lsaxton@washingtoninformer.com

Pew Research Center. 2010. "The Decline of Marriage and Rise of New Families" Pew Research Center and *TIME*. Social and Demographic Trends Project. Washington, DC. Retrieved from: http://pewsocialtrends.org

Raising Him Alone Campaign. 2009, 2015. "Raising Him Alone Campaign Kickoff" Baltimore, MD. Retrieved from: www.raisinghimsalone.com/kickoff.htm; http://www.raisinghimalone.com

RBG. 2012. "The History of Slavery in America" Active Interactive Multi-Media Tutorial. *RBG Street Scholar*. Updated on 2012. Retrieved on February 26, 2013 from: www.slideshare.net

Selten, Reinhard. 2005, May 23. "In Hild, M. & Laseter, T.: The Thought Leader Interview" *Strategy + Business*, Issue 39. Retrieved from: http://www.strategy-business.com

Scott J. Winslow Associates, Inc. "Slave Claims to be Plantation Owner's Wife" (PDF) Page 50. End-Scott Winslow Associates. Onlineslaes@scottsinslow.com. Retrieved on May 29, 2014 from: www.scottwinslow.com/images/file/auction-catalogs/50-END.pdf

WETA: Public Broadcasting Service (PBS). 2016. "Sharecropping. Slavery by Another Name" 2012 Twin Cities Public Television, Inc. Retrieved from: www.pbs.org

Seattle Area Population. 2014. Seattlearea.com. Retrieved from: Seattlearea.com/factoid/population

Sigle-Rushton, Wendy & McLanahan, Sara. 2004. "Father Absence and Child Well-Being"

Moynihan, D.P., Smeeding, T.M., & Rainwater, L. (Eds.). 2004. "The Future of the Family" Russell Sage Foundation.

SEARETHA SMITH-COLLINS

Simonson, G. 2008. "Moving in Circles: African and Black History in the Atlantic World" *Nuevo Mundo Mundos Nuevos* (en linea) Coloquois Puesto en linea el 19 Septiembre 2008. Retrieved from: http://nuevomundo.reves.org42303.

Soltan, R. 2004. "The Tween Market: Keeping Our Collections Attractive, Practical and Effective" Michigan Library Association Forum: Michigan Library Association: 3, 1. Retrieved from: http://journaldatabase.info/articles/tween_market_keeping_our_collections.html

Strauss, W. 2005. "Talking About Their Generations" *The School Administrator* (2005, September). "Generational Differences: Finding the Right Fit for Millennials, Gen-Xers and Boomers" (8, 62), 10–14

Strauss, W. & Howe, N. 1997. "The Fourth Turning: An American Prophecy" New York: Broadway Books.

Suburban Stats. 2016. "Population Information and Statistics from Every City, State, and County in the US" "Black or African-American Population in Seattle, Washington" Retrieved from: https://suburbanstats.org/race/washington/seattle/

TheUSGenWebProject. Grimes County Marriages, 1849-1871. Rootsweb/Ancestry.com.

Taylor, Dallas. 1982. "Grimes County Historical Commission, History of Grimes County, Land of Heritage and Progress" Retrieved on May 29, 2014 from: http://freepages.genealogy.rootsweb.ancestry.com/~meyer465/pafn94.htm

Taylor, Edward. B. "Defining Culture" Retrieved from: www.madisonian.net Texas State Historical Genealogy Society/Military Records (2013). Retrieved on June 3, 2012 from: http://www.lksfriday.comMILAM/

Turk, L.H. & Allen, E.A. 1956. "El Espaniol al Dia" DC Heath and Company; Boston (28).

Urban Dictionary. 2011. Central District. Retrieved from: follow@urbandictionary

W. Bruce Willis. 1998. "The Adinkra Dictionary: A Visual Primer on the Language of Adinkra" *Pyramid Complex*.

Wetzel, J.R. 1990. "American Families: 75 Years of Change" *Monthly Labor Review*, Retrieved from: www.bis.gov/mir/1990/art1full.pdf.

WGHB Interactive. The Power of Public Media. "Africans in America: The Terrible Transformation" PBS: Public Broadcasting Online (2007). Retrieved from: www.pbs.org/wgbh/aia/home.html.

WGHB Interactive. The Power of Public Media. "From Indentured Servants to Racial Slavery" Public Broadcasting Service Online: Teacher's Guide. Retrieved from: www.pbs.org/wgbh/aia/part1/1narr3.html

Wilson, B. 2013. "What Is a Pilgrimage?" Pilgrim's Tales Publishing. Reprinted with permission from: info@pilgrimstales.com

Wood & Torbert Families - John H. Stoneham, Ancestry.com. Retrieved on March 29, 2018 at: www.woodvorwerk.com/wood/g9/p9571.htm

Zinner, W. 2006. *On Writing, Well*. New York: Collins.

Photo Gallery

Aunt Juanita Green

Aunt Charlie Mae Green, Charles Pharms, Johnnie Mae Moten

Elbert and Oleatha Green (my parents)

Charles Ruby Green, daughter of Riley Green, Jr.

From left to right: Maggie James Holloway (Aunt Koosie), Ruth
Green (Aunt Ruthie), Juanita Green (Aunt Juanita), Charlie Mae
Green (Aunt Charlie Mae), Dorothy Green (Aunt Dorothy).

Elbert Green

The McGills

In the front, James (Jim) Green, Sr. holding baby Elnora Pittman
Sullivan, Back row from left to right: Andora Gordon McGill
(Aunt Fessie), Sirlina McGill Green, Ruth Green Pittman

Searetha Green Smith-Collins (approximately 9 years of age)

Maggie Samantha James Rosemond Holloway (Big Mama), 1988

The James Green, Sr. Siblings: Front row from left to right, Carson Holloway (Maggie, Aunt Koosie's husband), Dorothy Green, Maggie James Holloway, Charlie Mae Green, Ruth L. Green. Back row from left to right: Juanita Green, Elbert Green.

Elbert and Oleatha Green and their children and
grandchildren at their 50th Wedding Anniversary

Elbert Green's children, from left to right: Patricia Green,
Searetha Green, Elbert Green, Virgie Green, Melloniece Fuller

From left to right, Johnnie Moten Cunningham (Aunt Charlie Mae's Daughter), Leana Green Taylor (Precious, James Green, Jr.'s daughter), and Melloniece Fuller (Elbert Green's daughter).

Ruth Green's daughter's, Ruthie Mae and Elnora Sullivan's families visiting Uncle Elbert in Seattle and Canada in 1993, along with Patricia Green in the front row.

James Green, Jr. (Uncle Buddy)

Sharecropper's Abandoned Home in Cameron, Texas

Maggie Holloway (Big Mama, Aunt Koosie) and her
two daughters, Esther Mae Wells & Everlonia Bush

Dorothy Green Higgins

Dorothy Green

Reddie Mae Pittman Rosemond King

Reddie King (Ruth Green PIttman's daughter)

About the Author

Searetha Smith-Collins is a parent, author, educational strategist, and career educator. Currently a business owner, she has served as a teacher, principal, Chief Academic Officer, and executive educational leader in various parts of the country. She is a sought-after education consultant, speaker, and presenter. Searetha designs and offers seminars, and workshops on current topics related to societal change, education, and child development. She has a strong belief in the value of family and the underpinnings of hope and faith, which have sustained families and individuals throughout the generations.

Using long-standing experience, research, and practical explanations and examples, Searetha cleverly demonstrates how to nurture, support, and unite to co-create greatness from childhood to adulthood. She is passionate about children and holistic family experiences as foundational to our being. In this time of dramatic change, she offers ways to recraft a vision that leads to sustaining family, spiritual, cultural, and generational support and strength.

Searetha holds a doctorate degree in policy, governance, and administration, and a master's degree in curriculum and instruction from the University of Washington, Seattle. In her spare time, she has a fascination with fashion, interior design, writing, and exploring antique shops. Searetha lives with her family in Washington, DC.

CPSIA information can be obtained
at www.ICGtesting.com
Printed in the USA
FSHW010500300719
60526FS

9 781644 163023